COMMON GROUND

American University Studies

Series VII
Theology and Religion

Vol. 25

PETER LANG
New York · Bern · Frankfurt am Main · Paris

Emmanuel K. Twesigye

COMMON GROUND

Christianity, African Religion and Philosophy

PETER LANG
New York · Bern · Frankfurt am Main · Paris

Library of Congress Cataloging-in-Publication Data

Twesigye, Emmanuel K.
Common ground.

(American university studies. Series VII, Theology and religion; v. 25)
Bibliography: p.
Includes index.
1. Christianity and other religions—African.
2. Africa—Religion. 3. Salvation. 4. Love—Religious aspects—Christianity. 5. Rahner, Karl, 1904– . I. Title. II. Series.
BR128.A16T94 1987 261.2'96 86-27687
ISBN 0-8204-0408-X
ISSN 0740-0446

CIP-Kurztitelaufnahme der Deutschen Bibliothek

Twesigye, Emmanuel K.:
Common ground: Christianity, African religion and philosophy / Emmanuel K. Twesigye. – New York; Bern; Frankfurt am Main; Paris: Lang, 1987.
(American University Studies: Ser. 7, Theology and Religion; Vol. 25)
ISBN 0-8204-0408-X

NE: American University Studies / 07

Printed by Weihert-Druck GmbH, Darmstadt, West Germany

To

BULASIO and ESTHER JOY KALENZI

My Beloved Parents

Who Brought Me Up

In LOVE and the FEAR of God

THE TABLE OF CONTENTS

PREFACE

This book is a result of many years of serious research and reflection. It has been written primarily for scholars, teachers, and advanced college students in the fields of Theology, Philosophy, African Studies, Afro-American Studies, African Traditional Religion, Ecclesiology, Missiology and Comparative Religion.

Subsequently, the language employed in this book is explicitly academic and technical in nature. Footnotes are deliberately extensive and very detailed in order to provide more information not covered in the text. This was made necessary by the complex nature of the material, and the sensitive (if not controversial) central theme and thesis of the book. Similarly, I have included some long quotations from primary works not generally available to the readers. The main purpose of these quotations is to furnish outside evidence in support of my argument and position on very controversial issues.

The central focus as well as the central thesis of this book is that God's creative and redemptive activities are merely just two moments in time and space of the same free divine, universal, single, historical and continuous process of creation. This being the case, God's redemption as divine universal gratuitous salvation is viewed as the moment of the supernatural fulfillment of the initial historical process of creation, by the means of personal freedom, choice, responsibility, experience, love, knowledge, failures, disatisfaction, despair, fear, anxiety, sin, self-examination, repentance, forgiveness, transformation, growth and maturation.

In short, universal free supernatural salvation will be viewed in this book as the process by which God socializes and humanizes each individual human being, in free grace and freedom, into the very unique human being, that each one of us has been created by God to become.

Since this process of divine creation and humanization is historically visible as universal, subsequently, it will also be argued that God's free activity in both creation and redemption, in free loving grace is likewise to be viewed as invisibly correlatively universal in scope so as to coincide with this historical, universal human phenomenon ever living in God's loving omnipresence. Consequently, divine salvation will be viewed as the fulfillment and completion of the creation and humanization process wherever, and whenever this process occurs.

Subsquently, the authentic evidence for divine salvation has been identified as "unconditional love for God and the neighbor" since this unconditional love is required of all well socialized and humanized individuals as a prerequisite condition for full self-actualization and fulfillment as a complete human being.

In essence, the doctrine of God's universal salvation in unconditional loving free grace is not new. It can be found both in the Old and New Testaments, especially in the teachings of Isaiah, Jesus, John and Paul. Some of the Church Fathers like

Justin Martyr and Origen taught this doctrine very explicitly whereas many others taught it implicitly. The main trouble of teaching this doctrine implicitly, is a lack of systematic development of the doctrine and its serious implications for Christian theology, ethics, philosophy, ecclesiology and missiology.

Fortunately, this doctrine of free supernatural salvation has recently been taught by Karl Rahner (S.J.) who has been a leading Catholic theologian until his death in 1984. Rahner has taught this old doctrine under the ill-advised term of "anonymous Christianity." He made it quite clear that he used this term for lack of a more inclusive appropriate Christian term. However, I have adopted both his terminology and teaching as it stands without much modification. This was done deliberately so that the arguments and results of my study would not be overlooked or clouded by my modification of Rahner's teaching.

In this book I have employed Rahner's Christian teaching on "anonymous Christianity" as being representative of Western Christianity and attempted to show how Rahner's criterion for "anonymous Christianity" is adequately met and fulfilled by some members of the African Traditional Religion. Subsquently, I have made the claim that God's free creative, redemptive and fulfilling process, was also efficaciously at work in pre-Christian and pre-colonial Africa, in the same way it was at work in ancient Israel before the ministry of Jesus of Nazareth.

Therefore, the main claim being made in this book is that for the African, the African Traditional Religion has the same kind of validity which Judaism has for the Western Christian. Subsequently, the author's claim is that God's free process of creativity, loving, redemption and fulfillment is universal and not limited to any group of people in time or space. Africa is only used to illustrate this principle since inevitably it is always the one left out as "pagan" and "backward."

As an African Christian, a scholar, and an Anglican priest, I have tried to be objective and fair to the African Tradition. Nevertheless, my own standpoint as both a Christian and a minister is bound to have some indirect subjective influence on my work. However, the fact that historical Christianity is currently growing at the fastest rate in Africa, is probably evidence that the ground has been already prepared by God's redemptive grace in readiness for new Christian missions.

This book is a result of many years of research. The funding for the research was obtained from several sources of which the major ones are mentioned below in thankfulnesss and acknowledgement.

I am very grateful to many people and organizations in the United States of America, Europe, and Africa who made it possible for me to undertake programs of study leading to graduate degrees in Communications, Theology, and Philosophy, in addition to the provision of funds for the various research projects and publications. In Europe, the Africa Theological Fund deserves special mention, and in Africa, the National Research Council of Uganda and Makerere University also deserve special acknowledgement. I am grateful to my former teachers and advisors of whom the following deserve special mention: Professors Eugene TeSelle,

Walter Harrelson, Peter Hodgson, Jackson Fortsman, Michael Hodges, John Lachs, Donald Sherburne, and Robert Williams of Vanderbilt University. I am also very indebted to the Rt. Rev. David Birney, the late Urban T. Holmes, Professor of Theology and Dean of The School of Theology, University of the South for having introduced me to the late Karl Rahner and his thought on which much of this book is based, and also for making arrangement for my program of study in the U.S.A. and for the funding.

I am also thankful to the National Episcopal Church of the U.S.A., the Episcopal Church Women of Tennessee, The University of the South, Sewanee; Vanderbilt University, the Sisters of Saint Mary of St. Mary's Convent, Sewanee; and anonymous friends for their moral support, encouragement, and for funding my study programs leading to the graduate degree awards of MA in Crosscultural Communications from Wheaton College Graduate School in 1978, STM in Systematic Theology from The University of the South in 1979, MA and PhD in Theology and Philosophy from Vanderbilt University in 1982 and 1983, respectively. Without this support and education, this book would not have been written.

I am also very much indebted to professor John S. Mbiti my former teacher who introduced me to the positive study, appreciation, and interpretation of the African Religion. He also granted me a research fellowship in 1971 which led to the study and publication of "The Concept of Death Among the Bakiga of Western Uganda" in Byaruhanga (edited), <u>Research Occasional Papers.</u> Vol. II, Kampala: Makerere University Press, 1973. My study of the African Traditional Religion was shaped by Mbiti, Tempels and Alexis Kagame, all of whom have written almost definitively in this new, but fast growing field. My STM thesis entitled, "The Concept of Sin and Atonement Among the Balokole of Uganda" and now this book represents another serious academic effort by an African scholar to contribute to this formerly neglected, yet fertile field.

I am also grateful to Vanderbilt University for giving me funds to carry out research at the Harvard Center for the Study of World Religions. However, this book is also based on original research carried out in Africa since the research based on secondary sources alone would not have been adequate. Credit for the funding of the essential research trip to Africa in the Spring of 1982 goes to Beatrice, my understanding wife, who kindly agreed to let me use our own personal funds for the purpose of this essential research trip.

Without this essential original research in Africa, this book would not have been possible since little has been written on African metaphysics, ethics, ontology, and philosophical-theological anthropology which constitute the African material and background grounding. This African material is significantly important in the same way Karl Rahner's concept of the "Anonymous Christianity" is important for the book.

Equally important, and deserving of special acknowledgement and thanks, are my African informants and research assistants, particularly, those in East Africa where most of the field research material was gathered. I am very much indebted to the Rev.

Canon Wilson Baganizi, the then Provincial Secretary of the Church of Uganda for the special help and hospitality he rendered to me. He showed me some private research material, made travel and accommodation arrangements for me comfortable when I could hardly afford them! I am also grateful to his kind wife for the warm hospitality extended to me in their home.

Last, but not least I am most thankful to Mrs. Mary Howard Smith for typing the drafts of the manuscript, and the diligent Professor Dianne Harper for the invaluable many hours exerted in critiquing, typing and proofreading the various versions of the final copy. I am also very grateful to my kind wife, Beatrice T. Twesigye for proofreading the manuscript in its several revisions, and compliling the index, despite her greatly demanding duties as a mother of four young ones (Joy, Grace, Gloria and Peace) who would rather scribble on the manuscript to add a story of their own, in their own language to the book!

Nevertheless, they too, deserve thanks for leaving me alone on many occasions to work undisturbed even when they would have rather preferred to play ball with me or to play on the computer key board while I write! Thus to Joy Twesigye goes much credit and praise for her devotion in babysitting the children while Beatrice and I worked on the book, and also for offering to help with the various tasks such as collating the manuscript, and assembling the index.

Emmanuel K. Twesigye, Ph.D.
Associate Professor and Chairman
The Department of Religion & Philosophy
Fisk University
Nashville, Tennessee, U.S.A.

INTRODUCTION

It is almost certain that the late Karl Rahner has been the leading and most influential Catholic theologian for this century. Perhaps he is not the equal of either St. Augustine or Thomas Aquinas, but his impact on the Second Vatican Council, and on post-Vatican II Catholic theology is so great that it is difficult to assess it adequately at present. However, it can be said that like both saints Augustine and Thomas, he too has defined and reshaped the nature of Catholic theological reflection and ecclesiality. He has also introduced a new soteriological base and methodology which are fully grounded in philosophical-theological anthropology.

This theological starting point has enabled him to analyze and critique the well-established ecclesiastical exclusive, bigoted dogmas, such as that of *extra ecclesiam nulla salus*, and to reappraise them in a more constructive, ecumenical and contemporary manner. This innovative approach has been less dogmatic, and has its *modus operandi* in seeing all human beings, everywhere, as the universal concern of God both in creation and salvation, viewed as two moments of one divine act, and not two separate events in time or in divine action.

This being the case, Rahner then goes on to argue very convincingly that the God who created all human beings out of free, unmerited grace also loves them all by this same free, unmerited universal grace, which is efficaciously salvific by His unconditional love, and universal redemptive will for all human beings He has created. God's redemptive efficacious grace enables human beings to become more fully humanized and humane. This process of humanization is correlative with human deification and salvation. Both of these are the intention of God in both creation and salvation which are correlative with the divine act of calling humanity into being, and the constant divine action of calling human beings ever to become more humane and more loving.

It is very insightful of Rahner and theologically accurate to call this divine process of complete humanization of the human being, divine salvation, regardless of conditions, such as creed and religious affiliation. Nevertheless, Rahner being not only a Catholic priest but also a Western Christian theologian, has already had a given specific Western Christian context, and as such a Western Christian standpoint from which to discuss this central issue of humanity and salvation. Since according to Christianity, all supernatural salvation is of God through Christ as the divine *Logos* (Word of God) described in the Bible (cf. John 1-3; 10:9; 14:6-11; Acts 4:12), subsequently, for lack of better and inclusive Christian terminology, Rahner calls all those people "anonymous Christians" who experience divine salvation outside the conventional Christian Fellowship, Community or Church.

Consequently, the central thesis of this book is that Rahner's more inclusive Christian teaching on humanity, universal divine redemptive grace, and "anonymous Christianity are very meaningful and attractive Christian concepts which are at the same time compatible with the teaching, and the lived life in the African tradition. In otherwords, this book is largely a detailed African support for Rahner's and the Catholic Church's broad Christian affirmation that the concrete, temporal and historical human existence* is the very divine universal arena of creation and salvation. That this is also the arena of God's self-communication to all human beings in His unconditional love, and universal gratuitous efficacious grace, regardless of creed, color, ethnic origin, race, nationality or level of technology.

Obviously, this is a very meaningful and powerful Christian teaching, for all people, most especially those who are traditionally non-Christian, such as the Africans whose major population is still non-Christian. It will be shown in this work that the African modality of authentic human existence (Obuntu) is in harmony with Rahner's Christian teaching that whoever accepts God's implicit or explicit revelation, wherever it is given, and within its given mystery accepts both God (Ruhanga) and himself/herself as a finite special creature (Omuntu) of God whose very well-being as salvation lies in this very Incomprehensible, Creative, Infinite Mystery that Rahner calls God.

Consequently, an attempt has been made in this book to demonstrate that Rahner's Christian teaching on God, humanity and supernatural salvation as the divine humanization of the human being, is in fact similar, to the African understanding of authentic human existence (Obuntu) as the fullness of loving, humane, godly human life lived by individual human beings in the right social or communal living in full opennes, love, and fellowship with God, the neighbor as a fellow human being, both the living and the departed, most especially the ancestors.

This subject is especially significant and attrative to me as an African theologian and philosopher, because conventional Christianity in Africa South of the Sahara is still new, and remains largely a minority religion in a number of predominantly Islamic African nations. Therefore, it is important for us to study, explicate and adopt this previously unexamined revolutionary, constructive, Christian concept and teaching on "anonymous Christianity" in and for the African religious and philosophical systems of thought, teaching and practice.

By this venture, I hope to create more room in African Christian theology and philosophy for a more sympathetic understanding of both our departed ancestors, who died before hearing the historical Gospel of Christ, as preached by the historical Church, and also for those our relatives and countrymen, who

---

*Rahner uses the term "categorial" to denote concrete, temporal, spatial and historical dimensions of human existence in contrast to the transcendental or spiritual ones, which he regards as infinite, and unlimited, unlike these categorial dimensions of matter, time and space which categorize our own world.

This term will subsequently be used in this Rahnerian sense, and without any further quotation marks.

happen to be Muslims and subsequently, look at Christianity as just another "foreign religion" to choose from. Furthermore, in some countries like Uganda, on which much of this book is empirically based, there have been in the past serious wars fought in the name of God and Religion! Here Rahner's inclusive Christian teaching can become a corrective, and therefore, a harbinger of God's true salvation and peace in the current conflicts which are largely grounded in ethnic and religious sectarianism, bigotry and intolerance.

This study confronts this kind of religious hostility, bigotry and intolerance with the Rahnerian inclusive teaching on "anonymous Christianity," with emphasis on God's universal redemptive activity in gratuitous grace which is appropriated in faith and whose chief fruit is obedience to Jesus Christ's commandment of unconditional love for the neighbor (the neighbor being each human being; cf. Luke 10:25-37; Matt. 25:31-46; John 13:34-35.) By this method, it is made very explicit that these kinds of religious conflicts and wars have been misguided. Furthermore, it is demonstrated that they do not endear anybody with God, since they are uncharitable, violent and brutal in nature, and therefore, very contradictory to God's unconditional love for all human beings, which is also required of all God-loving human beings, being the very basis and quintessence of the supernatural human salvation in Christ (cf. John 3:16, 17; Rom. 5:5-11.)

The new religious understanding sought and portrayed in this book is one rooted in universal divine unconditional love, grace, inclusiveness, tolerance, forgiveness, and acceptance of life in its given complexity of racial, ethnic, cultural, idealogical diversity and religious pluralism.

Rahner's challenge and inclusive Christian teaching have great relevance for the world and Africa, today. For instance, his challenge can be restated as follows: that those engaged in religious discrimination, conflicts, hatred, violence or wars in the name of God, have in fact already lost Him/Her in so doing. For our God is the God of love, who commands us all also to love one another without conditions, and to do this by our manner of living as it finds its definitive expression in both word and deed. Subsequently, our own human worth and godliness or Christianity (both explicit and anonymous), are to be measured by our love for the neighbor as viewed by and through our acts of charity both spiritual and material.

Since God creates all human beings freely out of his gratuitous loving grace, the argument is that he also freely sustains them in this grace, and seeks to bring them to fulfillment in himself through his Word (Logos), who is the very divine medium of both creation and salvation, as the authentic human existence in universal divine redemptive grace and creative love (cf. John 1:1-5, 14.) This means that salvation also consists in our own free, positive self-actualization and fulfillment as finite creatures in this life as it is lived in the presence of God, the very Mystery of life as both its origins, and absolute future.

According to Professor John Mbiti's well documented study of the African religions and philosophy, there is already some fertile ground for rooting this new religious and philosophical understanding. For instance, Mbiti observes that for the African, God is regarded as both the ultimate human origin and destiny. The present, as the "now," is regarded as the perpetual divine unfolding of this ultimate destiny, and mystery of life as the absolute future with God, who is both the absolute beginning and the end of the human being. For the African, the human being cannot change this givenness of God-oriented life. It can only be either accepted in its givenness and mystery or be rejected to face the consequences of such a rejection, which is gravely regarded as the rejection of God himself and his will.

An attempt has been made to show that, despite Rahner's strong emphasis on this theme of anonymous Christianity, he is unlike Frederick Dennison Maurice or Origen in that he does not teach that everyone is or will be saved. It is shown in this study that there is still room for becoming eternally lost in Rahner's schema; since for him those conventional Christians who fail to love their fellow human beings are as lost to God as non-Christians who do likewise. Rahner's soteriology is, therefore, a faithful exposition of the Gospel of Jesus himself summed up definitively in the commandment to love unconditionally both God and the neighbor. Like St. John and St. Paul, Rahner says that our love for one another and our openness to life as it is given in its mystery of being is the evidence for godliness.

Rahner affirms that missionary work is still to be undertaken by the Church, contrary to Balthasar's claim that Rahner does away with missionary work, declaring pagans to be anonymous Christians! This mission is to proclaim God as both Love and Mystery, who desires that all human beings should love one another as part of their raison d'être.

Most of all, missionary work is to be undertaken in order to bring anonymous Christians to explicit confession of their hidden faith in God, and wherever possible, to bring them into the conventional Church to be strengthened and nurtured to spiritual maturity through the Church fellowship, teaching, and above all by participation in liturgical worship and the celebration of the sacraments, particularly penance and the Eucharist. Anonymous Christianity, though salvific, is still a deficient mode of Christianity, as Anita Roper and Klaus Riesenhuber clearly document.

Karl Rahner's concept of the anonymous Christian in relation to the African situation raises a number of serious questions for the Church, its theology and mission in Africa. For instance, should the Church in predominantly Islamic nations like Nigeria try to convert the Muslims, who far outnumber the Christians? Should the Church in Africa develop denominational traditions inherited from the missionaries, and should it repudiate them and try to create an African ecumenical Church based upon the uniqueness of their heritage and experience? Is polygamy a sin that excludes those engaged in it from salvation of the Church? Which one of these rival missonary churches is the true Church of God? Are all pagans and Muslims lost to God? What should one do to be sure of salvation? How should we live a good and satisfying life? These questions are significant for African spirituality and ecclesial life.

I shall undertake a study of Karl Rahner's theory of explicit and implicit anonymous Christianity, understood within his philosophical-theological anthropology as a whole, and try to relate this to the African religio-philosophical background. Such an inquiry will enable us, I hope, to answer these questions in a constructive manner.

In undertaking this study, I have briefly outlined the history of narrow and exclusive soteriological views in contrast to the inclusive ones. I have also outlined Rahner's concept of anonymous Christianity in its anthropological and philosophical-theological aspects and have examined the African religio-philosophical thought in its traditional expressions as regards the question of authentic human existence and salvation. Finally, the two systems of thought are brought into dialogue and synthesis, with Rahner's Christian teaching being tentatively regarded as the most suggestive statement of the case, and one that is at the same time most meaningful, attractive, inclusive and compatible with the African experience.

This is not a sell out of the African tradition. On the contrary, this approach is designed to give it a universal validity and credibility by demonstrating that what the West has already accepted as sound philosophical and Christian religious teaching, is in harmony with the precolonial and pre-Christian African traditional teaching and practice. This makes some of us question whether Africa itself might not be the actual origin of the main religious ideas which were later developed and systematized fully by the Hebrews, the Christians and the Muslims.

However, when conflict arises between Rahner's Christian exposition of either human existence or salvation and the African religious viewpoint, I attempt to allow the Scriptures and Rahner's inclusive Christian position address and challenge the African religious viewpoint. I also let the reverse challenge take place as well. Whenever necessary, I have also referred to other relevant views held by other major thinkers, both Christian and non-Christian, on the key issues under examination.

The scope of this book is broad, but the actual empirical data tends to be taken from the Bantu ethnic groups of East Africa. This approach is necessary to give the book a particular regional or ethnic focus, since Africa is so vast and varied. Uganda has received special attention mainly because that is where most religious and ethnic wars have been seriously fought, both in the colonial era, and in the modern post-independence period. The Martyrs of Uganda, Idi Amin and his legacy are all part of that unfortunate tradition.

My ability to speak and work with nine Bantu languages, including Swahili, Luganda and Runyarwanda has been a very great asset, since word study has been necessary in order to unveil the African ontology and metaphysics denoted by some African terms which might otherwise be missed, especially by foreign scholars. Since much of the African ontology and metaphysics is still oral, the study of local vocabulary, as well as the worldview, is imperative for this kind of book in order to arrive fully at both the explicit as well as the implicit African religious and philosopical understanding or consciousness on this important subject of what it means to be human "Omuntu", and the required process needed in order to create or transform imperfect human beings into authentic humanity or to understand what it is like to be an authentic human being possessing the completeness of humanity (Obuntu).

CHAPTER I

HUMAN EXISTENTIAL VULNERABILITY AS CONTEXT FOR THE QUEST OF SALVATION: AN OUTLINE OF THE PROBLEM OF NEIGHBORLY LOVE AND HUMAN PARTISAN EXCLUSIVENESS

The question of human existence, Karl Rahner contends, is the question of a meaningful human ultimate destiny.[1] This being the case, the question of human existence is intricately intertwined with the question of the Absolute Mystery which we call God.[2]

The Human Problematic

The correlation of the human existence and the quest for the Absolute[3] as the Infinite, Unconditioned yet loving, Transcendent personal Being[4] necessarily arises from the human limitless self-transcendence, as a historical free spirit in the world.[5] The human being finds himself or herself surrounded by infinite mystery, beauty and occasional joyous experiences as well as being dismayed and threatened by the forces of evil and destruction.

These forces of evil are perceived by the human being to be operative in this same world inhabited by the human being. These evil forces are attributed with the creation of chaos, discord, confusion, enemity, pain, disease, death, and therefore, the cause of human insecurity and despair, especially among those who are already overwhelmed by this sense of prevailing evil, finitude and its vulnerability.[6] This awareness and experience of finitude, vulnerability and insecurity in the world, leads the human being to the quest for salvation as primarily security, and wellbeing[7] in this wonderful world, yet infested with evil and its consequences in the form of pain, hatred, malice, finitude, destruction, death, and decay. Yet, the human being realizes that this is still the same world in which he or she is, nevertheless, called fully into active being.

Human Quest for Salvation and Exclusiveness of the Few Elect

Wherever humankind exists on this world[8] whether in Africa or America, Asia or Europe, it faces the very same problem of human existence and its ultimate meaning. This is particularly true since all human beings, regardless of who or what they are or where they are, are equally and radically threatened by guilt, evil, and most of all live in constant fear of the natural processes of finitude in terms of limitations, aging, disease, pain, decay and death.

Consequently, all human beings are all engaged in the same ultimate quest for meaning, a more full life, a future, love, happiness, wellbeing, success, harmony and peace. In short, all human beings, irrespective of creed, ideology, and religious affiliation, are all engaged in the same ultimate human quest for salvation.

Therefore, inasmuch as human beings are looking for security, better ways of survival to old age, better health, economy, and politics that makes it possible, such as the observance of international peace, human rights and freedom, they are all engaged in this same quest for salvation in its broad and wholistic dimensions.[9]

The Soviet Communists may undertake this ultimate quest in a seemingly very different manner, and under a very different label or terminology from the self-confessed Christian West, who undertake the same ultimate quest under other labels or even under the variety of the bigoted stereotyped terms such as, "democracy," Christianity," "Evangelicalism," "Charismatic," and the like.[10] On the other hand, the same quest for a more meaningful and a fuller life, which is the life of human existence in grace, and the right relationship with God as the Creator of the human being and the ultimate destiny,[11] may be undertaken differently by different peoples, such as the peoples of Asia and Africa because of their dissimilar historical, cultural and religious backgrounds. For instance, the Arabs might objectify their quest for the Divine and for salvation in their religion known as Islam,[12] (which translates as peace due to submission to God), whereas the Asians traditionally have done so through Hinduism and Buddhism.

In the same way, the Africans have traditionally objectified their own ultimate quest for divine salvation and authentic human existence in their Traditional Religion which permeates all their life, and all human activities to the very extent that the sacred and the secular had merged into one sacred realm of human life, and its activities could not be ever divided into the sacred and the secular, like the case in the West.[13]

The result of this African hallowing of the cosmos, life and its "mundane activities" has led to the African perception as that of being "incurably religious,"[14] as well as "superstitious"[15] and "animist,"[16] since most Africans seemed to believe that the divine power or Spirit could dwell everywhere and whenever it chooses, manifest itself anywhere, even including "mundane things," such as tops of mountains, gigantic trees, huge rocks, lakes, rivers, people and even animals.[17] This theophany was always understood to have a very specific meaning, directive and purpose for the people and the community.

One thing that is clear so far is that all human beings are aware of their vulnerability as human beings[18] and that they are variously engaged in dealing with this problem of meaning and concern for a fuller life.[19] Some of the solutions which have been prescribed have been political, economic, medical, philosophical and religious in nature. For instance, the enlightened Greek philosophers such as Socrates, Plato and Aristotle, taught that the main goal of human life was happiness;[20] whereas happiness was itself regarded as the result of the displined human life lived in the sober, contemplative state of virtue.[21] However, virtue itself was viewed as the result of the knowledge of the ultimate good[22] and its relentless pursuit.[23]

Implicit in this teaching is that the untutored ignorant masses were almost lacking in virtue and its correlative divine life, since they lacked the necessary knowledge required to enable them to become wise and virtuous.[24] This Platonic exclusion of the ignorant masses from happiness and salvation as union with God in intellectual or mental contemplation, and the virtuous life[25] resulting from it, also led Plato to exclude these same untutored, ignorant masses from responsible political process, and self-determination in the exercise of their human and political rights to vote or hold office in a democracy.[26]

Therefore, for Plato the philosopher is the representative of God in the society. Subsequently, Plato like the African tradition assigned the philosopher, a divine position which made him the ideal divine king and high priest, since he is the one close to God by virtue of possessing the divine secret of knowledge of the good which is the divine quintessence of God.[27] In another sense, the philosopher is God's human elect, prophet and missionary in a given society. Subsequently, in each era, God has given each society a local prophet to warn the people of worldliness, and evil, and to recall them to holiness through self-denial, purification, self-displine, charity and doing the good works which enhance the common good, and the general welfare of humanity and the world.

The Hebrews, on the other hand, had a different experience. They believed that they were the elect people of God out of all the peoples that God had created.[28] The writer of Genesis sees that the election of Israel in Abraham was for the redemptive purpose of the whole world and not just for Abraham's descendants:

> Now the Lord said to Abraham, "Go from your country and your kindred and your father's house to the land that I will show you. And I will make you a great nation, and I will bless you, and him who curses you I will curse; and by you all the families of the earth will bless themselves." (Gen. 12:1-4)

Despite this election for mission to the world, Israel as a nation forgot the wide-world mission that it had been entrusted with and had been elected to. Ironically, circumcision, which had been given to her as a sign of the covenant identity, and the Torah, which had been given to her as a tutor and guide into a fuller life of right living with each other and righteous communion with God, became a stumbling block and a barrier in Israel's relationship with the non-Jews. The Gentiles were viewed as a source of ritual uncleanliness. Salvation was then understood to include only those elect, and even then those among them who remained faithful to the election covenant.[29]

Inevitably, this position led to the kind of exclusiveness that was associated with Judaism in its claims to God and divine salvation. The Gentiles and all pagan nations were thought to be headed for perdition![30] Nevertheless, the Judaic religion, aware of its superior revelation and knowledge of God through the Torah and the prophets, made no effort to go out to convert the Gentile world in order to save them from perishing and barbarism.[31]

Judaism as a religion remained oblivious to its election to be God's universal salvific agency in the world. This remained generally true until the coming and ministry of Jesus of Nazareth about two thousand years ago. Jesus himself cannot be considered a religious revolutionary but rather a reformer and fulfiller of Judaism.[32] For instance, he recruited twelve men to represent the new Israel he was instituting. He did away with the burden of the law while keeping its esence.[33] He was too conservative to include a woman in his inner circle of twelve, nor did he include in it a Gentile. These inclusions would have been a revolutionary symbol of the universal nature of Jesus' message and ministry; but most likely these inclusions would have rendered Jesus' own historical ministry unacceptable and ineffective in the Jewish nation.[34]

However, Jesus himself did not do any significant "foreign missionary" activity during his earthly ministry to the non-Jews.[35] Nevertheless, his willingness to go to the Gentile world constitutes the post-resurrection ministry, as his commandment to the Apostles to make disciples of all nations, and to baptize them, clearly illustrates:

> And Jesus came and said to them, "All authority in heaven and earth has been given to me. Go therefore and make disciples of all nations, baptizing them in the name of the Father, and of the Son and of the Holy Spirit, teaching them to observe all that I have commanded you, and lo, I am with you always, to the close of the age." (Matt. 28:18-20)[36]

Nevertheless, it appears that if it had not been for St. Paul's conversion, and vigorous missionary activity to the Gentile world, and stubborn refusal to allow his Gentile converts to observe the details of the Jewish religious law and ceremonies,[37] the religious reformation of Jesus would have probably been contained within the Jewish religious heritage just as another puritanical sect within Judaism, just like the Pharisees and the Essenes.[38]

Consequently, Christianity *qua* Christianity as we know it today would have been non-existent![39] It is also most likely that the books of the New Testament as we have them today would have been fewer and different, as they would have been dealing with different problems, and since there would be no Gentile Christian community uninitiated into the Mosaic Law, there would be no need either for the Pauline type of letters or the incipient treatment of issues of Christian contextualization of the Christian faith and ethics in a Gentile world of "paganism" and Greek philosophy.[40]

Some materials in the Gospels themselves, such as the commissioning of Jesus to the Apostles to preach and convert all the nations baptizing them in the triune God, or the claims we find in the Gospel According to John in regard to Jesus as the beloved "Son of God," the creative "Logos" of "God become flesh" as "the truth," "the true light that enlightens every man" and the only "way" to eternal life, would most probably not have been written.[41] In any case, if Christianity had not broken away from Judaism, most likely the Gospels would not have emerged, and if they had emerged they would have been different both in content and purpose. They would have been unacceptable as they stand now, and they would have been most probably been suppressed as both blasphemous and heretical.[42]

Since incipient Christianity was rejected and persecuted by the Jews, and was consequently forced to assert its own identity as a separate religion, distinct from Judaism by which it had been born and nurtured, the problem of the new and the old and how they relate to each other began to emerge.[43] It is clear that the Judaisers within the incipient Christian Church wanted Christianinty subordinated to the old, namely, Judaism.[44]

However, radicals like Stephen and Paul saw a clear break between Christianity and Judaism, especially, as epitomized by the elaborate Mosaic Law. Christianity was regarded by the Christian radicals as "the new wine-skins,"[45] thus stressing the necessity for the new wine or Gospel message, to have its own autonomous new existence independent of Judaism. Paul and the radical Christian group saw Christianity as both the fulfillment and the superseding of Judaism by her new unique gift of God himself become flesh in the Incarnation and the divine grace through the abiding pentecostal Holy Spirit.[46] This divine gift of grace and the Holy Spirit enables humanity to live in a new era of the Christocentric abundant and fulfilling life in the love of God, and in the universal brotherly and neighborly love for our fellow human beings.[47]

The Untheological Absolutization of the Church

When the Christians began to view themselves as the new creation, and as the obedient elect children of God, they inevitably began to view the non-Christians, whether Jews or pagans, as the lost unless they were converted to Christ.[48] This was in their view, a revenge on the Jews who had rejected Jesus as their Messiah, and had trumped up charges of political sedition in order to get rid of him.[49] It is understandable how strong anti-Seminitic feelings would have arisen easily among the Gentile Christians.[50] Gospel passages such as the following would have been quoted to ground such hostile feelings as the vindication of Jesus' death upon the Jewish race:

> So when Pilate saw that he was gaining nothing, but rather that a riot was beginning, he took water and washed his hands before the crowd, saying, "I am

> innocent of this man's blood; see to it yourselves." And all the people answered, "His blood be on us and on our children!"[51] Then he released for them Barabbas, and having scourged Jesus, delivered him to be crucified. (Matt. 27:24-26)

Vatican II realized that much of anti-Semitic feelings arose from the hostile Christian attitude toward the Jews as responsible for the torture and cruel murder of Jesus on the shameful cross, and the Council repudiated this hostile attitude and misuse of scripture to justify it.[52] This is definitely a positive step in putting right this bad relationship that goes as far back as the very founding of Christianity itself by Jesus the Christ. It is also remarkable that the same Council, inspired by the spirit of Christ, nullified the old ecclesiastical bigotry of _extra ecclesiam nulla salus_.[53]

St. Paul struggled with the question of the Jews and Judaism in the Christian era. Paul had an open mind to realize that there is only one God who is Creator, Revealer, Savior, and Judge of all human beings wherever they are and to whatever religion they belong.[54] For Paul, as for Karl Rahner, God's gratuitous and efficaciously salvific grace as God's self-disclosure or divine salvific self-communication has been gratuitously given universally to all human beings, in the same way all of them have been also the victims of sin without any exception.[55] This includes the Jewish people as the very elect people of God, with the special privilege of the Torah as a guide and the warnings of the prophets, but without limiting God's activity to them _vis-à-vis_ the rest of the human world.

However, with the exception of philosophically inclined apologists like Justin Martyr and Clement of Alexandria, most of the Church Fathers, particularly the Latin ones such as Tertullian and Cyprian, tended to care less about non-Christians whether they were Jews, Greek philosophers, or mere pagans. For Tertullian, the Christian faith had nothing to do with the Greek Academy.[56] Philosophy was looked at as an enemy of faith and not as its ally, as Justin Martyr, Origen, Augustine and later St. Thomas, thought and taught.[57]

It is certain that, whereas the Greek fathers were interested in speculative, philosophical theology on controversial topics such as Christology, salvation and God's being, the Latin Church Fathers with a few exceptions, were less speculative, more dogmatic, and generally they were rather more concerned with Church structure, hierarchy and discipline.[58] The result was that the Latin Western Church was characterized by the preoccupation with ecclesiology, authority, unity and the threat of schism, whereas the Eastern Church was generally engaged in the intellectual quest for grounding and understanding of the Christian faith and doctrines.[59]

Given those main traits in the Church, it is not surprising, therefore, to find that Justin Martyr and Origen taught a broader and more inclusive view of Christian salvation.[60] For instance, Justin Martyr taught that Greek philosophy contained salvific truth for the Greeks, who adhered to it and lived faithfully in accordance with it like Plato and Socrates. He claimed that the truth found in this philosophy which men like Socrates and Plato taught was the same salvific truth of the cosmic divine Logos that was later made historically manifest in the incarnation of Jesus of Nazareth.

Since truth is the one divine, salvific grace in the divine Logos, who is the pre-existent Christ, Justin Martyr affirmed that all those who possess this divine truth and cherish it can be, therefore, termed Christians.[61] But as we have seen, the Latin Church Fathers such as Tertullian and later Augustine rejected such a view of salvation of non-explicit Christians, without accounting for the divine activity or lack of it outside the Christian Church. Bishop Cyprian made this view impossible to hold when he expounded extra ecclesiam nulla salus in his attempt to quell a Novatianist schismatic revolt that had sought unsuccessfully to dethrone him, and had consequently gone into schism in protest against his cowardice and flight into hiding during the severe mid-third century Roman imperial Christian persecution in North Africa.[62]

Therefore, the doctrine of extra ecclesiam nulla salus, though later ratified by the Church, should be viewed within its proper context of the Church's internal political rivalry, jurisdictional conflicts and discipline, rather than a broader theological spectrum of God's universal creative grace and salvation that is operative everywhere, inside and outside the historical Church. Extra ecclesiam nulla salus was even used by the Catholic Church for some time to exclude Protestant churches from divine salvation, as they were regarded as schismatic and lacking in efficacious salvific grace![63]

This doctrine illustrates the human problem of pride, egocentricity and bigotry that manifests the exclusive claim of truth and salvation. Contemporary examples abound. For instance, recently Mr. Bailey Smith, the President of the U. S. Southern Baptist Convention, said that God does not hear the prayers of either the Jews or the Muslims![64] According to him the Jews and the Muslims are outside of both God's communion and divine salvation (unless they convert to conventional Christianity and preferably become "born again").

Similarly, in economic and political systems, the East and the West discredit each other endlessly in the name of truth, freedom, religion, ideology and might.[65] The problem here does not seem to be primarily that of either faith in God or its absence. The real problem here, again, is that of human sin. The human sins of pride and bigotry make it hard and nearly impossible for one to love and accept the other as he/she is without any conditions or reservations and seek to live in mutual co-existence, harmony and dialogue, rather than live in mutual suspicion, malignant competition, hatred and confrontation.[66]

The absurdity in this case lies in the fact that, whereas the West generally claims to be God-fearing and Christian,[67] often it forgets the very grounding and essence of Christianity, which is Jesus' commandment to love God and the neighbor as ourselves.[68] There is no doubt that the neighbor to be loved, in this case, includes the Soviets, Iranian fanatic shiite Muslims and "pagan" Africans.[69] In the case of Uganda, which will be the main focus of this book, the neighbor includes the Catholics, Muslims, Anglicans, "Balokole," "pagans," and perhaps, most of all, members of the other tribes and the other political parties.[70]

The Problem and Central Thesis

The problem of human existence is the problem of meaning in the face of apparent prevailing evil and chaos in the world in which we are called into being by the infinite and supposedly loving God to live as finite, vulnerable human beings who are capable of experiencing evil in the form of pain, loneliness, failure, despair and death, whereas he/she is also capable and aware of the possibility of joy, hope, happiness, friendship and fellowship with God and fellow human beings as the main objective and goal for human authentic life, or the human *raison d'être*.[71] But at the same time, because of human self-transcendence and moral self-evaluation, the human being realizes that there is a contrast in what one is *vis-à-vis* what one ought to be.

This awareness causes internal guilt in addition to the external threats of pain, chaos, and extinction of one's being in the form of accidents, homicide, robbery, rape, hunger, poverty, disease, slander, broken relationships, isolation, loneliness, anxiety, crises of identity, and perhaps most of all the omnipresent threat of death. In short, this predicament constitutes the universal human problematic and the human existential condition.

In Africa, however, we have additional problems, such as the fear of evil spirits, witchcraft, and ostracism by the family or clan if one fails to behave in accordance with the culturally and religiously prescribed patterns of acceptable behavior. There is also the fear and hatred of strangers, such as the members of other tribes and races. There is also bitterness against some former Western imperialist and colonialist countries for their former harsh rule and, in some cases, previous cruel activities in Africa.[72] The bitterness of slave trade has largely sunk into oblivion, though the Arabs and the Western nations that engaged in this inhumane trade have not been entirely forgiven. The colonial forced labor in Kenya and some other parts of Africa was resented by the Africans as a new form of slavery,[73] since its essence and objective was free or cheap African labor for the white settlers who owned vast plantations.

Until recently, Uganda, like most of Africa south of the Sahara, was largely non-Christian.[74] However, the people in this area had the understanding of God that enabled them to live humanely in the community. This pre-Christian understanding of both God and humanity still remains the very grounding of African values and the definitive guide for human interaction. This is still true at present for Uganda, which has now largely accepted Christianity, at least nominally.[75]

My central thesis, which is based on Karl Rahner's Christian philosophical-theological anthropology (and understanding of God as the Creator-God and the Infinite cosmic Mystery, whose universal self-communication in efficacious gratuitous grace enables the gratuitous divine salvation of all human beings everywhere, regardless of time and space),[76] is that whoever has accepted to be "Omuntu,"[77] that is, to be a responsible and/or an authentic human being, and has, therefore, accepted and acquired the "Obuntu,"[78] or full humanity as manifested in being humane, has both fully accepted God and Christ as the divine cosmic Logos,[79] who is the full embodiment of authentic humanity (Obuntu).[80]

Karl Rahner contends that such a person has exercised personal faith, hope, and love for God and fellow human beings, and he/she is therefore truly an heir of divine gratuitous salvation through the divine cosmic Logos, who is similarly, the preexistent cosmic Christ, and is therefore a "Christian."[81] But since this person may not even be aware of the existence of such a label,[82] and may even reject "Christian" as a description of his or her condition as a full human being fully open to the Absolute Mystery and life itself, which is the condition of grace and salvation, Karl Rahner affirms that he or she is therefore to be correctly termed an "anonymous Christian" and similarly, his or her state to be termed "anonymous Christianity."[83]

If divine salvation is properly viewed as a present condition of human life, and not a reward to be obtained in the future life for the good life lived on this earth,[84] then it becomes imperative for us to re-examine the world in order to see more of God's ceaseless activities of gratuitous grace in continuing creation, sustenance, transformation and renewal.[85] Both creation and salvation are God's freely willed and universally executed activities in the world by his unconditional love in gratuitous creative and salvific grace.[86]

Therefore, we cannot limit God's universal gratuitous salvation by our partisan exclusive theology to our own revival group, charismatic movement, church denomination, race, or political-economic ideological grouping or even East or West.[87] God's free creativity pervades the whole universe, and similarly, his gratuitous universal love and salvific will in gratuitous grace to divine salvation[88] as well-being, wholeness, a peaceful life, joy, and hope for the abundant life for all people who truly respond to this divine invitation to gratuitous supernatural salvation that presupposes faith, hope and love in personal freedom on the part of those people who respond positively to God.

Unconditional Love for the Neighbor as the Criterion for True Christianity

As part of the central thesis of this book, it will be strongly argued that the true criterion for true Christianity, whether explicit or anonymous, is our unconditional love for our concrete neighbors and other persons we happen to encounter during the course of our ordinary routine of day-to-day living.[89] This is held as the essence and grounding of true Christianity and evidence of our love for God, since by virtue of the incarnation God has become man, therefore, symbolically becoming our temporal neighbor, being incarnate in every person that there is in the world.[90] Consequently, the question of "Who is my neighbor?" has been only settled for explicit Christians, and it still remains to be answered for anonymous Christianity.

Hence the continued urgency for Christian missionary activity among the non-Christians including the "anonymous Christians," even if they were known.[91] There is no doubt that "anonymous Christianity," though efficaciously salvific, is still a deficient modality of Christianity and human existence, as it is usually lacking in the fullness of unconditional love, explicit knowledge, confession of faith in Christ, fellowship and nurture of the historical Church and Sacraments. Therefore, the humble task of the Church's missionary activity is to remedy these deficiencies wherever and whenever it is possible.[92]

Since the historical Church is not to be regarded as the equivalent of Noah's Ark of divine salvation in this world,[93] it is therefore, to be viewed as a symbolic historical presence of Christ as the Logos incarnate in historical process, yet without losing the prior nature of its cosmic transcendental dimension which is universally at work in the whole cosmos, implementing God's gratuitous creative processes, and effecting its creative advance to greater self-actualization, positive fulfillment, personal maturity in creative growth and transformation, in divinely guided personal freedom.[94]

NOTES

1. This is, as far as we can tell, the main distinguishing mark of a human being as opposed to other animals, especially the higher primates such as chimpanzees and other apes. For instance, the latter are considered as lacking the necessary capabilities that would lead them to ask such questions as: Who am I? Where did I come from? And where is my existence heading? If these animals ever ask these kinds of questions, then they will cease to be mere animals. According to Rahner, they will have become human, no matter what else they might look like! For a human being is a creature that possesses the capacity to ask these self-transcending questions.

2. Cf. Karl Rahner, _Foundations of Christian Faith_ (New York: Seabury Press, 1978), pp. 44 ff, 85-89; _Spirit in the World_ (New York: Herder and Herder, 1968), pp. 406-408; _Grace in Freedom_ (New York: Herder and Herder, 1969), pp. 183-196, 203-207 and 229 ff. Rahner argues that the proper name or term given to the Infinite Mystery is not considered important. What is considered important is our attitude and response to this Mystery. That is why the rejection of the term "God" does not necessarily lead to atheism as long as the person remains open to life, the world and its mystery. Cf. Rahner, "Atheism and Implicit Christianity," _Theological Investigations_ 9:145-164.

3. This theological method of correlation is the chief means by which relevant theology addresses questions and problems raised by being a human being in the world. Karl Rahner uses it but the most famous utilizer and expounder of this method remains Paul Tillich; cf. _Systematic Theology_ (Chicago: University of Chicago Press, 1967) 1:59-66, where Tillich summarizes his method of correlation in theology. For Africa, this method means that Christian theology should address the questions of polygamy, spirits, ancestors and evil, most especially as it manifests itself in poverty, witchcraft, tribalism, corruption and political irresponsibility.

4. The God of human worship has to be not only Creator, Mystery, Ground of Being and Knowledge, but he also has to be personal and responsive to human prayer and needs. The God of religion who is worthy of human worship cannot be conceived as merely an impersonal, static omnipotence. Therefore, Karl Rahner argues that ideally the God of worship should be conceived as both Transcendental and Incomprehensible Mystery without becoming impersonal as the Immutable God of St. Thomas almost sounds; cf. _Prayers and Meditations_ (New York: Seabury Press, 1980), pp. 5-14; and _Foundations of Christian Faith_, pp. 42-89.

This kind of approach avoids the kind of religious problem that arises with Tillich's conception of God as the Ground of Being with the implied impersonality of this Ground. Worship tends to reject or ignore a philosophically conceived God lacking in personal warmth toward the human worshippers. Therefore, the dilemma of Christian theology as meaningful "God-talk" that is theologically and philosophically acceptable without losing the religious personal appeal for the ordinary worshippers. Maybe this is why some people find anthropomorphic religious language very appealing, especially in liturgical worship.

5. According to Karl Rahner, the quest for God is a result of self-transcendence and the "supernatural existential." This is God's prior gratuitous orientation of the human being in creation toward the supernatural destiny in the beatific vision; cf. Rahner, Foundations of Christian Faith, pp. 75-80; "The Experience of Self and the Experience of God," Theological Investigations 13: 122-132; Hearers of the Word (New York: Seabury Press, 1960), Chs. 5 and 11; "The Existential," Sacramentum Mundi: An Encyclopedia of Theology, ed. Karl Rahner et al. (New York: Seabury Press, 1968-1970) 2:304-307. Rahner argues that the human being is a Spirit because of personal freedom and self-transcendence. This Spirit as a human being is historical because it is emergent in history. In light of evolution, it can be said that "the ape" became human when "it spoke," if language is considered as the evidence and unique tool of human abstract thought, self-transcendence and communication.

6. It can be argued that evil is, particularly felt by human beings because of this superior structure for abstract thought, self-transcendence and self-evaluation. The human being is usually aware of personal moral responsibility, unlike most animals. The human being is also able to ponder and speculate about such evils as war, famine, disease, poverty, slavery, injustice, political repression, corruption, pain and death. This capability tends to make the human being feel more vulnerable and overwhelmed with evil, the result being usually the kind of despair (Angst) which Soren Kierkegaard very ably and vividly described in his works, particularly in The Concept of Dread and The Sickness unto Death. The animals have a natural instinct for survival. Therefore, they are radically sensitive to danger.

However, they feel no dread or despair as Kierkegaard describes it, as a general pervasive dread which is not a specific fear of this or that object that one could, therefore, remedy by the removal of those specific objects that are the effective cause of fear. Therefore, it appears that dread (Angst) is a constitutive element of being in the world.

7. It is perhaps due to this sense of dread and vulnerability that the human being lives in the perpetual quest for salvation as wellbeing and security vis-à-vis evil with its tragedy and destruction that seem to abound in the world. It was Feuerbach's contention that if the human being was not aware of evil and his or her finitude and vulnerability in this world, there would not be any need for religion, which he saw as the conscious quest for salvation by an illusory immortal God from the threat of evil, pain and death; cf. The Essence of Religion (New York:

Harper & Row, 1967), pp. 16 ff.; Essence of Christianity (New York: Harper & Row Publishers, 1957), pp. 13 ff.

8. Humankind and life in general, both zoological and botanical, exist only on this planet, earth. So far, scientific explorations of space and the cosmos have not yet been able to detect the existence of any other kind of life in this wide cosmos apart from the terrestrial one. However, the search continues, and it is not impossible that, in the future, space scientists may find other intelligent beings in the cosmos if these beings do not discover us first! Nevertheless, it is imperative for humankind to realize the uniqueness and invaluable nature of this life and find ways to improve its quality and to preserve it, as it can be eternally lost by human blind hatred for each other and nuclear war, that would probably produce massive nuclear radiation and long-term pollution that would lead to the indiscriminate extinction of living organisms, thus the extinction of life itself.

9. Contrary to the naive teaching of the Balokole (the saved ones) of Uganda, who teach that for salvation, only the spirit matters and nothing else, salvation in its broad or holistic understanding includes the totality of the human being, as the individual is always a unity and not a loose collection of parts. Therefore, divine salvation should be viewed more broadly to include better health of both body and mind, personal freedom, and general wellbeing. That is, one should not be threatened by extreme poverty, starvation or lack of basic freedoms. Jesus' ministry was basically oriented to the poor and the ignorant. He healed the sick, taught the ignorant crowds, and fed the hungry. Similarly, we too who are his followers are called upon to imitate his example as we try to follow his teaching and to keep his commandments; cf. Matt. 25:31-46; Karl Rahner, "Anonymous Christians," Theological Investigations 6:231-249.

10. Karl Rahner argues that it is not the label for oneself that matters; that what really matters is our attitude and response to the Mystery and the life given to us, and how we live it in this world. Our own actions definitely speak louder than our words. Therefore, whether a person calls himself or herself a Christian or an atheist, it is of little importance. What really counts is what a person is and the quality of the life he or she is living as a result of personal free choice to become that person; cf. Rahner, "The Theology of Freedom," Theological Investigations 6:178-196; "On the Dignity and Freedom of Man," Theological Investigations 2:235-263; and "Atheism and Implicit Christianity," Theological Investigations 9:145-164.

The major problem of labels, or terms such as "Evangelical," "Marxist," "Communist," "Mulokole" and the like, is that they are already stereotyped in such a way that the individual so labeled tends to lose his or her unique individuality. Such labels or terms are generally misused by becoming exclusive passwords for certain groups to exclusive divine destiny, usually excluding the majority of humanity, leaving them to damnation. At least the

Balokole still make this claim openly in order to scare non-Balokole into conversion! This is obviously an inappropriate method of evangelism, since the Good News of the Gospel is that God loves all people and wills to save them all through the mediation of Jesus Christ. Therefore, Christian conversion should be a response of love in faith to God and his salvific activity in Christ, not a reaction out of fear. Unfortunately, most religious labels today engender either religious fear or partisanship and not the love for God.

However, it is always comforting to remember that none of these religious or political labels ever capture all the truth. The truth is too big to be captured by any one of these labels. Therefore, they all remain relative, including the Balokole, who claim such an absolute position in the Ugandan religious situation. Indeed, the extreme Balokole religious exclusiveness can be regarded as a kind of Christian Pharisaism or bigotry.

For the debate of salvation within the Anglican Church of Uganda on the position of labels such as Balokole and "Sinners" in regard to this divine salvation, see the following articles and Letters to the Editor in <u>New Day</u>, a bi-weekly newspaper published by the Church of Uganda, Kampala: The Rev. E.M.K. Baluku, "A Challenge to the Balokole" <u>New Day</u> 4 January 1968; J.T.H. Deborrah, "One-Sided Challenge," <u>New Day</u> 1 February 1968; the Rev. Canon A. J. Binaisa's Letter to the Editor, <u>New Day</u> 1 February 1968; the Rev. Enos T. Bagona, "The Devil's Sermon," <u>New Day</u> 15 February 1968; C. C. Galiwango, "Canon in Darkness," <u>New Day</u> 25 April 1968; the Rev. E. Wamala, "Clergy are not necessarily called by God," <u>New Day</u> 9 May 1968 (front page headline in thick black print); Willis B. Shalita, "Their Acts Differ from Their Words," <u>New Day</u> 9 May 1968; Joseph Kisubika's argument that "Jesus was a Mulokole" in "The Saved Are Sinners Too," <u>New Day</u> 6 June 1968; Dan Lukwago, "Roman Catholics are not God's Chosen People," <u>New Day</u> 4 July 1968; Keith Konyogonya's interview of Bishop Festo Kivengere as the leader of the Balokole revivalists in Uganda, <u>New Day</u> 18 July 1968 (front page with a continuation on page 6); M. Y. Musoke. "There are Two Types of Sinners," <u>New Day</u> 1 August 1968; and an editorial on 1 August 1968 that summed up this debate and closed it formally with a theological explanation of salvation which is inclusive and embraces even non-Balokole. See also the Rev. Kauma's <u>New Day</u> readers' lecture on "Salvation," 4 December 1969.

Since the Balokole could not accept that even the non-Balokole of the same Anglican Church could be heirs of eternal life in God, it should not be surprising, then, that they regard other Christians such as the Roman Catholics as eternally lost. Therefore, for such extremists, the Rahnerian inclusive Christian concept of "anonymous Christianity" would be viewed with suspicion and probably considered as a kind of anti-Christ treatise that should be repudiated by the "faithful Christians" on the grounds that "nobody is saved unless he/she is born again."

11. Within a Rahnerian understanding, salvation in this context is human life that is lived in the world in divine grace and harmony with one's <u>a priori</u> destiny. This life has to be charac-

terized by the awareness of one's dependency on God for one's being, origin and destiny. Life lived in movement toward one's true destiny is the life of salvation, and salvation is realized in this finite life. That is life faithfully oriented and moving in hope towards fulfillment in the utlimate divine destiny that still lies in the Mystery of the Future; cf. Wolfhart Pannenberg, What Is Man? Contemporary Anthropology in Theological Perspective (Philadelphia: Fortress Press, 1970), pp. 54-67.

12. For instance, "Islam" is an Arabic word which means "total surrender" or "submission," and in this case, it means total submission to God. Therefore, those Christians who sing the popular revival hymn, "All to Jesus I surrender... I surrender all," can be termed Muslims, that is, people who have surrended all to God! The Quran (Koran) and the "Sharia," which constitute the Islamic scriptures and the Islamic law, respectively, do reveal a close similarity to the Old Testament and the Mosaic law. Under Rahner's theory, the same God inspired the emergence of both types, inasmuch as both types do contain a degree of divine revelation and answers to human existential questions.

13. In African traditional religion there is no division between sacred and mundane. God has created everything, and though God is transcendent, he is also present everywhere in creation directly or indirectly, by means of mediation through nature or human ancestral spirits and phenomena; cf. John Mbiti, African Religions and Philosophy (London: Heinemann, 1969), pp. 1-3, 88-100; Introduction to African Religion, pp. 65 ff.; and Newell S. Booth, ed., African Religions: A Symposium (New York: NOK Publishers, Ltd., 1977), p. 7.

For the African, the ordinary is the conveyor of the extra-ordinary for those willing to see with their inner eyes of faith and having willing ears to hear the silent divine Word of the Invisible, Transcendent Mystery, locally known as "Ruhanga" in Kigezi, Ankole, Bunyoro and Toro, and "Katonda" in Buganda and Busoga. Ruhanga or Katonda literally means and translates "The Creator." It has to be noted that in this part of Africa God is God only if he is "The Creator" creating ex nihilo. However, this Creator-God is not a static "Pure Act" of St. Thomas. He is too transcendent to act in the world directly most of the time, so he acts through a chain of mediators and delegates like a mighty Celestial King.

14. See, e.g., John Mbiti, African Religion and Philosophy, pp. 1-3, 6, 20 and 343. However, Western missionary Christianity is beginning to change this picture, as it has attacked and still continues to attack traditional religion and its values in order to westernize the African as evidence of successful Christian conversion. This mistaken evangelical missionary method has been destructive to African values. As expected, the reactionary voices of skepticism and even atheism are beginning to be heard at the universities and among the educated youth. Therefore, in this respect, Christianity has brought damnation and destruction to Africa.

The high rate of breakdown in family discipline and rising cases of divorce, prostitution and selfishness, mainly among Western educated Christians who live in towns and earn more money, which they spend on themselves trying to compete with the white missionaries and ex-colonial officers in living styles, can always be traced back to the introduction and growth of Western Christianity and Western education. Christianity has the negative potential of secularizing the pre-Christian religious Africa, thus causing a religious crisis rather than "causing salvation." Consequently, the main effective remedy and preventive measure against this impending calamity is to contextualize Christianity in African religious milieu rather than seek to destroy it, as the C.M.S. missionaries tried to do in Uganda; cf. F.B. Welbourn, East African Rebels: A Study of Some Independent Churches (London: C.M.S. Press, 1961), pp. 3-14 and Chs. 2-5, 9. Chapter 9 is particularly important, as it deals with the "Missionary Culture and the African response," and in this case revolt and schism as the African response to this apparent cultural imperialism of the Western Christian missionaries in East Africa.

15. See Mbiti, African Religion and Philosophy, p. 13, for a detailed discussion of these Western ethnocentric derogatory descriptions of the African people and their religion. He points out that terms such as "ancestor worship," "primitive," "totemism," "savage," "fetish," "magic," "pagan," "Satanic," "hellish," "superstition," "animism" and the like, previously used to describe African religion by Western writers, are inaccurate, racist, derogatory and unacceptable both academically and to the African people as such.

16. Ibid. Animism as a belief that everything has anima (soul) in it is probably a close description of most African people, since they view the world as pervaded by divine energy or powerful spirit that can be accessible to people, especially kings, priests, elders, medicine men and women, mediums and diviners. It is also believed that evil people, such as witches and evil magicians, can gain access to it too, and use it to do harm to people and their property. Nevertheless, the belief in a "world-soul" pervading the universe cannot constitute a religion, as it is just one of the numerous major beliefs in African religion.

This energy pervading the universe has been called "vital force" by Placide Tempels in Bantu Philosophy (Paris: Presence Africaine, 1959). Mbiti rejects Tempels' "vital force" as the center of African philosophy and says the concept of time is the center; African Religion and Philosophy, pp. 14-15. However, both points of view should be treated together as mutually correlative, since together they explain much of African metaphysics better than does either one of these views in isolation. Janheinz Jahn, Muntu: An Outline of the New African Culture (New York: Grove Press, 1961) and Alexis Kagame (Fr.), La Philosophie Bantu-Rwandaise de l'Être (Brussels: Academie Royale des Sciences Coloniales, 1956) follow Tempels alone in their analysis of African philosophies, as Mbiti's theory of time as the basis for African metaphysics and ontology had not yet been put forward.

17. For East Africans God is considered to be omnipotent, but whether he is also omnispatial is not clearly thought out. Consequently, it is thought that, although divine presence is pervasive in the world, it only manifests itself occasionally in a specific place such as a high mountain, big river, huge rock, even in an animal such as a huge snake. Wherever this divine presence reveals itself in its varied mystery, it is always for the same benefit of human beings, i.e. to awe or amaze them and motivate them to worship Ruhanga as the Creator of this wonderful mystery. See Mbiti, Concepts of God in Africa (New York: Praeger, 1970), passim.

18. For instance, all human beings experience dread (Angst) and usually have a religion and generally fear to die.

19. Fuller life (as in John 10:10) and its quest can be considered to amount to the quest for salvation whether it is carried out by religious or by secular means such as "Marxism" or "Secular Humanism;" see Jurgen Moltmann, What is Man? Christian Anthropology in the Conflicts of the Present (Philadelphia: Fortress Press, 1971), pp. 46-96. See also note 11 above.

20. Cf., e.g., W.K.C. Guthrie, The Greek Philosophers: from Thales to Aristotle (New York: Harper & Row, Publishers, 1960), pp. 6-12 and 153 ff.; Bertrand Russell, A History of Western Philosophy (New York: Simon Schuster, 1945), pp. 178-189. Happiness is the general goal of authentic human activity unless there is something wrong in the doer to obscure in his or her mind the ultimate good. In this sense, then, sin can be termed free human self-actualization in the world in such a way that happiness is made impossible most of the time for oneself and others around him or her.

21. Ibid. It was argued that virtuous acts did not cause virtue in the doer, but rather the doer was already in a state of virtue which enabled him/her to perform virtuous deeds. This argument is similar to that of Jesus when he stated that people are known by their fruits, as good fruits are borne of a good tree while a bad tree yields bad fruits (see Matt. 7:16-20). This argument is important in the debate on salvation and grace, as it can be used to support Karl Rahner's view that Divine salvation is freely given to human beings everywhere in grace prior to their actions of faith, love and virtue, as these spring from the already present state of grace, which is prior to any human activity. See Rahner, "Reflections on the Experience of Grace," Theological Investigations 3:86-90; "Concerning the Relationship of Nature and Grace," Theological Investigations 4:165-188; "Some Concepts on Uncreated Grace," Theological Investigations 1:319-346; and his articles on "Existential," " Supernatural," "Grace," and "Potentia Oboedientialis" in Sacramentum Mundi: A Theological Dictionary, 5 vols. edited by Karl Rahner and Herbert Vorgimeler.

22. *Summum bonum*, variously identified with God or as God. Plato's God as seen in the *Timaeus* was a mere architect, such as a carpenter or potter fashioning an item from pre-existent materials. The idea of the good transcended Plato's God as it was all perfection and all-inclusive. The good, according to Plato, was mediated by beauty as its immanence in this flux world of becoming; see *Phaedrus* 250e. However, Plato's followers such as Plotinus modified his concept of God by combining the Idea of the Good with Plato's Architect God. The result was a good Creator-God taught in Neoplatonism, the kind that St. Augustine learned from Porphyry. See St. Augustine's *City of God*, Book VIII, particularly Chapter 8, which deals with the *summum bonum* in the context of Platonism.

23. For Socrates and Plato, philosophy was considered as ground for practical ethics. Knowledge was pursued, not as an end in itself, but as a means to virtue and happiness; see note 20 above. Even today education is positive if it leads to a positive modification in behavior as a result of the knowledge acquired through learning or instruction. Knowledge which does not lead to this internal modification or internal relation in the knower or learner is not worth acquiring. True knowledge, like truth, is power for willful human self-realization and transformation either positively or negatively in freedom. Guilt is a result of negative knowing self-realization. Without knowledge there is no possibility for guilt, because guilt is due to the awareness of the contrast of what is *vis-à-vis* what ought to have been.

24. The "rudes" or the masses were left to perish in ignorance, as not everyone could become a philosopher. It is not surprising, therefore, that both Socrates and Jesus were alike in that both saw their mission as teaching divine salvific truths to all who cared enough to listen and follow their teaching. It is ironic that both of them were accused of impiety and subsequently put to death, and that both went to their deaths willingly and calmly. See Plato's *Crito* for the execution of Socrates, and Matt. 25-27 or Luke 22-23 for the passion story of Jesus.

25. This is the main grounding of Platonic and Christian mysticism. In this mysticism there are usually three stages of theosis. The first stage is self-purgation from base or bodily desires that distract the mind from concentration. The second stage is a disciplined contemplation of God until the thinker is finally lost in the object of his or her thought. This is the climactic unitive stage and it is very much like Hegel's "Absolute Knowledge," in which there is the abrogation of the distinction between object and subject, thought and thinker. See Hegel's *Phenomenology of Spirit*, the section on the "Absolute Knowledge;" St. John of the Cross, *The Ascent of Mount Carmel*; and the anonymous *The Cloud of Unknowing*.

26. It can be argued that Plato was right. The current troubled politics and economies of the Third World could be largely attributed to a lack of Philosopher-Kings! The military

tyrants heading most of these nations are the very opposite of the Philosopher-King. Furthermore, it can be argued that democracy cannot yet be possible in the Third World, particularly Africa, where functional literacy is barely twenty percent. The ignorant masses cannot be considered responsible governors of their own nations, as democracy implies. Instead, they need a good, learned, skilled and capable guide in the form of their nation's political leader.

For instance, the notorious Idi Amin of Uganda was a bare elementary school dropout, and he proved that without education he could not rule the country insightfully, despite his supposed great military power. President Nyerere of Tanzania, his opponent, on the other hand, has a Master of Arts degree. Could it be mere coincidence, then, that even in actual battle, Nyerere was able to defeat the semi-literate Idi Amin and drive him out of Uganda in 1979? Probably not. The excesses of Idi Amin could be attributed mainly to ignorance, tribalism, greed, sin, and personal sadism.

27. In East Africa political order and religion were very much part of each other. They were both thought to have been given to humanity and sanctioned by God, as the myth of Kairu, Kahima and Kakama in Western and Southern Uganda illustrates. Therefore, to these people Plato's king, who is also a kind of high priest by virtue of his divine knowledge and exemplary virtue, would probably be most welcome. For concepts of theocracy and divine kingship held in this area, see: A. G. Katate and L. Kamugungunu, Abagabe b'Ankole (Kampala: E.A.P.B., 1955); S. M. Kiwanuka, Kings of Buganda and A History of Buganda; M. Beattie, Bunyoro; Nyakatura, Bunyoro-Kitara; Paul Ngorogoza, Kigezi n'Abantu Bayo; and Apollo Kagwa, Ba Ssekkabaka Be Buganda.

28. See Gen. 12:1-4, 15:7-18; Exod. 6:4 ff., 19:5 ff; Isa. 42-55. The election of Israel by God was purely out of God's free grace and universal will to save the world and not just those special elect people who were to be his main historical symbol of grace and salvation in the world (cf. Rom. 1-4). For this divine unconditional salvation of Israel, and therefore, other people too, see Gerhard von Rad, Old Testament Theology (New York: Harper & Row, 1957) 1:121-135.

29. See Ezekiel 18, where individuals are to be punished for their personal transgressions of the divine statutes. As regards universal salvation beyond the covenant, it can be said that in general, the Jewish prophets and priests had little interest, as Israel's credo in Deut. 25:5-9 very clearly proves. Israel became too preoccupied with the covenant and its demands of holiness to be concerned with the possible conversion of Gentiles. (After all, the covenant was considered a birthright and Judaism was synonymous with Jewish. As a result, foreign mission to the Gentiles in this case was thought either as unnecessary, since it meant Jewish imperialism, or as a matter to be left to God; cf. Isa. 55:5.)

30. As they were excluded from the covenant, the Torah and its guidance; see Psalms 9, 10; Isa. 16:8, 10:25; and Joel 3:12. However, there were exceptions to this Jewish exclusiveness regarding salvation; for instance, the Gentile Cyrus mentioned in Isaiah 44 as one who helps to rebuild Jerusalem and the temple, is portrayed as God's "Messiah" for the Jews now in exile. He and others like him are unconsciously used as illustrative examples of how God's work of gratuitous universal grace and salvation transcends the covenant people and their Jewish borders. Similarly, it can be argued that today God's salvific work in gratuitous grace transcends the baptismal covenant and its narrow borders of the historical Church. This is my main contention in this book.

31. Yet God's mercy and salvation are, nevertheless, to be mediated to these Gentiles; cf. Gen. 12:1-4; Zech. 8:7-23; and most of all the dramatic story of prophet Jonah, the reluctant missionary to Nineveh. The book of Jonah can be viewed as a symbolic commissioning of Israel to foreign mission among the Gentiles, to convert them to God's mercy and by so doing humanize them more, thus sensitizing them against inhumane acts of injustice and cruelty.

The assertion here is that the barbarian heathens were cruel because they lacked the knowledge of a merciful, loving God and that it is, therefore, impossible to know God in this way and remain a "barbarian" or "savage" at the same time. This is because people generally try to behave like the God they know and worship. For instance, if God is known to be loving and merciful, as in Christianity, the worshippers of this God will, likewise, try to love one another and be merciful to other people. This is why Christian missionary activity to the world is a must, since it is the divine historical means of humanization of the world by means of unconditional neighborly and brotherly love.

32. Cf. Matt. 5:17: "Think not that I come to destroy the law or the prophets; I am not come to destroy but to fulfill..." (KJV). See also the kind of reforms Jesus is concerned with as recorded in Matt. 5-7, such as the rejection of the Mosaic law of <u>lex talionis</u> (Matt. 5:38) as seen in "an eye for an eye and a tooth for a tooth" (Exod. 21:24). However, Jesus inaugurated a new era when he commanded his followers to love one another without counting the cost (Mark 12:30-31, 33; John 15:12, 17), because it is this very commandment that has led to the Christian transformation and revolution in the world, both directly and indirectly, to enhance human freedom and dignity.

33. Paul himself was compelled to argue that Jesus' commandment to love God and one's neighbor is not only the summary of the law but is its very essence and energizing power. Therefore, in agreement with both Paul and John, one can say, like Rahner, that whoever loves unconditionally, whether he/she is a self-labeled "atheist," "Muslim," or "Humanist," he or she has fulfilled the requirements of God's law in grace and is an heir to supernatural salvation and eternal life (cf. I John 4:7-21), since without God's grace no one can either fulfill the demands

of the law or express love without conditions attached to it for personal ends. See Paul's insightful analysis of the nature of this unconditional love (agape) in I Cor. 13; see also Anders Nygren, Agape and Eros (London: MacMillan, 1939), which deals in great detail with the subject of love and its role in the Christian faith.

34. This is one of the reasons why Jesus should be considered a reformer rather than a religious revolutionary. If Jesus had included a woman within this inner circle of the twelve Apostles, the current heated debates on the ordination of women within the Anglican and Catholic Churches would have been entirely out of place! However, since the Apostolic ministry was opened to Gentiles who were originally not included among the twelve Apostles, why should it not be open to women too? After all, women have a valid claim to the Eucharistic ministry if it is the confection of the elements into the body and blood of Jesus Christ and to distribute them to "the worshippers of the Son of Mary"!

It could be argued that Mary brought Jesus into the world and through this act of chastity, faith and obedience to the Theotokos, all women have been symbolically cleansed and elevated in grace and status, in both religious and secular affairs. But the Church has been slow in realizing this in the same way that it has been slow in seeing God's salvific activity among non-Christians. Consequently, it could be said that the historical Church is suffering from spiritual myopia due to self-imposed excessive conservatism, exclusiveness, pride, sin, fear and either superstition or prejudice as regards human sexuality. For the angry and radical feminist reaction to this state of affairs, see: Mary Daly, Beyond God the Father: Toward a Philosophy of Women's Liberation (New York: Beacon Press, 1973); Rose Mary Radford Ruether, The Feminine Face of the Church and New Woman, New Earth: Sexist Ideologies and Human Liberation (New York: Seabury Press, 1975).

35. It seems that Jesus understood his ministry to be primarily the fulfillment of Judaism; c.f., e.g., Matt. 5:17, 27; 15:21-28; Mark 7:24-30. It could also be pointed out that the incident at Gerasa (Gadara) recorded in the Synoptic Gospels (Matt. 8:24-34; Luke 8:26-39; Mark 5:1-20) further illustrates that, though Jesus cared and healed the demoniac, he did not care enough for the local non-Jewish populace, their culture and their property, since he allegedly killed about 2,000 of their herd of pigs! If this incident took place as it is described by Luke, then the New Testament commentators cannot fully absolve.Jesus of insensitivity to non-Jewish culture by saying that this was a symbolic cleansing of the Gentile land for Christian missions, as some of them suggest, such as Nineham in his commentary on Mark. The Gospel should not be preceded by the destruction of animals nor of food, since these are not the idols to be destroyed by the Gospel of Christ.

I suggest that modern missionary activity should try to save both the demoniacs and their pigs, except where the pigs are objects of worship! Christian missionary cultural imperialism that kills pigs to prove that the demoniacs have been healed and cleansed cannot, therefore, be encouraged. Unfortunately, much of the African cultural heritage has been destroyed by the Western Christian missionaries, due to the confusion of Western culture with the essence of Christianity. But the two are different. Since Christianity can survive outside the original Jewish milieu, it can also successfully adapt itself and flourish outside the Western culture. This means that the African or the Asian does not have to become westernized in order to become a Christian. It also means that the demons in Africa or Asia have to be exorcised without the unwarranted "destruction of pigs."

36. These can be understood as the words of the risen Christ as he is known and experienced by the Church in his abiding presence through the Holy Spirit. In this sense the words and the commissioning of the Church to the venture of world mission stem from the Church's nature and self-consciousness as the visible and historical embodiment of the risen Christ, whose mission has taken on a new universal dimension as a result of the resurrection and God's original universal salvific will (cf. John 3:16).

Pannenberg, in reference to this great commision of the Church to world mission, skeptically asks: "Do we really have to baptize everybody?" See Human Nature, Election and History (Philadelphia: The Westminster Press, 1977), p. 36. The answer to this question is the concern of this book. But in short, the answer of Karl Rahner is "No." After two thousand years since the beginning of Christianity, according to David Barrett's recent statistical study, all baptized Christians constitute just a bare 33 percent of the world's total population, which in 1986 was estimated to be about 5 billion people; see The World Christian Encyclopedia: A Comparative Survey of Churches and Religions in the Modern World, A.D. 1900-2000 (London: Oxford University Press, 1982).

Barrett's gloomy discovery was that Christianity, while growing in numbers, was declining in percentage of world population, because the world population was growing faster than Christianity itself. So how can we ever baptize everybody? Does it mean that all those unreached people are excluded from God's grace of salvation? Rahner's answer is again, "No." Rahner argues that, God being both Creator and Savior, the historical limitation of the Church cannot limit the divine universal and supernatural salvation even if it tried; for wherever full humanity is realized, there is God's redemptive grace present to make it possible. This is true, irrespective of time and place, for these temporal historical limitations are not binding to God the Transcendent, Omnipresent Mystery.

37. See Acts 9:1-23, 15:1-35; Galatians; and Rom. 2-4. Paul, a self-styled Apostle to the Gentiles, seems to have successfully transformed the nature of Christianity and its theology from a narrow Jewish base and adapted it for a universal (Catholic) creative advance into the whole world.

38. Such as the vanished Essenes of Qumran Community. Juda-

ism at the time of Jesus was already divided into doctrinal parties or sects, such as the Sadducees and the rigorist Pharisees who, contrary to the Sadducees, believed in the resurrection, spirits and angels; see Acts 23:6-9.

39. Because our present Christianity is basically Pauline, especially in the Protestant churches, which adopted Paul's principle of <u>sola gratia</u>, particularly as taught in both his letters to the Romans and the Galatians, and Martin Luther being the most keen and famous exponent of this Pauline doctrine. However, modern Roman Catholic theologians like Kung and Karl Rahner agree with this doctrine; cf. Rahner, <u>Grace in Freedom</u> (New York: Herder & Herder, 1969), pp. 101-111; <u>Foundations of Christian Faith</u>, pp. 116-170; see also the literature in note 21 above.

40. For example, see Rom. 1-4; 1 Cor. 5-10; Galatians; Hebrews; and the Johannine epistles which deal with heresies originating from Greek and Oriental dualistic philosophies. If Christianity had remained Jewish, such problems as those that these epistles were written to address, would probably not have arisen, and consequently, the Epistles as we have them in the New Testament today would not have existed!

41. This claim is based on the fact that Orthodox Judaism was becoming increasingly strictly monotheistic. Consequently, Jesus would have been understood, not as God become incarnate, as John puts it (John 1:1-4, 14), but rather as a "divine man" (theios-aner), "Son of Man" as Mark puts it (cf. Mark 2:10), with the divine power and messianic mission to Israel and beyond, since he was God's eschatological gift of grace and salvation to all nations (Luke 2:30-32) for the glory of Israel, which would become the new central focus (Zion) for the world as the terrestrial symbol of divine light and salvation in the world (cf. Gen. 12:1-4; Isa. 51:1-16, 52:9, 53:12, 55:5 and 59:16-61:3). Main-line Christianity insists that such a bringer of divine salvation should be God himself, as orthodox Christology and soteriology teach. It is mainly, therefore, on the question of the divinity of Christ that other universal religions such as Islam part company with Christianity; see the Quran (Koran), "Suras" (or chapters) entitled "Mary," "Christians," "Infidels," "God," "Jesus," "People of the Book," and "Judgment."

42. For Israel's requirement for a monotheistic conception of God, see the "Shema"; "Hear O Israel... I am the Lord your God... You shall not have other gods besides me..." (Deut. 5:1-21, Exod. 20:1-17). The oneness (<u>monos</u>) of God is the core of the "Shema" or the decalogue; see Bernhard W. Anderson, <u>Understanding the Old Testament</u> (Englewood Cliffs: Prentice-Hall, Inc., 1975), pp. 356-357; von Rad, <u>Old Testament Theology</u>, pp. 239 ff.

43. See Acts 15:1-35; Paul's letter to the Galatians and the Romans.

44. Ibid. Peter had a big problem of indecision (Gal. 2:11-21). But he must have overcome it adequately for him to be able to undertake a foreign missionary venture in the cosmopolitan city of Rome, where he reportedly perished in Nero's Christian persecution in 64 A.D., being crucified upside down at his request, according to popular but unvalidated tradition; Eusebius, The History of the Church from Christ to Constantine, trans. G.A. Williamson (Minneapolis: Augsburg Publishing House, 1965) 25:1, pp. 104 ff.

45. A doctrine taught by Jesus but without any further elaboration as it is recorded in the New Testament; see Matt. 9:17, Mark 2:22, Luke 5:37-38. Stephen's address and martyrdom (Acts 6-7) played an indirect key part in Paul's conversion and theological formation. In this sense Stephen was a forerunner of St. Paul almost in the same way that John the Baptist was a forerunner of Jesus (cf. Mark 1:1-15 and compare it with Acts 6:1-9:31).

46. See Rom. 3-11; cf. Heb. 1-5. St. Augustine, like Justin Martyr, could say that what was unique in Christianity was the incarnation of the Logos in a particular individual man, Jesus. See The City of God, Book VIII; Confessions, Book VIII; and Justin Martyr's Dialogues and I Apol.

47. Cf. II Cor. 5:16-20; I Cor. 13; John 10:10, 15:12-17; and 1 John 4:7-21.

48. With the exception of Paul (cf. Rom. 2-4), statements such as "I am the Way, and the truth and the life; and no one comes to the Father but by me" (John 14:6) and the claims in John 6:35-40 and 10:1-18 were possibly meant by the evangelist to exclude non-Christians or unbelievers from Christ's benefits and God's eternal life. But it is also possible that such exclusiveness had an apologetic and evangelistic purpose, namely, to frighten non-believers into faith, and not to deny them divine salvation that John has previously announced to be universal in scope (John 3:16).

After all, Christ as the creative Logos of God mentioned in the prologue was also the Life-Giver to all the world, to whom he was now adding even more life to make it fully abundant (John 10:10). So then it appears that, in the final analysis, John does not intend to deny anybody God's salvation in Christ. It is precisely because Christ is the only "way, and the truth and the life" and no one ever goes to God except through Christ, that we can be sure that all God's salvation is through Christ and that all those who have known the truth and have lived according to it are correctly termed "Christians" whether they know it or not, hence "anonymous Christians" even to themselves!

49. See, e.g., Luke 23:1-5. However, for the Christians this failure of justice and the apparent triumph of evil and death was overcome by the resurrection, which proved that the power of God is stronger than that of evil. Similarly, the power of God to

save is stronger than the power of evil and destruction.

50. Cf. "I believed in Him so strongly that I wanted to take an army and destroy the Jews who crucified Him, if I had not been prevented by the imperial power of Rome from doing so." This is an extract quoted from King Abgar's letter (inauthentic) cited by Eusebius, op. cit., p. 68. Josephus' Book of Antiquities is strongly anti-Semitic. For instance, he is happy that Christ's murder was vindicated by severe famine and a prolonged Roman siege of the City of Jerusalem that finally destroyed the city, including the temple, in 70 A.D.

51. I have myself heard an anti-Semitic sermon preached on this text. The preacher claimed that the current Jewish diaspora and persecution, especially by Hitler, is God's punishment on them for having murdered the innocent Jesus as a criminal and having spared Barabbas the murderer, saying, "Let his blood be upon us and our children."

52. See "The Declaration on the Relationship of the Church to Non-Christian Religions," The Documents of Vatican II, trans. and ed. Walter M. Abbott and Joseph Gallagher (Chicago: Follett Publishing Co., 1966), pp. 660-668. Anti-Semitism is condemned in strong terms: "The Church repudiates all persecutions...mindful of her common patrimony with the Jews, and motivated by the gospel's spiritual love...she deplores the hatred, persecutions and displays of anti-Semitism directed against the Jews at any time from any source" (pp. 665-667). See also notes 19-30 above for the vital information regarding previous Christian persecutions of the Jews based on the charge that the Jews were Christ's murderers to be punished by both God and man.

53. Ibid. This is to my mind the greatest decree of the Council, as it did away with the Tridentine adaptation of Cyprianic Church exclusiveness and bigotry of extra ecclesiam nulla salus, which was the grounding of the Roman Catholic non-ecumenical dogmatic theology. St. Thomas also expounded a strict form of this dogma of extra ecclesiam nulla salus; cf. Summa Theologiae III, qq. 1 ff., especially 8 and 60-65. He excludes heretics, schismatics and non-Christians (non-believers). For Thomas, predestination to salvation includes predestination to these sacraments that were considered essential for salvation (cf. Summa Theologiae III, qq. 60 ff.). However, Thomas complicates the issue when he says that the faithful Old Testament community belongs to this same redemptive church (cf. Summa Theologiae III, q. 3).

54. Cf. Rom. 1-5. Paul considers God as "One," "the Creator" and source of all revelation, salvation and judgment. There is no partiality with God. God's love and salvation are unconditional (Rom. 5:6-8) and salvific for all human beings. Since none is excluded by God from salvation, nor should we on his behalf by our own narrow mindedness, pride, bigotry, and failure to love the neighbor as ourselves (Mark 12:29-31; I Cor. 13). The doc-

trine of *extra ecclesiam nulla salus* was rightly repudiated by Vatican II, since it put a false limit and condition on God's universal, unconditional, gratuitous, supernatural revelation and salvation (see previous note, above).

55. Ibid. See also Karl Rahner's writings mentioned in note 21. In addition, see Karl Rahner and Joseph Ratzinger, *Revelation and Tradition*; Karl Rahner, *Kerygma and Dogma* (New York: Herder and Herder, 1969); "The Order of Redemption within the Order of Creation," *The Christian Commitment* (New York: Sheed and Ward, 1963), pp. 38-74; "Nature and Grace," in *Nature and Grace* (New York: Sheed and Ward, 1964), pp. 114-149.

56. For a fuller treatment of this controversy, see: Henry Chadwick, *Early Christian Thought and Classical Tradition* (New York: Oxford University Press, 1966), pp. 1 ff.; Tertullian, *de Praescr*. 7; Justin Martyr, *Apol*. 46.

57. This controversy over philosophy and its role in Christian theology still rages on, especially among Protestant theologians. For instance, Karl Barth rejected the alliance between theology and philosophy and attacked both Emil Brunner and Paul Tillich on this matter and the question of "natural theology," to which philosophical theology gives basis and logical validation. See: Karl Barth, *Church Dogmatics I* for this debate; Brunner, *The Christian Doctrine of Creation and Redemption, Dogmatics II* (Philadelphia: The Westminster Press, 1952); *Revelation and Reason* (Philadelphia: The Westminster Press, 1946); *Natural Theology*, comprising "Nature and Grace" by Emil Brunner and the emphatic "No" in reply by Karl Barth (London: Geoffrey Bles, 1946). For Paul Tillich's basic position, see his collected essays on the subject in *What Is Religion?*, trans. James Luther Adams (New York: Harper and Row Publishers, 1969) and *Systematic Theology* 2:71-162. Tillich's position is that philosophy is a tool and resource for doing theology without being held captive by it.

Hegel's attempt to turn theology into philosophy (cf. *Phenomenology of Spirit*, section on Absolute Knowledge; *Christian Religion: Lectures on the Philosophy of Religion, Part III; The Revelatory, Consummate, Absolute Religion*, trans. and ed. Peter C. Hodgson (AAR: Scholars Press, 1979) represents another extreme, approached cautiously by most theologians.

If we adopt the helpful Aristotelian axiom that virtue lies in the middle, it will then follow that in the debate above, Brunner and Tillich have a more moderate stand and therefore a better position than Barth and his followers. Karl Rahner, whose thought underlies most of this book, is very much like Tillich as regards this debate; cf., e.g., "Theology and Anthropology," *The Word in History*, ed. Patrick T. Burke (New York: Sheed and Ward, 1968); "Philosophy and Theology," *Theological Investigations* 6:77-81; "Philosophy and Philosophising in Theology," *Theological Investigations* 9:46-63; "Christian Humanism," ibid., 187-204.

It is unfortunate that, as regards this debate, the Anglican Church of Uganda has decided to fall within the line of Tertullian and Karl Barth. For instance, during my recent philosophical-theological inquiry for this book, I was counseled by one bishop that the Bible warns against philosophy, and he went on to read to me Colossians 2:8, "See to it that no one makes a prey of you by philosophy and empty deceit, according to human tradition ... and not according to Christ." This position is typical of the whole Ugandan Church leadership. Consequently, at the moment the Major Seminary itself at Mukono offers no course in either philosophy or fundamental theology.

Unfortunately, Uganda and the rest of Africa will not be able to do much in constructive African theology unless local philosophy and Western religious philosophy have been carefully studied as a possible medium of God's revelation and vehicle for local theological contextualization. Like Justin Martyr, Origen and Augustine found Platonism a useful tool in explaining their new Christian faith to their contemporaries; St. Thomas found Aristotelianism handy for his theological task in the Middle Ages; and presently theologians like John Cobb and Norman Pittenger have found a modern theological tool in Whitehead's Process Philosophy. The African Christian thinkers need the right philosophical tools in order to accomplish their own theological task of contextualizing the Christian faith that has been received from the foreign Western missionaries and former colonialists, into the local indigenous cultural context, in order to render this Christian faith essentially meaningful.

It is hoped that this process will unmask the potent power of the Gospel and thus enable it to transform us as Africans more effectively into the very authentic human beings that God intends us to be as Africans, as such, and not poor imitations of our former Western imperialists, colonialists and/or the white foreign Western missionaries. God created us Africans to be Africans and not something else. Therefore, the task of the Gospel should ideally be to enable us to become the true Africans God wants us to be. This is, indeed the very essence of the good news of God's incarnation in Christ for us and nothing else.

58. The West was characterized by Rome's political and administrative centrality and pride of being the capital of the Roman Empire, and therefore, the pivot of the known civilized world. Lacking in the Eastern Greek tradition of speculative philosophy, the Church in the West began to imitate the administrative structure of the civil Roman Empire and to pattern the Church hierarchy, authority and structure accordingly. It is not surprising, therefore, that the institution of the Papacy developed in Rome and probably in competition with the Roman Emperor! The Petrine texts (Matt. 16:17-20; John 21:15-17) were used later on to prove the validity of the Papal position and not prior to this institutional development; cf. Philip Schaff, History of the Christian Church 2:121-193, 228-619.

It has been suggested by African historians that, because of this Latin authoritarian ecclesiology and Roman imperial repression, North Africa welcomed the conquering Arab Muslims in the seventh century in order to free themselves from Roman imperialism that had become synonymous with Christianity. There is no evidence that local Christians put up a fight to resist conquest or the subsequent Islamization. This in part accounts for the disappearance of Christianity in Latin North Africa, whereas it survived in Egypt and Ethiopia. In Egypt and Ethiopia, the Coptic (native) Christianity survived as evidence to the validity of this phenomenon.

59. Consequently, whereas the Eastern Church was generally not threatened by schism and rebellion as the Latin Church in the West, it was threatened by heresy. See, e.g., J.N.D. Kelly, Early Christian Doctrines (New York: Harper & Row, 1960), pp. 223-400.

60. See Justin Martyr, Apologies and Dialogue with Tripho, which develop an acceptable divine universal salvation based on the universal efficacy of divine truth available in God's cosmic Logos. However, Origen developed this position further to an unacceptable conclusion when he speculated (too much) in his teaching on "Apocatastasis" that all free moral creatures, that is all human beings, angels, evil spirits and even the devil, will all finally repent, and share in the supernatural gratuitous grace and divine salvation (cf. Hom. in Lev. VII:2, de Princ. IV, 4:9). Clement of Alexandria and Gregory of Nyssa taught (to some extent) this kind of universalism, whereas St. Augustine and St. Thomas repudiated and negated it in their own teaching and affirmation of predestination; see, e.g., Augustine, De diversis quaestionibus ad Simplicianum I, q.2; De spiritu littera, 52-66; De natura et gratia; De gratia Christi, 13-27; De gratia et libero arbitrio; De corruptione et gratia 11:26 ff.; De praedestinatione sanctorum; St. Thomas, Contra Gentiles III, Chs. 147-163; Summa Theologiae I-II, qq. 110-113, I q. 23.

Again, neither of these extremes, that is, complete universalism or strict predestination, is tenable. The truth appears to lie between these two extremes, i.e. God's gratuitous universal will to save should be combined with the human free will and freedom either to accept or reject this divine unconditional proffer of gratuitous salvific grace, thus enabling full human self-actualization and self-determination in personal freedom in the presence of God and his gratuitous salvific grace that enables us to be and to become what we choose to become. Consequently, the human being can accept full responsibility for one's actions without blaming the bad ones on the devil and attributing all the good ones to God, thus absolving oneself of any responsibility for either category of deeds, as the Balokole in Uganda try to do.

Many would assert that predestination, like fatalism, has no place in Christianity, as it disregards God's universal love and will to save, while downgrading human dignity and responsibility by the very act of denying the reality of human freedom, irrespective of sin and historical or environmental conditioning. What constitutes a human being is freedom and whatever negates this freedom of both human self-transcendence and action, both limits and negates humanity. Therefore, the fewer the negations the better, since the God whom we worship and imitate in Christ is the power as well as the lure for positive self-actualization, whereas evil and its destructive power is the resistance to this process and even the reversal of this positive process.

61. See also Eusebius, Hist. Eccl. I, 4, where "pre-Christian" men such as Abraham, Moses, etc., are said to be "Christians."

62. Cf., e.g., Cyprian's harsh administrative and episcopal treatment of his opponents in schism: "The spouse of Christ ... preserves us for God...enrols into the Kingdom the sons she has borne. Whoso stands aloof from the Church...is cut off from the promises of the Church; and he that leaves the Church of Christ attains not to Christ's rewards. He is an alien, an outcast, an enemy. He cannot have God for his father who has not the Church for his mother. If any one was able to escape outside Noah's ark, then he also escapes who is outside the doors of the Church" (De Catholicae Unitate, 6). See also Epistle LXVI.7, in which he claims that the bishop is the symbol of the Church and 35, therefore, all Christians desiring salvation should obey their bishop, for "the bishop is the Church!"

The doctrine of extra ecclesiam nulla salus was formulated in this ecclesiastical internal strife, schism and rivalry. It is seen by many as a negative, bitter, revengeful castigation of rivals by denying them salvation, and as the most unchristian attitude toward an enemy, as it ignores Christ's commandment to love our neighbors and even our enemies, too (cf. Matt. 5:43-48; Mark 12:29-31; John 15:12-17; 1 Cor. 13; 1 John 4:13-21). See also notes 52, 53 and 58.

63. Ibid. See also Vatican "Decree on Ecumenism," Documents of Vatican II (ed. Abbott), pp. 336-371, and "Declaration on the Relationship of the Church to Non-Christian Religions," ibid., pp. 656-672.

64. See, e.g., front page, The Tennesseean and The Banner, Aug. 31, 1980; Time, Sept. 29, 1980, p. 85 (among other publications and television news headlines).

65. See Reinhold Niebuhr, The Nature and Destiny of Man 2:86 ff.; Jurgen Moltman, Man: Christian Anthropology in the Conflicts of the Present, pp. 47-96; Paul Tillich, Systematic Theology 3:382 ff.; Karl Rahner, "Atheism and Implicit Christianity," Theological Investigations 9:145-164.

66. Failure to love the neighbor is perhaps the primary cause of some major political and economic problems in the world today. For instance, the division of West-East ideological conflicts, nuclear arms race, and the division of rich and poor nations, imperialist and dominated nations in the world, tribalism, most coups d'etat, and repressive governments can all be attributed mainly to this failure in unconditional love for the neighbor.

67. E.G., the United States of America's motto is "In God We Trust." And Uganda's motto is "For God and My Country," despite

the kind of ungodly and unpatriotic state of affairs that has prevailed there for a long time!

68. See notes 32 and 33 above. Christian unconditional love can be said to be the origin, essence, grounding, uniqueness and objective of Christianity. It is possibly this emphasis on unconditional love that makes Christianity the "Absolute Religion," as it enables reconciliation between an individual and his neighbor in free love and unmerited forgiveness, and in so doing gains fellowship with God (cf. 1 John 4:13-21; Mark 12:29-31; Rom. 13:8; 1 Cor. 13; Gal. 5:14, and James 2:8).

69. This acceptance would possibly help to neutralize political, religious, cultural and racial prejudice and our unwillingness to treat those who are different from us as human beings. Love is believed to transcend most barriers to human relationships if given an opportunity to function well.

70. The problems of Uganda, such as the religious wars of the last century, exclusive tribalism in the Church, employment and politics, and Catholic-Anglican rivalry and hostility, are clear evidence of failure in Chrisitian unconditional love (Agape). Idi Amin's ascendance to power in a coup d'etat of January 25, 1971, and his consequent repressive regime and ruthless mass murder of rivals and the Christian elite (including the Most Rev. Jenani Luwum, the Anglican Archbishop of Uganda) that left the world aghast, is a clear illustration of this point. If Christians, who are about 80 percent of the Ugandan population, had loved each other and their Muslim neighbors (who are just about seven percent), Idi Amin, an evil, illiterate Muslim, would probably not have risen to power in Uganda.

Idi Amin's rise to power and consequent misrule of Uganda, and consequent overthrow, with President Nyerere's help, was a lesson to Ugandans and their African neighbors about the folly and futility of human greed, pride and malignant tribalism against the efficacy of love, unity and cooperation. (Continuing instability in Uganda is also evidence that some people never seem to learn their lesson well from history, therefore, they are bound to repeat it to their own chagrin. Cf. Toward a Free and Democratic Uganda: The Basic Principles and Policies of the National Resistance Movement (N.R.M.), (Kampala-Uganda, n.d.). For more details of the history of conflict in Uganda, see Henry Kyemba, The State of Blood: The Inside Story of Idi Amin's Reign of Terror (London: Paddington Press, Ltd., 1977); see also AF Press Clips, Bureau of African Affairs, U.S. Dept. of State, Washington, D.C., May 25, 1982, XVII No. 21, and June 4, 1982, XVII No. 22; articles on Uganda by Charles T. Powers for an update on the Ugandan situation. It is not surprising, therefore, that Powers himself was arrested, imprisoned and beaten during his journalistic assignment to Uganda in May 1982.

Nevertheless, love (Agape) can overcome most of this hostility and conflict. Indeed, obedience to Christ's commandment to love the neighbor is the healing salvific divine power that Uganda perhaps needs most today and not more weapons, revolutions or even money! It can almost be said, again, that "All we need is love," as was correctly observed and sung by the Beatles during the world social and political unrest of the 60s.

It should also be pointed out here that the rivalry and hostility between the Roman Catholics and the Anglicans, the two major Christian denominations in Uganda, is so bad and thoroughly unchristian that the two church bodies in Uganda are usually thought of as two mutually exclusive religions!

Nevertheless, it is only love that can reconcile even these two neighbors, who should know better, but rather choose exclusiveness, as they both individually claim to be the only authentic Church of Christ and faithful custodian of the Gospel. (See, e.g., Tom Tuma and Phares Mutibwa, eds., A Century of Christianity in Uganda, 1877-1977, published by the Church of Uganda, 1978; F. B. Welbourn, Politics and Religion in Uganda (Nairobi: East African Publishing Co., 1965); J. F. Taylor, Christianity and Politics in Africa (London: Harmondsworth, 1957); J. J. Taylor, The Growth of the Church in Buganda (London: S.C.M. Press, 1958); and Roland Oliver, The Missionary Factor in East Africa.

71. It can be affirmed that the presence of evil in the world is the main problem. Plato himself speculated that since there is evil in the world, God must be either Good and less powerful to get rid of it or Omnipotent but lacking in goodness! For this discussion, see John Hick, Evil and the God of Love (New York: Harper and Row, 1978), pp. 25-27, 32 ff., 72-75. The whole book should be read for its treatment of evil in the world while the Christian claim is that it was created and is controlled by the same God who is Good and Omnipotent.

For other views on this topic, see St. Thomas, Summa Theologiae I, qq. 2-3, 9-10, 47-49; De Malo I. 1; Contra Gentiles III, Chs. 7-9, 18; Summa Theologiae II q. 42; Sent. 44:1, 2, 6; and Whitehead, Process and Reality, ed. David Griffin and Donald W. Sherburne (New York: MacMillan, 1978), pp. 340-351. See Whitehead's treatment of evil here and in his other works such as the Adventures of Ideas (New York: MacMillan Publishing Co., Inc., 1967), pp. 284 ff. His doctrine on the "Divine Lure" helps me to see how God can offer gratuitous salvific grace to human beings and enable them to move towards positive, maximum self-actualization of themselves in complete personal freedom and self-determination (cf. pp. 25, 184-189, 224, 259, 263-277, and 334). The problem of evil is a serious one for both believers and theologians. It is perhaps the main philosophical-theological argument against the existence of God; at least against the loving omnipotent God as Christianity teaches. For instance, during my recent trip to Uganda, where people have suffered a great deal, I heard comments such as this: "God has gone away on leave!"

72. There was generally a mass murder of natives during the last century by Western imperialist nations in many parts of Africa during the conquest of Africa and the establishment of the colonial governments. In East Africa, the Germans used brutal force to overcome African resistance in the southern part of

Tanzania (then known as Tanganyika) and later on to put down the Maji Maji rebellion. In Uganda, King Kabalega's nationalist resistance was crushed by the British, who enlisted the help of their Buganda allies. This was also generally true in Kigezi. But perhaps the most injustice was done to the Kikuyu, who were conquered and deprived of their fertile land by the British settlers. This injustice led to the well-known Mau Mau nationalist liberation movement and prolonged war in Kenya, in which thousands of innocent Africans perished; cf. Rosberg Nottingham and Karaari Njama, Mau Mau from Within (London/Nairobi: Oxford University Press, 1968). For a complete history of East Africa in its socio-economic and political context, see R. Oliver's History of East Africa, 2 vols. They are a standard reference text for this area.

73. Ibid. Most of the forced African labor was required by the British settlers in Kenya and the Germans in Tanzania before World War I, when they lost their territorial possessions in Africa following their defeat in the war.

74. The Portuguese Roman Catholics undertook missionary activity in Africa in the 17th century without much success, as they demanded that baptized African kings and individuals should swear allegiance to the King of Portugal; see Stephen Neill, A History of Christian Missions (New York: Penguin Books, 1977), pp. 197-200. It is also known that some Portuguese missionaries involved themselves in African slave trade in order to support their mission, and as a result they were resented and finally rejected together with their religion by the Africans in the Kongo Kingdom and Angola where they were working.

Effective African missionary activity in the interior of Africa did not take place until the second half of the 19th century. Unfortunately, this is also the time when European imperialist nations were invading and conquering Africa. The fact that missionaries were soon followed by the imperialists in Africa has given rise to the dictum: "The Cross before the Flag!" See Stephen Neill, op. cit., pp. 368-389; C. P. Groves, The Planting of Christianity in Africa, 4 vols. (London: Lutterworth Press, 1948-1958), vol. 1 and first half of vol. 2; Kenneth Scott Latourette, A History of Christianity (New York: Harper & Row, 1975) 2:1302-1333.

75. Uganda is possibly the most Christian and Anglican country in Africa; cf. Stephen Neill, op. cit., pp. 368-389; Adrian Hastings, African Christianity (New York: The Seabury Press, 1976), pp. 29-32. It was no coincidence that the first Papal visit ever to an African nation was a visit to Uganda by Pope Paul VI in 1969. The Ugandan martyrs were also canonized by the Pope at this visit. He also consecrated the African Saints' and Uganda Martyrs' Shrine at Namugongo, which has become an African Holy Christian Center for Christian pilgrimage.

With the exception of the nomadic cattle-keeping Karamojong of Northeastern Uganda, who have been recently decimated by famine because of severe drought and the loss of their cattle, there are almost no more "pagans" in Uganda. Nevertheless, the traditional religion is not yet dead. Ironically, it has become the very grounding for Christianity; cf. J. Mbiti, African Religion and Philosophy, pp. 219 ff., 360 ff. Most of all, the African world view, metaphysics and ontology are still deeply grounded in African traditional religious culture, and whereas Christianity tends to divide the Africans, the traditional religion tends to reunite them.

76. See notes 4 and 21 above.

77. Omuntu is the local Ugandan Bantu word for the people of Kigezi, Ankole, Bunyoro, Toro, Buganda and others, meaning "a human being." It is neutral as regards gender. Here, the claim is that salvation consists in our full acceptance to be what we were created to be, namely, human beings qua human beings and not some other super beings such as angels or any other immortal spirits (if there be any). See notes 11 and 58 above.

78. In Uganda and Rwanda, "Obuntu" is regarded as the essence of "Omuntu". The "Obuntu" are abstract human qualities that make a person humane, such as love, understanding, being considerate, kindness, generosity, wisdom, politeness, bravery and the like. "Omuntu" without "Obuntu" is the kind termed "wicked," "savage," "cruel," "witch," "anti-social," "mean," "hater of people" and the like.

79. Logos is used here in the sense of John 1:1-4, 9-10,14. That is the Word that was in the beginning with God, the medium of creation, life, light, illumination and truth (John 14:6) that became enfleshed (Incarnate) in Jesus of Nazareth (John 1:14).

80. This statement suggests that Jesus should be viewed as the archetypal human being to whom humanity should look for what true humanity should be like in its essential quality. The qualities of humanness (Obuntu) mentioned in note 78 were definitely manifested in their fullness in his life. Hence the example and origin of the commandment to love the neighbor and even the enemy (Mark 5:43-48). Jesus vividly epitomized the fullness of this unconditional love and humane quality when he asked God his Father to forgive his executioners as they mocked him and nailed him to the cross (Luke 23:34). This view is in full harmony with Emil Brunner, Karl Barth, Rahner and others who say that Christian anthropology presupposes Christology (cf. Brunner, Man in Revolt, pp. 98 ff.; Barth, Church Dogmatics III:II; Rahner, Foundations of Christian Faith, pp. 178-219. See also Eph. 4:13, which states that Christ is the measure of our humanity).

81. See notes 11, 33, 36 and 48. See also Karl Rahner, "Anonymous Christians," Theological Investigations 9:145-164; "Reflections on the Unity of Neighbour and the Love of God," Theological Investigations 6:231-249; Foundations of Christian Faith, pp. 311-321; "Observations Concerning Anonymous Christianity," Theological Investigations 12:163 ff.; Grace in Freedom, pp. 81-86; Anita Roper, The Anonymous Christian, with an after-

word, "The Anonymous Christian According to Karl Rahner" by Klaus Riesenhuber, S.J. (New York: Sheed and Ward, 1966); Donald Maloney, "Rahner and the Anonymous Christian," America 23 (1970), pp. 348-350.

82. Ibid. See also note 10 above.

83. See notes 10, 11, 36, 48 and 81 above.

84. See notes 7, 11 and 37. See also John 3:16-17, 10:10; Rom. 5-6; and 2 Cor. 5:17. Divine salvation is here viewed as a present reality, though it remains future-oriented in anticipation of fulfillment and perfection. Rahner suggests that if salvation is not present now, neither will it be present in the future, namely, after death, for death is the final and irrevocable eternal ratification of our personal free historical life by God. This is also the final divine judgment of our personal lives as they acquire eternal divine approval or disapproval and hence enter the state of eternal blessedness for those whose lives are deemed worthy, or eternal isolation and remorse for those who were unloving, uncaring, the foolish and the wicked; cf. Matt. 25; Karl Rahner, Foundations of Christian Faith, pp. 311 ff.

85. Modern theologians emphasize that God is ceaselessly active, creating something new, saving and transforming the old (2 Cor. 5:17). God is the ground of all creativity, transformation, novelty and advancement in improvement; cf. Alfred North Whitehead, Process and Reality, Part I, Chs. 2, 3; Part II, Chs. 2, 8, 10; Part III, Ch. 1; Part IV, Chs. 1, 4; and Part V, Chs. 1, 2; Lewis S. Ford, The Lure of God: A Biblical Backgrond for Process Theism (Philadelphia: Fortress Press, 1978), Chs. 1, 2, 3; Whitehead, Adventures in Ideas, Parts II and III; Science and the Modern World (New York: MacMillan Publishing Co., 1925), Chs. 7-13; and Religion in the Making (entire book).

86. Cf., e.g., John 1:1-4, 14; 3:16-21; Rom. 1-5. As creation is entirely the work of God, so is supernatural salvation. St. Augustine saw no room for Pelagianism in supernatural salvation; cf. De Gratia Cristi. See also notes 21, 31, 36, 48, 53-56 and 81 above. The human being can just respond in freedom and grace to God's prior proffer of salvation in grace with either a "Yes" and acceptance, or rejection and therefore with a "No" to this divine gratuitous proffer of grace and salvation.

87. As it tends to be the case! See notes 10, 12 and 82 above.

88. Ibid. See also note 86.

89. See note 8 above. The love of neighbor is towards a concrete person and not a mere abstraction. Cf. Matt. 25:31-46.

90. See, e.g., Matt. 5:43-48; Mark 12:29-31; and especially

Luke 10:25-37. The Good Samaritan here can be a Muslim or even a Communist as regards our own modern global context.

91. Ibid., and see also notes 10-12, 81 and 85 above. The missionary task of the Church is the announcing of the Good News that, by virtue of the incarnation, all human beings have become friends and "blood brothers and sisters" in Christ, and that we are therefore, to love all human beings as we love ourselves and members of our immediate families.

This approach makes sense in Africa, where the family ties are still strong and obligatory for each family member. However, it may be ineffective in the West, where family life and family ties have been disrupted, often in the name of individualism, personal freedom and self-fulfillment.

If unconditional love for the neighbor is adopted as the criterion for salvation and true Christianity (cf. notes 32 and 33 above), then "anonymous Christians" can be discerned on this basis.

92. Cf., e.g., Karl Rahner, "Anonymous Christianity and the Missionary Task of the Church," _Theological Investigations_ 12:161-178; "Observations on the Problem of the 'Anonymous Christians'," _Theological Investigations_ 14:280-294; "The Commandment of Love in Relation to the Other Commandments," _Theological Investigations_ 5:439-467; and "Reflections on the Unity of the Love of Neighbour and the Love of God," _Theological Investigations_ 6:231-249; _Grace in Freedom_, pp. 81-86, 183-264.

93. See notes 53, 59 and 62.

94. Cf. John 1:1-4, 9-14; Isa. 55:11; and note 84 above. See also, e.g., Karl Rahner, "Nature and Grace," _Nature and Grace_ (New York: Sheed and Ward, 1964), pp. 114-149; _Grace in Freedom_, pp. 203-265; "The Order of Redemption within the Order of Creation," _The Christian Commitment_ (New York: Sheed and Ward, 1963), pp. 38-74; "The Theology of Freedom," _Theological Investigations_ 6:178-196; "On the Dignity and Freedom of Man," _Theological Investigations_ 2:235-263; _Hearers of the Word_, Chs. 5-11; Alfred North Whitehead, _Adventures of Ideas_ (London: MacMillan Publishers, 1933), IV, V, VI-X, pp. 69-86, 103-174, 284 ff.; _Process and Reality_, Part V; _Religion in the Making_ (New York: MacMillan, 1926), II-IV, pp. 47-160.

CHAPTER II

KARL RAHNER'S CHRISTIAN ANTHROPOLOGICAL AND PHILOSOPHICAL FRAMEWORK AS A BASIS FOR A BROAD CHRISTIAN REFLECTION ON AUTHENTIC HUMAN EXISTENCE AND SOTERIOLOGY

Having outlined the history and development of some of the familiar narrow and exclusive soteriological doctrines in the previous chapter, we now turn to the problem of salvation itself. Since Karl Rahner has been the greatest expounder of the acceptable modern Catholic Christian doctrine of God's gratuitous universal salvation to include the non-Christians,[1] he will subsequently be accepted and treated as such for this book. Accordingly, he will be regarded as the normative spokesman, expounder and defender of the modern Christian inclusive doctrine of supernatural salvation, particularly as it finds its logical expression and climax in his teaching on "anonymous Christianity."[2]

Rahner's theology is grounded in his philosophical-theological anthropology.[3] This anthropological starting point is very advantageous for his theological task, which is the interpretation of human existence as it is lived daily before God and fellow human beings in the community. This anthropological method enables Rahner to discern better and to explain more insightfully God's universal gratuitous self-communication in grace to all human beings he has created, in order to draw them to the self-realization in a more complete manner and towards the ultimate destiny of their being and fulfillment of life in his mystery.[4] By so doing, Rahner is again enabled to discern more meaningfully and insightfully the co-extensive nature and correlation between the divine act of creation and that of salvation as two moments of the same divine creative process and not two separate events in time and space.[5] Consequently, Rahner is able to perceive that creation requires salvation as its guidance to positive self-actualization, maturity, wholeness, health, wholesome self-enjoyment, joy, and happiness as fulfillment. This is why he insists that salvation must be a present reality for those to be saved, since divine salvation is not to be regarded as just the fulfillment in the distant future, but rather that it is chiefly the radical divine humanization of the individuals here and now in this categorial world.[6]

Since for Rahner anthropology is the starting point for Christian theology, including revelation and soteriology, we should look at his anthropological framework in order to appreciate his theology, and in our case his concepts of universal divine revelation, gratuitous grace and salvation, which are the three basic concepts underlying his great Christian inclusive teaching on God's gratuitous universal salvation and "anonymous Christianity."

The Human Being as a Mystery

Karl Rahner affirms that the human being, like God in whose image he or she has been created, is similarly a mystery.[7] Consequently, the human being is a mystery to himself or herself and to those around him or her. Rahner contends that, because the human being is a mystery, he or she asks infinite questions of his or her origin, destiny and about his or her being as a person. Similarly, the human being asks questions of humanity in general. But in the end, no definitive answers are found because, like God, the infinite cosmic creative Mystery, the human being is likewise a mystery. Rahner puts this point simply in the following terms:

> Man is a mystery ... What do we mean by man? My reply, stripped to its essentials, is simple: Man is the question to which there is no answer.[8]

For Rahner, therefore, human knowledge and self-investigation cannot exhaust this human mystery, as it is infinite. In this respect it could also be argued that the writer of Genesis, who declared that "God created man in his own image, in the image of God he created him; male and female he created them..." (1:27), was also in a sense trying to say the same thing, but in his own way.[9] Rahner is conveying this same message of Genesis in a more contemporary language, utilizing modern philosophical anthropology, in order to make this divine Word relevant and revelatory for the modern man and contemporary theology, which seeks to address the contemporary human existential questions in a meaningful manner that will enable God's Word of invitation to a fuller life to be heard.

Rahner, like the writer of the book of Genesis, sees human uniqueness as divine and purposeful. This human uniqueness points back to the majesty, skill and power of God the Creator as well as pointing to the affinity between God as the Creator and the human being as the creature, the very affinity that enables meaningful, effective communication and fellowship between God and the human being to take place. Rahner explicates this affinity between God and the human being as follows:

> Man is a mystery. He is more than this. He is the mystery, not because he is open to the mystery of the incomprehensible fullness of God, but also because God has expressed this mystery as his own. Assuming that God wanted to express himself in the empty void and that he wanted to call his Word into that void, how could he do anything other than create in man an inner hearing of the Word and express his Word in such a way that the self-expression of that Word and its being heard become one?[10]

For Karl Rahner, then, the human being is God's unique creature that is able to "hear God's Word." In other words, the human being is a creature radically oriented to God as its main constitutive characteristic elements.[11] This prior divine ontological attunement of the human being to its origin and destiny in the Infinite Mystery, is, for Rahner, the distinguishing mark of human beings from the rest of animality of which the human being is part.[12] This election of the human being by God to be a special creature in creation and to be God's categorial representative in the world is symbolized by the special human features which participate in divine qualities to which they have affinity, the chief one being human self-transcendence to an Infinite Horizon which Rahner calls God.[13] The other unique features of the human being include the capacity for unrestricted creative love, which is, according to the Bible, the main definitive quality of God,[14] intellect,[15] spirit, freedom, language, a refined neurological system, a well-developed and well-coordinated body.

However, since the human being is a historical being and has evolved like and along with the rest of the creatures, there is also some human sharing in animal qualities. The human being, despite his/her being akin to God in respect to the transcendental qualities, biologically still remains akin to the animals. For instance, the human being has physical needs just as the other animals do, such as the need for food, shelter, security, sex, reproduction, the nurture and protection of the offspring. Similarly, the human being sometimes gets angry, irrational and brutal. Perhaps even worse than the other animals, the human being is capable of being deliberately, calculatingly, and maliciously mean, sadistic, cruel and destructive. This survival of some malignant animality in the human being, and the human failure or misuse of his/her higher faculties, is called evil because the human being has already been elevated by God to a higher level where love, humaneness and moral responsibility are expected as the universal characteristics of the authentic mode of human behavior.[16]

At this level, humanity is faced with either the acceptance of this gratuitous divine election and elevation in grace to be human beings who are loving, free, moral, responsible creatures accountable to each other and to God, or to sink back into the animality whence humanity has emerged by way of evolution, thereby rejecting God's salvific love and personal freedom, and thereby also rejecting personal moral responsibility as the accountability that is correlative to this exercise of freedom which is constitutive of authentic humanity.[17] Human beings find themselves in a dilemma of choosing in accordance with their higher ideals, because the human being still has within him/her an irrational animality that is usually stronger in its impulsive drive towards mere physical satisfaction, which is most often in sharp contradiction to the perceived divine ideals. Consequently, the human being is racked by guilt when he or she becomes aware that the animality has taken control instead of the divine. St. Paul expressed vividly this very human problem when he wrote of his inner tormenting conflicts and moral struggle as follows:

> So I find it to be a law that when I want to do

> right, evil lies close at hand. For I delight in the law of God, in my innermost self, but I see in my members another law at war with the law of my mind and making me captive to the law of sin which dwells in my members. Wretched man that I am! Who will deliver me from this body of death? Thanks be to God through Jesus Christ our Lord! So then, I of myself serve the law of God with my mind, but with my flesh I serve the law of sin (Romans 7:21-25).[18]

Dualistic philosophical and religious conceptions of humanity that perceived the human being as consisting of spirit and matter that were mutually opposed to each other, as in Platonism,[19] were trying to provide a logical solution to this problematic nature of humanity, which is aware of its own noble and divine ideals and goals, yet does not achieve them because of the hindrance that is experienced by the human being to be a constitutive element of human nature itself.

The popular Platonic idealistic solution to this human existential paradox was that the human soul is divine, eternal and good, but it finds itself trapped in the human body, which is oriented to insatiable pleasure and the satisfaction of physical needs, particularly of food and sex.[20] Therefore, the soul should seek to be freed from this degradation of embodiment in matter that was perceived to be evil. Consequently, for the Platonists, death was to be regarded as a welcome event for a philosopher, as it led to the totality of knowledge, freedom and the beatific vision.[21]

However, for Karl Rahner this Platonic solution is unacceptable to orthodox Christianity. He says that there is no possible division of humanity into the constitutive elements such as spirit and matter (that can be joined together or separated) without destroying the unity of the human being. For Rahner, the human being is an indivisible unity, and that applies to him or her as both matter and spirit, animal and divine, sinner and redeemed, human and divinized.[22]

Rahner rejects all attempts to simplify the question of the nature of the human being into a narrow, comprehensive, final statement such as the popular Aristotelian definition of "animal rationale" or "animal politicus." Rahner insists that the human being is more than he can be described or defined. For instance, the human being is not just rational (as in any case many people are irrational) but is also very intuitive and emotional. A rational person without any kind of intuition or emotion would be more or less a living version of a computer or a robot and not a human being.

To be a human being means more than intellectual ability. That is where Descartes' "cogito ergo sum" fails, too.[23] For instance, what happens when Descartes falls asleep? Does he cease to be since "cogito" has ceased? What about those who are either too young or are mentally handicapped and unable to cogitate; do they possess being or are they even considered to be human beings?

Since human beings are aware of themselves apart from

"cogito," therefore, intellect in "cogito" cannot be the definitive, inclusive definition of a human being. Moreover, that definition would exclude children, the senile, those in sleep or mentally retarded from the category of humanity. Ideally, therefore, we need a definition of the human being that keeps the beasts out, but yet is inclusive enough to permit the inclusion of those individuals who are for some reason unable to cogitate.[24]

Modern depth psychology and psychiatry, especially Freudian, has uncovered the fact that much of the human behavior and activity is controlled by the unconscious mind.[25] This subconscious control is supposedly done in the same way that bodily coordination and involuntary activity are carried out by the involuntary nervous system. This makes it clear that it is inaccurate to say that the human being is characterized by intellect as great thinkers such as Hegel, Descartes, St. Thomas, Aristotle and Plato affirmed. Rahner, like Emil Brunner and Reinhold Niebuhr, affirms that the main uniqueness of the human being is not the intellect but rather human self-transcendence.[26] This human self-transcendence includes intellect, intuition, imagination, emotions, self-awareness and personal freedom.

However, Rahner goes on to affirm that the human being, as God's image, still remains an infinite mystery to himself or herself and to scholars (be it philosophical or theological anthropologists, social and natural scientists such as physicians, biologists, psychologists and psychiatrists). Consequently, Rahner counsels us that the human mystery is an inconceivable complexity and, being such, we should not try to over-simplify it in order to understand it. This is because such a move would amount to a falsification of humanity in order to make it comprehensible to ourselves by a dishonest intellectual amputation of those human complex dimensions that appear either transcendental and non-verifiable by an empirical experiment and inquiry or because they appear to be mere religious formulations claiming divine supernatural revelation as their undemonstrable basis. Rahner sums up his insightful observations on this question as follows:

> Man as we know him today, man of metaphysics, of abstract thought, the creator of his own environment, the space-traveller, the moulder of himself, the man of God and of grace and of the promise of eternal life, precisely this man who is radically distinct from any animal and who at the moment of man's origin...very slowly, took a path that led him so far away from all that is merely animal, yet in such a fashion that he carried with him the whole inheritance of his biological pre-history into these realms of his existence remote from the animals, was there when man began to exist.

Then Rahner goes on to link together creation and biological evolution as one moment of God's creative activity in the following manner:

> . ... what now is historically and externally manifest, was then present as a task and as an active potentiality. Because how his biological, spiritual and divine elements are present in him, they are also plainly and simply to be affirmed of the beginning...Today there are plenty of theories which consider that they must amputate man of one of these dimensions of his existence, in order to understand him...However, ...only a very complex answer...can be a correct one and that any simplification of the problem can lead to error.[27]

Consequently, Rahner affirms the infinite mystery of the human being, origin, development, and ultimate destiny in the infinite Mystery that he calls God. This again implies that the human being is by essential nature a mystery from the very beginning to the end, and that we should not be so presumptuous as to claim the complete knowability of humanity nor to disclaim as illusions the human transcendental dimensions which are elusive to the mind as the materialists tend to think.[28]

The human question, which is well stated by the Psalmist, "What is man, that thou art mindful of him?" (Ps. 8:4, K.J.V.), is therefore, a puzzling question to which there is no definitive answer yet. However, the kind of tentative answer given to this question can be definitive for human existence. For instance, if the human being is understood to be essentially a laborer, as Marxism tends to do, then it follows that the authentic life of a human being is similarly thought to consist in work, and consequently, the human worth is to be measured by the value of one's labor or of the product. Conversely, when the human being is understood to be "a child of God" as in Christianity, then all human beings gain incalculable value and infinite worth as "God's children," fellow brothers and sisters whose chief objective as an authentic life is the contemplation of God and to seek to live in unrestricted love, fellowship and harmony with all human beings.

Furthermore, the human being ideally has to live in respect and in thoughtful preservation of the rest of God's creation and the world on which human life is contingent for life-support, and divine revelation through self-awareness, knowledge, beauty, wonder and mystery which result from the human encounter with this wonder-filled world and God's mystifying cosmic creation in general. This leads us then to the inevitable affirmation that the human being cannot be known nor can he or she know himself or herself as a unique mystery in isolation. Consequently, the human being is only known as such, only within this total background of interrelations in the total context of the world and the totality of God's creation.

The Human Being as the Creature That Asks Questions of Origin and Destiny

Karl Rahner puts great emphasis on the fact that all normal human beings ask endless metaphysical questions, such questions of origins and ultimate destiny as the following: Who am I? Where did I come from? Why am I here? Does human existence have any meaning or purpose? Is death the ultimate end of human life? Is there personal life beyond the grave, and if not, how is a good or virtuous person who suffers in this life for the sake of truth vindicated? These questions and the like are unique to the human being and Rahner attributes them to human self-transcendence and human mystery.[29]

The fact that the human being is a mystery to himself or herself leads to the endless self-quest and self-investigation in order to understand one's own existence. Self-understanding is sought so that the human being can become his or her own responsible master, in terms of informed and deliberate self-determinative self-actualization in personal freedom and positive choice. Consequently, it could be said that most of the human knowledge, particularly in the sciences, is concerned with the human self-investigation, such as the investigation of the human structure and its processes, human existence and its interpretation, or the investigation of the world for better human masterly control and exploitation.[30] In other words, the human being is engaged in the process of self-discovery, self-understanding, self-improvement and even self-deification into a god, for the primal human temptation of eating the fruit of knowledge for self-deification and mastery is endemic in the human being and in human existence, in which God sometimes appears as a kind of absentee monarch.

However, despite this self-investigation the human being never gets any definitive answers, and consequently, he or she remains in the perpetual quest for the full definitive truth. But since God is the definitive eternal truth and the source of life and its fulfillment, the human being finds himself or herself dealing with the questions of God as the Ultimate human Origin as the Creator and the Ultimate Destiny as Savior and the Source of human self-fulfillment. Rahner insists that the human questions of origin or destiny may be silent and non-verbal, but they are always there. Whenever human beings are faced with danger, pain, loss of property or friends, and perhaps most of all, when they are confronted with death face to face, what they experience or express is this concern for the ultimate meaning of human existence and its final destiny.[31]

For Rahner this ultimate concern lies at the core of human existence and it cannot be ignored. It is so important that it marks off humanity from animality. For instance, no other animal ever asks: What am I? Where did I come from? or, Is death the end of my life? If ever any animal, whether ape, dog or dolphin, asks such questions, it will have become human no matter what else it looks like, as this is the chief characteristic uniqueness of humanity *vis-à-vis* animality. For Rahner these metaphysical questions arise only in the human being because it is only the human being that possesses the divine gratuitous gift of self-transcendence and abstract thought.

However, Rahner does not offer any evidence for this assertion. Nevertheless, in support of Rahner one could probably argue that, since such an abstract thought requires the use of language, whether verbal, sign, or another system of conventional coding and decoding of thought, information, and messages or the instruction of others, we should expect to notice such an advanced activity among the animals should it ever occur. For instance, cultural anthropologists have been able to study cultures of the so-called "primitive peoples" and it has been almost always observed that, in these underdeveloped or non-technological societies, the most important cultural dimension is religion.[32]

Archaeology, too, testifies that all pre-historical homo sapiens were real human beings like us as they had some form of religion, which is the major indication of their capability for abstract thought, self-transcendence, awareness of their human existential predicament and quest for supernatural salvation.[33] The ancient Egyptian pyramids and mummies are probably a good illustration of this characteristic human orientation to some form of supernatural salvation as the fulfillment of this earthly life.

It can also be said that the Christian fundamentalists, who reject all forms of the theory of human biological evolution from a lower form of animal life slowly to the present sophisticated state of human neurological structure and human existence, do so not just because the book of Genesis contradicts this evolutionary theory, but also because they feel threatened by the realization that their Destiny is inevitably and essentially correlatively bound up with their Origin. They correctly reason that, unless God is their Creator and Origin, he cannot be their Destiny either.[34]

However, what is often forgotten in this argument is that God need not create directly each individual human being in order to be each individual's Ultimate Origin and Destiny. God can choose to work through secondary agent causes such as natural laws, history, and the human beings as free moral agents, in order to modify and transform an already existing thing or to bring into being another individual human being into the world.

God cannot be limited in his mystery or infinite mode of activity in the world by human restricted and stereotyped concepts or expectations. For instance, most of the Jews who heard the message of Jesus were skeptical mainly because of their own stereotyped conceptions of what an eschatological Jewish Messiah should be. Consequently, they rejected him as their Destiny and fulfillment, precisely because of their lack of faith in God's mystery and activity that did not seem majestic and impressive enough in correspondence with their beliefs and expectations. Jesus was mocked and rejected because of his humble origins as the son of Joseph, the local carpenter, and his wife Mary, the potter.[35] Similarly, it can be argued that today some people make the mistake of seeing only the human being's humble origins from the lower forms of life, and stumble in their own faith because they fail to see that this humble human origin is itself rooted and ultimately originated in God himself as the very creative Mystery that grounds all life as its origin, sustenance, fulfillment, perfector and ultimate Destiny.

The human questions of both ultimate Origin and Destiny are of paramount importance for the human being, as they determine and orient the human being's total existence in accordance with and towards the perceived destiny, in order to realize this perceived destiny for self-fulfillment and the definitive, irrevocable, climactic crowning of one's life or the attainment of salvation.

Since the perceived destiny determines the nature and course of one's total existence, therefore, it is important for the human being to ask these vital questions, as they constitute the meaning, direction and fulfillment of human existence in the ultimate Destiny, which Rahner identifies with the beatific vision and union with God.[36]

However, some confessed destinies of the human life are sometimes explicitly different from this Rahnerian ideal and even appear to be in complete contradiction to it. For instance, Marxists try to visualize their own destiny in a "utopian" communist classless society, whereas the Christians and Muslims anticipate their own destiny as being in heaven with God (if they are found worthy and in hell if they are judged to be unfaithful!).

Therefore, one's perceived destiny and the attempts to realize it can be considered the vital guides for human action and behavior in the present and the "lure" as final cause for future activity arising out of human free personal choice. It is also the principle of limitation to multiple alternatives that present themselves for choice in every personal free human action. Consequently, the human destiny as perceived by the human being is of fundamental importance as the focus and grounding of human life as it is lived in the present and in the future. Without this vision and hope for the future, "utopian" whether in the Marxist sense or in the religious sense, it is a necessary dimension of human life that empowers and directs human life in all its sophisticated categorial manifestations, particularly in the religious, political and economic realms.[37]

In other words, it is impossible for a human being to live a fully meaningful life unless it is lived in accordance with and toward the realization of this perceived destiny, whether be it a utopian dream of a humanitarian vision of universal brotherhood-sisterhood or life in heaven. There must be something very valuable, meaningful and loved enough for the human being to live for; otherwise life becomes purposeless, and consequently becomes aimless, drifting along, and a mere struggle for survival just like the animals, whose existence seems to be to eat, reproduce, and avoid pain or danger, lacking any observable sense of purpose, direction or destiny. Karl Rahner argues that most people find this definitive ultimate Destiny in the infinite nameless Mystery, and therefore they are "Christians," since they do so through cosmic Christ as the universal divine Logos that mediates gratuitously the very divine life, love, truth and hope that make humanity authentic, and human life exciting, worth living, and fulfilling. In this context, idolatry and inauthentic human life can be said to derive from a false destiny which is other than the real ultimate Destiny in the divine infinite Mystery, the Abyss known as God.[38] Similarly, Rahner argues that the life of salvation menas an authentic human life which is lived faithfully in hopeful anticipation, in harmony and movement towards a definitive fulfillment in the ultimate Destiny as Infinite Mystery, Absolute Future, Creator and redemptive personal God of human adoration and worship.

However, according to Rahner this process is not always conscious or explicit to all human beings and that some people fulfill God's law and then meet the requirement for salvation even in that state of unawareness and therefore appropriately belong to the community of salvation as unaware members, or "anonymous Chrisitans." This Rahnerian might appear to relativize historical Christianity and to demean Christian missionary activity. But this is merely a superficial impression, as a close study of Rahner reveals him to be apologetic, biblical and conservative both in soteriology and ecclesiology.

Human Infinite Self-Transcendence as Prior Orientation to Ultimate Destiny

According to Rahner, human self-transcendence is infinite in its nature, scope and horizon. He affirms that this infinite human transcendence is by its nature given in creation by God and not satisfied in itself. It has been attuned by God to find its fulfillment in the infinite Mystery, which is presented to the human being as the ever-inviting and tantalizing, receding Horizon of pure knowledge, happiness, love and self-fulfillment. This inviting, attractive, ever-receding Horizon as human beings come eagerly toward it, this infinite Horizon of human self-transcendence and human existence, yet tantalizingly unobtainable and ever-receding, is identified by Rahner as God, the infinite incomprehensible Mystery that as final cause is the lure, energizer and ultimate Destiny of all authentic human existence.[39]

Rahner argues that the structure of human self-transcendence is a complex divine gratuitous gift, as it is the main distinguishing feature between the human being and the lower animals close to us. The kind of affinity between us and the apes is such that we both have similar anatomical structure, the same embryonic developmental stages, similar metabolism, and it could be argued also that these apes have a degree of intelligence, as they can learn human sign language, be taught to behave appropriately or even be trained to perform fantastic feats in a circus.[40]

In short, these apes are capable of some limited intellectual activity. Nevertheless, they have not become human! For to be a human being requires more than an intellectual ability; otherwise robots and computers would have surpassed men and women in their human quality if intellectual activity was the criterion of humanity. But they remain machines, as apes remain apes, despite their programmed fantastic feats.[41]

However, although these apes posess a measure of intelligence, it is so limited that, even if it were fully developed to its maximum capacity by training and instruction, the ape would still fail to achieve self-transcendence. Therefore, the chimp might look impressive in human clothing, eating at a table with a spoon, smoking a cigar, watching television, riding a bicycle or doing some other human-like activity, but since it is unable, individually or with others, to reflect upon the meaning and end of these activities, or to reflect upon the meaning of life and existence in general and its ultimate Destiny, therefore it remains just a mere sophisticated ape. It can also be said that as long as this is the case, the chimp will always remain a dumb beast, doing things and living by programming or instinct and not by reflective, responsible personal moral free choice and self-determination, as is the case of human beings, who in contrast can be said to be essentially free, knowing and morally responsible creatures.[42]

Reflection is regarded by Rahner as a unique human quality that constitutes the core component of the general structure of human self-transcendence. The human being is able to transcend his or her bodily limitations, and by an act of the mind he or she can go beyond them to reflect, pray, judge, imagine, dream, fantasize and even to innovate and invent new things. Consequently, Rahner describes the human being as "a free historical spirit" by virtue of this quality of unlimited self-transcendence.[43]

The human being as a free spirit is therefore not bound by space or time. Rahner asserts that these limitations of the categorial world are transcended by the human mind in its act of self-transcendental reflection. In the act of reflection, the human being as free spirit is able to transcend all the categorial limitations of time, space and matter. For instance, he or she is able to traverse space, irrespective of the magnitude of distance involved, and is able to visualize mentally what is taking place in another location as an interested invisible spectator or even keen participant. In the same way, the human being is able to move forwards in time to peep into the tantalizing mystery of the future and backwards into history to enjoy reliving the joyous experiences of the past, while avoiding and repressing the painful memory and anguish of the unhappy ones.[44]

It is also precisely because of this same human quality of self-transcendence and consequent human capacity to transcend time, therefore, being able to reflect and speculate on one's utimate future. But this ultimate future lies carefufully hidden in the divine encompassing impenetrable Mystery, that is why also the human being is the only creature in the known cosmos that is able to suffer from undifferentiated anxiety and despair (Angst).[45] The human being is able to suffer in this way because of his or her logical mind which demands a logical conclusion in connection with the human Ultimate Destiny in the infinite Mystery, yet he or she cannot get one, for any conclusion is enshrined in this very Mystery that is infinitely impenetrable to the human finite mind.

Therefore, the human being, being aware of his or her finitude and unable to foresee the future, worries about his or her mysterious future, and particularly, he or she fears the impending inescapable death, not just because of the unpleasant, painful or slow manner it might occur, but chiefly because the human being is frightened to face the unknown final destiny that lies beyond the grave. Feuerbach, too, made this important observation, but concluded that human religion and human concepts of the Immortal, Redemptive God were merely a result of human finitude and the fear of death.

The result was the human quest for salvation and immortality in a benevolent, omnipotent and immortal God, and in Feuerbach's view, human beings created such an ideal God in their own imaginative minds and projected him externally into the sky by the same process of self-redemptive objectification, and hypostasization of the projected human being's ideals and expectations into their God, as the object of worship, imitation, norms, and most of all, salvation.[46]

This is the kind of false God that Feuerbach and his followers, such as Karl Marx and Sigmund Freud, correctly saw as an illusion to be exorcised from the human minds and human mode of existence.[47] Any gods that are created by the human being, either by careful artistic work in clay, concrete or wood, or by the act of the mind and projection, are all equally repugnant idols and false gods to be got rid of. The real God who is the Creator is always the infinite Mystery that underlies all mystery in the world, and even the very human quest that leads to the misguided fashioning and creation of a concrete image as a god is itself prompted by the human awareness of the cosmic infinite Mystery and the desire to make it more accessible by concretizing it into a visible and tangible god.

The maker and worshipper of the idol, however, soon realizes that the transcendent Mystery is greater than his or her idol. As a result, he or she makes more and supposedly more capable idols until he or she is overcome by despair at the inability of these (false) gods to offer him or her the desired security and salvation. Then follows the inevitable realization that only the transcendent Mystery or God can save him or her from the existential vulnerability, the threats of evil and chaos, loneliness, disease, pain and death.[48]

Rahner argues that human self-transcendence, which is the capacity for human self-possession as self-consciousness and total self-awareness as a historical, material and spiritual being, and as historical material being, rooted in this historical or categorial world, yet transcending it, simultaneously as spirit, to investigate the origins in the past and to survey the future as hidden Destiny in infinite Divine Mystery, this human structure of self-transcendence is not the ground or driving human force to invent God as the human being's Creator, Savior and Destiny. But rather, it is the very ground for divine self-giving revelation to the human being, as God the Creator, Savior and ultimate human Destiny. Rahner affirms that human self-transcendence is God's gratuitous prior orientation of every human being to divine Destiny which is the beatific vision, and sin is the human resistance or personal free contradiction of this Destiny.[49]

Furthermore, Rahner affirms that the human being as a free

historical spirit in this categorial world is characterized by personal freedom. This is not just "transcendental" freedom to move forwards and backwards in time and space, by means of the act of the mind in reflection; it is also the "historical" or "categorial" freedom of movement, expression, worship and association.[50] It is because the human being has intellect, personal freedom and knowledge that he or she is able to become a moral being, responsible for one's choice and its attending consequences, whether good or bad.[51] Without this human knowledge, real personal freedom and free choice, there would not be any meaningful human moral responsibility. Similarly, without human moral responsibility there would not be any guilt, since guilt is due to knowledge and the moral awareness involved in the contrast of what is _vis-à-vis_ what should have been. Guilt is therefore a product of human knowledge, personal freedom and awareness of moral failure.

Animals, therefore, have no guilt, since they do not have the kind of personal freedom and the knowledge that moral responsibility presupposes. Similarly, the young and the mentally handicapped may have no consciousness of guilt, since they have no moral responsibility. Otherwise human maturity and authenticity can be measured by this personal moral responsibility, as this is the true indication of how well the human being has lived his or her life in personal freedom, harmony and pilgrimage towards the definitive destiny in God, who is the author of human life, knowledge, freedom, self-transcendence, moral and structural order in the world.[52]

These open and infinite dimensions not only orient the human being to his or her eternal quest and mystical journey to fulfillment in the beatific vision in God, but they also open up the possibility of dialogue with God, since these dimensions themselves are divine qualities and, as such, open media for such a dialogue between God and the human being and channels of self-revelation in grace and gratuitous supernatural salvation for the human being.[53]

Human a priori Openness to the Infinite Mystery

The fact that the human being is created by God as a self-transcending creature is an _a priori_ human existential. It is the main constitutive feature of the human being _qua_ human being. As an _a priori_ human structure it leads to permanent human openness and orientation to God as the Infinite Mystery, the Ground and ever-receding Horizon of human knowledge and self-transcendence. Karl Rahner describes the human transcendental experience as an _a priori_ human openness to God as the Infinite Mystery and Ground of reality. He puts it as follows:

> We shall call transcendental experience the subjective, unthematic, necessary and unfailing consciousness of the knowing subject that is co-present in every spiritual act of knowledge, and the

> subject's openness to the unlimited expanse of all possible reality. It is an 'experience' because this knowledge, unthematic but ever-present, is a moment within and a condition of possibility for every concrete experience of any and every object ...This transcendental experience, of course, is not merely an experience of pure kowledge, but also of the will and of freedom. The same character of transcendentality belongs to them, so that basically one can ask about the source and the destiny of the subject as a knowing being and as a free being together...There is present in this transcendental experience an unthematic and anonymous, as it were, knowledge of God...Transcendence is always oriented towards the holy mystery.[54]

It is quite clear, therefore, that for Rahner the human being is like Heidegger's *Dasein*, which is by its essential nature oriented and open to Being and Being's lumniosity and self-disclosure on *Dasein's* open receptive region and through *Dasein's a priori* structures (existentials) of language, reflection and mood.[55] The human being is as essentially attuned to God in creation just as ears are attuned and receptive to sound and eyes to light. The human being was created in God's image to love, worship and contemplate God, the Infinite Mystery, in whom the human being finds authentic happiness, rest, beatitude and fulfillment.[56]

In addition, the human being, being a self-transcendent, free historical spirit oriented to the Infinite Mystery, and as a knowing, moral, responsible agent, is tormented by guilt due to the awareness of moral failure, weakness, sin and its consequent internal and social tension and disharmony, mainly as a result of human pride, greed, selfishness and excessive love for material things and wealth at the expense of the neighbor and God. But if God as the *summum bonum* is ignored, then the human being becomes the miserable creature that is self-immersed and lost in the material world, groping in the dark (tripping on worldly things lying in and around the dim path), but nevertheless striving forward toward the beckoning divine light of God's gratuitous salvation that shines beyond. The human being is consequently driven forward to God by divine love and personal guilt that seeks forgiveness, cleansing and restoration to wholeness by the holy, loving and redemptive God.

Since every normal human being experiences love, personal freedom, mystery, choice, responsibility and guilt, and since the human being is ever in quest for meaningful self-expression and perfection in these dimensions, and since the human being is always in search of forgiveness and cleansing from personal guilt incurred in the process of living, by failure to realize and to actualize oneself to the maximum possibility in each case, it can therefore be affirmed that the human being is ever oriented in receptive openness to God in Christ as the source and mediation of all genuine forgiveness and cleansing from guilt and sin, and also as the enabler, lure, mover and energizing power of the human being to move ever forwards in growth towards perfect self-realization and the categorial self-actualization of faith, hope, love in personal freedom and responsibility.

Rahner's concept that the human being is a finite categorial being, who as spirit is a mystery like God the Creator and Infinite Mystery, is inseparably bound up with the idea that the human being by a priori essential constitutive nature and structure, an ontological receptive openness to this Infinite Mystery to which the human being is oriented and attuned a priori in creation.

The Human Being as the Hearer of the Divine Word

Rahner's anthropology has its focal axis, grounding and climax in the notion that the human being who is essentially a self-transcendent being as a free historical spirit (characterized by self-conscious self-presence and reflection, personal freedom, knowledge, choice, moral responsibility and guilt), this finite creature, yet infinite as spirit in virtue of unlimited self-transcendence, and its a priori orientation to holy Mystery, and receptive openness to this Mystery, this complex human being is "the Hearer of the Divine Word."[57] In short, this is the main grounding of Rahner's philosophical anthropology and theology. This is also the main basis for Rahner's theology of God's universal free self-communication in unconditional love and gratuitous grace to all human beings, everywhere and throughout the ages for their gratuitous salvation inasmuch as they heard and responded positively to God's word.

Rahner sums up his argument on the human being as hearer of the (divine) Word in the following manner:

> We started with the question of what our first metaphysical question about being had to tell us, in its aspect, about the nature of man as the possible subject of a revelation. The answer has been that it belongs to man's fundamental make-up to be the absolute openness for being as such. Through the 'Vorgriff,' which is the condition of the possibility of objective knowledge and of man's self-subsistence, man continually transcends everything towards pure being. Man is the first of these finite knowing subjects that stand open for the absolute fullness of being in such a way that this openness is the condition of the possibility for every single knowledge...capable of freely acting and deciding his own destiny.
>
> Man is spirit i.e. he lives his life while reaching unceasingly for the absolute, in openness toward God...Only that makes him into a man: that he is always already on the way to God, whether or not he wills it. He is forever the infinite openness of the finite for God.[58]

Because of Vorgriff as human infinite self-transcendence, and also because the human being is a finite historical spirit oriented to the Infinite Divine Spirit to which it is irresistibly drawn by virtue or orientation and prior affinity, as St. Augustine himself realized through this personal experience, the human being is ever restless and in search of union with God as the ultimate destiny of human life and its definitive fulfillment. Rahner himself puts it this way:

> Man is spirit and, as such, he always already stands before the infinite God who, as infinite, is always more than only the ideal unity of the essentially finite powers of human existence and of the world. He does not only acknowledge God in fact, but in the daily drift of his existence he is man, self-subsistent, capable of judgment and of free activity, only because he continually reaches out into a domain that only the fullness of God's absolute being can fill.[59]

The human capability to seek God and apprehend his implicit self-disclosure in the world, its wonders, beauty and mystery as divine revelation, is the human openness to the world, the search for knowledge, truth and its ultimate origin and basis, and the perpetual human quest for a meaningful life, love, health, comfort, happiness, and on the other hand for deliverance from the threat of evil, chaos, pain and death. But this is not all. Karl Rahner, like St. Augustine, further affirms that God made the human being in such a manner that at the core of his or her being there is a void, oriented as infinite openness towards fulfillment in the Infinite Mystery and, as such, filled only by God as this Infinite Mystery.

This being the case, other mistaken attempts to fill this infinite void with finite things fail, as our own experiences or those of St. Paul and St. Augustine clearly demonstrate.[60] As both of these saints realized, human life is incomplete, restless and ever searching for its completion and fulfillment, which can only be found in God.

This inner void experienced by the human being is for Rahner God's ontological ordering of the human being in such a way that the human being remains permanently oriented and open to God and his Word (Logos) that are desired at least implicitly by the human being as the human fulfillment. Rahner explicates that God calls his Word into being in this void at the center of the human being and the human being hears this divine Word, not as an alien coming from outside but rather as intimately personal, since it is heard coming from the center of the human being. The Word of God is heard from within because God is not an external object nor alien to the human being.

For Rahner, God is always present and presented to the human being as the Ground and Condition of being, self-transcendence, knowing, personal freedom, moral choice and responsibility. God's knowledge is given to the human being in undifferentiated, prethematic, noncognitive and unobjective anonymous manner as the ground and horizon of all human knowing, as it is the intelligibility itself and without which nothing is knowable. It is also the luminosity of Being that enables all beings to be seen as they are by and within its light and background.[61]

For Rahner, the human being is both able to hear God's silent word and to see the cosmic divine revelation by looking at the world reflectively and by reflecting upon life and human experience. Furthermore, the human being is able to discern God's Word as the message for human life now and also as being directive and determinative for future action and positive self-realization. For Rahner this personal discerning inner eye and "mystical experience" is the main goal of humanization as divinization in Christ. He also argues that Jesus and the prophets manifested the nature of this quality to which every human being is called, namely, to be able to hear God's Word in and through the world, human existence and the prevailing state of affairs be it social, economic, medical or political. Jesus and the prophets were able to see God's invisible hand in history, creating, directing, saving and judging and to hear his silent Word because they were in full receptive attunement to God through the inner mystical or transcendental dimension as spirit which is by grace able to ascend to God.

According to Rahner, God's Word, which is implicit in every human being as noncognitive, undifferentiated intuition of the Transcendent Mystery and Ground for knowledge and truth, quietly guides in free grace the human being toward the ultimate Destiny and fulfillment in God as this Mystery. However, sometimes this pre-thematic and uncognitive revelation of God comes to human full consciousness and becomes objective. Then the silent, implicit Word of God becomes the explicit, verbal, proclaimed and written Word of God, but without exhausting or replacing that portion of the cosmic divine Word that remains for many people implicit, unthematic and anonymous.[62]

The Scriptures, creeds and doctrinal dogmatic formulations as systematic cognitive propositional statements of faith have to do with the divine Word as objectified and thematized by the human being as the hearer of the divine Word in its unthematic *a priori* intrinsic existence in the human being as the condition of human knowing, freedom, self-transcendence, choice and responsibility, and also as the ground energizer and lure for human beings to reflection, self-examination and self-evaluation in social, moral, religious dimensions as well as temporal terms, namely past, present, and future dimensions. However, it is erroneous for anybody to claim that only the thematic divine Word really counts as divine revelation and that there is no divine revelation apart from the Holy Bible, as most reformers seemed to be affirming by their doctrine of *sola scriptura*, since this *sola scriptura* principle did not even admit that the Koran and the Hindu or Buddhist holy books were themselves scriptures and, as such, a component part of this *sola scriptura*.[63]

God's Word is infinite and, therefore, unlimited to certain books whether written by prophets or saints, including the Bible and the Koran themselves. God's Infinite Word cannot ever be written down in its totality, and therefore, only portions or fragments can be heard as addressed to specific human beings or human existential conditions at a specific time and in a given place.[64] The Word of God is personal to the hearer(s). Since every human being is unique, it should be logical also to assume that each human being hears God speak personally and differently so as to address the individual's personal uniqueness, and to call his Word into existence in the infinite void that exists at the center of the human being as the eternal receptive openness to the divine Mystery, and prior ontological attunement in readiness for the reception of the Divine Word.

The Word of God itself, as understood by the writer of the fourth Gospel, cannot be itself written down as it is God himself, in creative and redemptive action as the medium and instrumentality of both divine processes, which are simultaneous intertwined actions of God constitutive of this world, with the human being as the main center, focus and example of this divine free and unmerited action. What can be written, then, are words and actions of God in salvation history, as God in Christ is the Word and cannot be written down.[65]

However, these sacred writings as Scriptures can be loosely called the Word of God, since they came into being through the inspiration and motivating of the Word of God which was heard by the godly men and women and recorded as they personally heard it and understood it themselves in their own uniqueness, time, culture and general prevailing circumstances as background context for this hearing, interpretation, understanding and writing.[66] Like Karl Barth, Karl Rahner affirms that the written Word becomes the true living Word of God when its readers or hearers hear God speaking to them, addressing them individually or collectively in challenge, direction for the future or in judgment. When this divine speaking and human hearing take place, then, one can truly say that God has spoken his Word and likewise, that these pieces of religious literature are inspired Holy Scriptures and that they are God's word.[67]

Karl Barth himself was very perceptive of the heresy and theological problem of claiming that <u>sola scriptura</u> implied that God's salvific Word had been captured and somehow transcribed into the Bible as holy Scripture. His solution for this complex problem was his doctrine of the Word as by its essential nature threefold: "The Written Word," "the Incarnate Word" and "the Proclaimed Word."[68] Whereas this solution is a noteworthy theological attempt at arriving at a consistent and comprehensive understanding of God's Word, it is too restrictive to answer many contemporary questions.

In Rahner's view God's Word must be recognized as infinite, universal, and omnipresent to everybody as it is co-present with God as the Speaker addressed to every human being as the hearer of this divine Word that calls everything into being and to life, love, happiness, hope, personal freedom and responsibility. This is also the silent Word of God in the inner life of the human being that calls him or her into question and judgment, and similarly, divine forgiveness. This is the divine creative, sustaining and transforming Word of God that is universally present, silently, anonymously, and ceaselessly at God's work of creation and salvation as guided creative self-actualization in harmony, and movement towards fulfillment in eternal Destiny and Mystery as God. All this is the work of God out of his pure gratuitous, efficacious grace and universal salvific will. His will is that all human beings should live in accordance with his grace, which is given through the inner directive Word, love, faith, hope, and be saved.[69]

Therefore, God's Word cannot be captured and be encapsulated in a book or pamphlet. Otherwise, God would have sent a book into the world instead of sending his Word, which is infinite yet personal, and as personal became a person, in order to communicate more effectively and concretely with human beings, who are historical and categorial creatures. Jesus as the Christ was and is God's Word addressed to human beings in a historical and categorial context.

However, this historical mediation of God's Word in the world cannot be considered to represent the totality of God's Word, since there is still a transcendental, universal dimension of the divine Cosmic Word that transcends these temporal-spatial dimensions. It could also be argued that Jesus, as the Incarnate Word of God in historical process, was no doubt aware of this Infinite dimension of God's Word and that is one of the main reasons why he never wrote a book himself either about God or about his message of God's kingdom. Rather he challenged his audience "to hear the Word of God by opening their inner, mystical ears and eyes so as to hear God's voiceless, silent Word uttered, and to see his invisible, mysterious, protecting and guiding hand at work in the course of the world's history and in the ordinary events of human daily life and/or history."[70]

It follows, therefore, that Rahner's human being, like Heidegger's <u>Dasein</u>, is not just an <u>a priori</u> receptive openness and readiness in the world for the reception of God's free-willed self-disclosure as revelation and illumination for himself/herself and on behalf of the whole world, but also that the human unique structures of language, mind and mood become the divine revelatory media and channels of God's Word in which language finds its expression in and through the human thought and emotions, which then become adapted as God's means of making his voiceless silent Word heard, perceived and loved by the human being to whom it is addressed both universally, as the transcendental Logos in human transcendence, and historically in Jesus Christ and the Church as his categorial embodiment and mediation in this historical and categorial world's processes.

Since the human structure is the revelatory vehicle and medium of the divine Word which is addressed to the human being, and the human condition in the world, Rahner argues that it could also be affirmed that the human being who is the hearer of this divine Word is also in a sense its co-speaker with God, since without the human being the Word remains unheard and remains without voice, thought and language for self-expression.

The human being as this medium of God's Word, as the creature whose constitutive unique structure is the revelatory instrumentality of God, the human being is then probably deservedly described by Rahner as "the hearer of the divine Word." According to Rahner, this remains true whether the human being is explicitly aware of it or not, since to be a human being is to be a hearer of God's Word that calls all human beings into existence, invites them to actualize themselves towards a more complete humanity and humaneness as made possible by divine grace finding expression in faith, hope and unrestricted love for fellow human beings and God, who is correlative with humanity and whose love is, similarly, co-extensive with the love for humanity. According to Rahner, God cannot be found nor can he be loved apart from humanity, for humanity is the expression, representation and the Incarnation of God in historical process and this categorial world.[71] In the Incarnation, God not only speaks in a human Word to address himself to humanity in its categorial historical form and unique modality, but also "became man" and the archetypal human being. Thus, he concretized his abstract Infinite Word of grace, love and creative transformation in human history.

Since God's Word has become a human being, and since divine revelation is deposited in every human being by God in creation, therefore, to be the hearer of the Word and/or to accept God's revelation, the human being must accept himself or herself in his or her _a priori_ mystery and listen to his or her inner voice so as to hear God speak. For God and his Word have become incarnated in the center of humanity and therefore in each human being. God and his Word as the pre-existent cosmic Logos or Christ and the Holy Spirit as their energizing power are no longer alien to the human being, since they have their dwelling in the inner core of humanity, not as foreign objects but as the very ground for human life itself, which is constituted by hearing the Word of God, which calls all things into being and quietly guides them to their respective fulfillment in their prior divinely given destinations unless they rebel and choose otherwise.

Consequently, all human existential life is lived in the presence of God's Word of invitation to life in its fullness. Therefore, the human being lives in the daily open possibility of hearing this God's Word of invitation to a fuller life as salvation in grace, and to respond in individual, personally accountable and consequential freedom with either "Yes" or "No" to this universal, unconditional divine proffer of gratuitous salvific grace. Furthermore, since God in his Word and through the power and mystery of his Holy Spirit has become human, Rahner is right to affirm that we can only seek God as we seek humanity, and that we can only find truth about ourselves as we find truth about God, since the Divine and the human have become co-extensive correlatives in the Incarnation and by virtue of the "Hypostatic Union."[72]

The Supernatural Existential and Gratuitous Divine Universal Salvific Grace

Rahner's anthropology and theology have one basic essential theme, pivot, grounding and destiny, namely, the supernatural gratuitous grace in love as prior to creation and as reason for creation, creation's raison d'être and ultimate Destiny. In this sense creation is good, infused by grace and destined to fulfillment in God both as its free Creator and Destiny, and this being especially true of human beings as knowing, transcendent, moral, free, responsible and loving creatures rendered by the supernatural existential so as to respond in personal responsible freedom to God's proffer of himself in grace.

This Rahnerian starting point renders frivolous the question why the good creation should be in need of God's salvific grace, while at the same time it puts an end to the debate between extrinsicists and intrinsicists regarding the supernatural and human nature.[73] Rahner's theory of the supernatural existential as God's free gift of grace to the human being in creation as a permanent ontological divine elevation of the human to supernature, and as prior ordering and permanent ontological receptive openness, readiness and attunement to God's Word in gratuitous grace for positive self-actualization and self-determination in personal freedom and in the midst of this divine encompassing efficacious grace, explains that the human being is created with an "obediential potency" oriented and elected to divine destiny in the beatific vision, yet without putting a demand on this supernatural grace as a condition for the human fulfillment in this destiny, or without making grace an alien force that overrides human personal freedom, choice and responsibility for one's being and destiny.

According to Rahner, the human supernatural existential is a neutral divine proffer of supernatural grace which allows the human being to exercise his or her personal consequential freedom to either accept it or reject it in this same freedom.[74] In this way the human being determines himself or herself to a fuller meaningful, fulfilling life as it is offered to him or her by God in love and mystery, and therefore to happiness, love, fellowship, community and salvation or its negation in personal freedom and consequential self-imposed isolation, loneliness, a lesser mode of life, minimum self-actualization, meaningless misery, and damnation. The supernatural existential, therefore, is the impartial divine instrumentality for free actualization of salvation or damnation.

The existence of the supernatural existential is vital for Rahner's works, as it is the grounding for his understanding of God's universal divine self-communication to every normal human being for revelatory and salvific purposes in gratuitous grace. According to Rahner, the supernatural existential allows every reflective human being, in grace and responsible personal freedoms, to respond to the divine immanent revelation and divine Word deposited at the center of his or her inner being, ever calling him or her to a fuller life, love, hope, forgiveness, healing, wholeness, happiness, perfection and definitive fulfillment in the *visio beatifica* with either a "Yes" or a "No." Those who answer *"Yes"* to this invitation to supernatural salvation are Christians, since they do so through the Word which is Christ.

Those who are unaware of this title as descriptive of their surrender to God as the Mystery, source and Destiny of life and salvation, or those who resent this title for past unfortunate associations and misunderstandings, yet completely surrendering themselves to the fullness of life, unrestricted love and Mystery in which these are wrapped up, especially in the future dimension, these people are termed by Rahner "anonymous Christians."[75]

Anonymous Christianity

Rahner's theology can be said to be basically an explication of divine universal gratuitous, salvific grace that finds its logical climactic expression in the concept of "anonymous Christianity," which for him is the response to God's universal divine self-communication in his pre-existent Cosmic Word and gratuitous grace for the salvation of all human beings wherever they are, irrespective of religion, technology, culture, literacy, education, economy, color, race and time.[76] This "anonymous Christianity" as the divine proffer of universal efficacious salvific revelatory gratuitous grace is co-extensive with human history.

Therefore, in this manner, preceding and transcending the divine historical election of Israel, the giving of the Torah by Moses and the Scriptures, the Incarnation of the Word in historical process, and the emergence of the Church as its historical embodiment and mediation in this categorial world. Consequently, God's salvific activity in supernatural grace, like creation, is universal, unconditional, free and not to be limited either by human sin of selfishness, pride, sadism, hatred and exclusiveness by such doctrines as *massa damnata* or as *extra ecclesiam nulla salus* or narrow double predestinarian views as found in Calvinism and in groups such as the Jehovah's Witnesses.[77] Since for Rahner salvation implies the completion and fulfillment of the human being as such, it cannot be limited either to the Church or to certain religions, as this doctrine would leave the majority of the human race incomplete and unfulfilled as human beings, which is contrary to reality as observed in the world, namely, that there are people who do not claim to be "saved" nor to be "Christians," yet these same people have accepted themselves as human beings and live a full human life, open to the world, its mystery and the future, and most of all they live in unrestricted love for their neighbor, which is the authentic mark of supernatural grace and salvation. Rahner puts it this way:

> According to the Christian view of things, even though a person is co-conditioned by original sin in his situation of salvation and sin, he always and everywhere has the genuine possibility of en-

> countering God and achieving salvation by the acceptance of God's supernatural self-communication in grace, a possibility which is forfeited only through his own guilt. There is a serious, effective and universal will of God in the sense of that salvation which the Christian means by his own Christian salvation. In Catholic dogmatics God's salvific will is characterized as universal in contrast to the pessimism in Augustine or in Calvinism; that is, it is promised to every person regardless of where or at what time he lives, but this does not just mean that a person in some way or other is kept from being lost.[78]

In the same place, Rahner goes on to argue very constructively in the following manner:

> Salvation in the proper and Christian sense of God's absolute self-communication in absolute closeness and hence it also means the beatific vision ...But this salvation takes place as the salvation of a free person as such, and hence it takes place precisely when this person in fact actualizes himself in freedom, that is, towards his salvation.

Rahner goes on to argue very insightfully that whoever has turned to God as the Infinite Mystery, experienced from within and/or as seen in the world that leads to the human infinite questioning and wonder, whoever has accepted his or her own humanity in its given mystery, contingency, vulnerability and finitude, whoever seeks to live in unrestricted love, peace and harmony with his/her fellow human beings and the world, that that person has surrendered himself or herself to God and God's gratuitous salvific grace, whether he or she knows it explicitly, as in the case of a confessing Christian, or is still unaware of it and therefore an "anonymous Christian."[79]

This can be regarded as a good criterion for salvation, since it has to do with the quality of categorial human life and the way it is daily lived before God as the transcendent Holy Mystery in the world and in relation to one's fellow human beings, the community and the world, as the rest of this book will attempt to show, taking the Central and Southern Bantu people of Uganda as the main focus. Therefore, the main task in the rest of this book will be to try to demonstrate that these Bantu people traditionally live a life that is both oriented and receptive to God, while at the same time seeking to live in neighborly love and to enhance peace and harmony within the community. The main criterion by which they will be measured to see if they fulfill Rahner's criteria to be termed "anonymous Christians," and therefore, heirs of divine salvation, will be the practical expression of unconditional love for the neighbor.

NOTES

1. See Chapter I, notes 9, 10, 21, 36, 39, 54-58.

2. Ibid. See also note 6 below. I consider "anonymous Christianity" to be the logical apex of Rahner's theory of divine gratuitous grace. For Rahner, universal supernatural salvation is dependent on God's universal salvific will, which is correlative to his universal, supernatural, gratuitous, efficaciously salvific grace as the means to achieve God's universal will to save every human being. In this sense, every human being is elected to supernatural salvation and will only lose it by his or her personal free will to defect and live in contradiction to this divine Destiny. Consequently, Rahner argues that every human being is a potential Christian.

This approach seems to make more sense than that of Anita Roper, who declares that everybody is an "anonymous Christian," i.e., see The Anonymous Christian, p. 126, where she writes:

> Every human being is a Christian, and he is one not always expressly but very often anonymously. This statement, which summarizes what we have said so far...All men are Christians in some way, although the ways differ widely. That is a fact.

To Roper's position I can only repeat Kierkegaard's apt critique, namely, that "If we are all Christians, the concept is annulled...and so Christianity is 'eo ipso' abolished." See "Attack upon 'Christiandom'" in A Kierkegaard Anthology, ed. Robert Bretall (New York: The Modern Library, 1946), p. 447; see also "What It Is to Become a Christian," which is Kierkegaard's conclusion of the famous Concluding Unscientific Postscript, and/or Training in Christianity, "The Offence," C, Supplement 2, pp. 108 ff.

3. The major philosophical anthropological works being Spirit in the World and Hearers of the Word. Rahner starts with anthropology in order to do theology because the human being is the given and God is the implicit in this given (the human being), which is the only explicit. He also believes that the divine revelation has been deposited in the human being by God in creation, and therefore, the human being is the cipher of God and, as such, revelatory of God, particularly since, by virtue of the Incarnation and Hypostatic Union, God has become irrevocably united and inseparable from the human being; cf. Foundations of Christian Faith, pp. 24-70, 212-227.

For Rahner, it can be stated that without anthropology, theology is impossible, for theology is a theistic and meaningful study of humanity and a theistic interpretation of human existence in light of the Incarnation; see "Theology and Anthropology," Theological Investigations 9:28-45, and "Philosophy and

Philosophising in Theology," Theological Investigations 9:46-63. See also Chapter I, note 57, for a full discussion of the validity of this theological starting point.

4. For Rahner, salvation is not a future fulfillment in the beatific vision. It is the manner of human life now as the movement towards this divine Destiny; cf. Rahner, Foundations of Christian Faith, pp. 97-105, 142-170, and Pannenberg, What Is Man?, pp. 54-67. See also Chapter I, note 11.

5. Contrary to the historicization and the popular literal interpretation of Genesis 1-3, found among some Christian fundamentalists.

6. See note 4 above. Rahner defines salvation as the humanization of the human being. This humanization is making humanity more loving and humane. In this sense, the Incarnation is a complete humanization of humankind, and as such, its divinization, since authentic humanity is impossible to achieve without divine help in the form of the supernatural grace that elevates the mere human nature (which tends to be more inclined to animality from which it previously has emerged in evolution) to a supernatural level, where it is oriented to Mystery and to seek fulfillment in God as its ultimate Origin and Destiny.

According to Rahner, these two levels exist simultaneously together in the human being right from the beginning, since he regards grace not as something added to the human being later, as an ornament or an attire, but rather as constitutive of the human being in terms of the supernatural existential that is a permanent divine proffer of grace to the human being. See: Foundations of Christian Faith, pp. 39 ff.; "The Order of Redemption within the Order of Creation," The Christian Commitment (New York: Sheed and Ward, 1963), pp. 38-74; "Nature and Grace," Nature and Grace (New York: Sheed and Ward, 1964), pp. 114-149; "Concerning the Relationship between Nature and Grace," Theological Investigations 1:297-317; "Some Implications of the Scholastic Concept of Uncreated Grace," ibid., pp. 347-382; "Reflections of the Experience of Grace," Theological Investigations 3:86-90; "Nature and Grace," Theological Investigations 4:165-188; "The Existential," Sacramentum Mundi 2:304-307; "Grace," ibid., pp. 412-427; "Potentia Oboedientialis," Sacramentum Mundi 5: 65-67; "Salvation (Universal Salvific Will)," ibid., pp. 405-409.

7. Cf. Karl Rahner, Prayers and Meditations, pp. 115-116.

8. Ibid., p. 17.

9. It is conceivable, therefore, that if Rahner were writing Genesis today, it is most probable that he would say: "God created man in his own mystery," instead of saying that "God created man in his own image." Rahner, unlike Barth, starts with anthropology in order to do theology mainly because he believes that the human mystery points back to its Creator/Origin, which

Rahner identifies as the transcendent incomprehensible Infinite Mystery that is known as God in the English language.

10. Karl Rahner, Prayers and Meditations, p. 115.

11. See Hearers of the Word, Chs. 5-13; Spirit in the World, pp. 65-77, 279-298, 387-408; The Foundations of Christian Faith, pp. 24-132.

12. See Chapter I, notes 1, 5 and 6.

13. See note 11 above and Chapter I, note 4.

14. Cf. John 3:16; Rom. 5:8; 1 Cor. 13; John 4:7-21. "Beloved, let us love one another; for love is of God; and he who loves is born of God and knows God. He who does not love does not know God for God is love" (1 John 4:7-8).

15. If we characterize God as love, then intellect becomes a secondary quality of God, contrary to St. Thomas and Hegel, who tend to view God as primarily intellect. (Cf. Summa Theologiae I:1 qq. 3, 4 and 12; Hegel's Phenomenology of Spirit; and Lectures on Philosophy of Religion: The Christian Religion.)

16. For instance, all normal human beings are aware of moral norms and all human societies have an ethical code of some kind to regulate moral behavior. This cannot be said to be true of the rest of the animals.

17. Human moral responsibility presupposes human freedom as ground and condition of that responsibility arising out of personal free choice. Without freedom, Rahner argues, the human being is incomplete and cannot be morally accountable as such; cf. Rahner, Grace in Freedom, pp. 203-265, and Prayers and Meditations, p. 74; see also Alfred North Whitehead, Adventures in Ideas, pp. 43-86.

18. This can be described as St. Paul's dualistic way of describing the conflicts he experienced within himself, between the animality and the divine constitutive elements of his human nature. He correctly identifies animality with the bodily or physical desires but, like the Platonists, wrongly assumes deliverance as salvation to be apart from the troublesome body; hence his cry, "Who will deliver me from this body of death?"

The Incarnation should affirm to Christians that divine salvation does not consist in the abolition of the human body or escape from it; rather, that salvation consists in its healing, and positive orientation and response to God, and to seek to live in unity and harmony with the neighbor and the power of the Holy Spirit.

19. E.G., see Plato's Crito and Phaedo; see also W.K.C. Guthrie, The Greek Philosophers, pp. 86-121; Gordon H. Clark, Thales to Dewey: A History of Philosophy (Boston: The Riverside

Press, 1957), pp. 70-77.

20. Ibid. Food and sex are usually singled out as the two basic physical needs that govern most of human behavior, and consequently, affect the human spirit and in some cases even become a great hindrance to moral responsibility and personal spirituality. Freud's emphasis on Id as the undifferentiated sexual driving force underlying most human activity and problems can be brought in to support this observation. Children's orientation to food and play is perhaps another illustration that can be used to support this dipolar theory of the basic human needs that dominate human life.

Since the philosophers wanted to govern their own lives, they were therefore bound either to repudiate these bodily desires as the Platonists did, by rejecting the body, or by celebrating it as the Hedonists did. Therefore, for many dualistic Christians, such as the Balokole of Uganda, the greatest commandment is perceived to be "Thou shalt not commit adultery" rather than "Love your neighbor as yourself." Similarly, the greatest sin is perceived to be sexual rather than failure to love the neighbor unconditionally.

21. See note 19 above. The body was regarded as the prison and as the tomb for the soul and consequently death as its release from this misery and bondage. This dualistic unchristian anthropological philosophy entered into Christianity through the early Church usage of Greek philosophy to explicate and contextualize the Christian faith to the Hellenized world of their day. However, this does not necessarily make it either any more Christian or acceptable to us. For a corrective, see Karl Rahner, _Hominisation_, pp. 32-111.

22. Cf. Karl Rahner, _Spirit in the World_, pp. 135-142, 248-252; _Hearers of the Word_, Chs. 5-13; _Foundations of Christian Faith_, pp. 24-175; _Grace in Freedom_, pp. 113-116; _Opportunities for Faith_ (New York: Seabury Press, 1970), pp. 92-122, 194-198.

23. _Cogito ergo sum_ perceives the human being to be essentially an intellect. This view of humanity follows from the Thomistic view of God as "Perfect Intellect" or, as Hegel clearly puts it, "Absolute Intellect" or "Pure Thought thinking itself;" cf. "Absolute Knowledge" which concludes _The Phenomenology of Spirit_.

24. A proper definition of a human being is required to solve the ethical debates involved in abortion, euthanasia and genetic engineering. Careless and irresponsible definitions of the human being should be avoided, as they can be socially, politically or religiously harmful (i.e. Nietzsche's philosophy, and particularly, the notion of the _Ubermensch_, was used by the Nazi fascists as their blueprint for life and action.) Slavery and economic exploitatioin of some people by another group is usually based on and justified by some crude definition of humanity. For instance, some South African white racists rarely feel guilty for their ruthless oppression and exploitation of the

black populace because, according to their own understanding, the blacks are inferior to the whites and therefore not deserving the same human rights, employment, pay and services as the whites. This is the anthropological grounding of the legal racial segregation system known as apartheid in present South Africa. Similarly, the Arab Muslims justified their enslavement of the Africans on the religious grounds that it was all right to enslave infidels. It appears, therefore, that human beings will live and behave according to what they understand themselves to be and how they perceive their humanity and that of others.

25. S. Freud's studies and discoveries have opened up the unconscious mind and have made it accessible to scientific investigation. He divides the mind into three sections. The biggest section of these three he called "Id;" this is the unconscious region in which the basic animal (physical) instincts of human nature jostle together with no pattern of determined order or sense of value. The other two are "Ego" and "Superego;" these determine which of Id's demands is satisfied and which one is rejected if its satisfaction would lead to social disapproval and the ostracization of the individual. Freud found that these rejected drives did not vanish entirely, but rather they vanished out of sight into the unconscious mind, but showed up now and again in the acceptable guise of dreams and fantasies, or even manifested themselves destructively in pathological ways such as neuroses. Cf. Freud, New Introductory Lectures on Psychoanalysis, An Outline of Psychoanalysis, pp. 5 ff.

26. See Emil Brunner, "The Christian Understanding of Man," in The Christian Understanding of Man, pp. 141-178; Reinhold Niebuhr, The Nature and Destiny of Man 1:1-92. See also notes 22 and 23 above.

27. Karl Rahner, Hominization: The Evolutionary Origin of Man as a Theological Problem (New York: Herder and Herder, 1965), pp. 108-109.

28. Ibid. See also Rahner, Prayers and Meditations, pp. 17, 115-116.

29. See Chapter I, notes 1, 5 and 6.

30. See Karl Rahner, "The Problem of Genetic Manipulation," Theological Investigations 9:225-252, and "The Experiment with Man," ibid., pp. 205-224. This human knowledge and self-mastery creates ethical problems arising from potential abuses, such as those involved in abortions, sex changes, genetic engineering, and the prior determnination of the sex of the fetus even before conception. If these processes are not properly controlled and protected, the human being can do irreparable harm to the unborn future generations. If the technological being begins to create himself or herself according to his/her own fancy, humanity may be put in danger of either usurping the role of God or inflicting irrevocable harm on itself, if not self-destruction altogether in

the case of a major nuclear war or accident involving other deadly chemical weapons.

Knowledge is by itself intrinsically good and to be acquired by all human beings. However, the evil person who has access to unlimited knowledge is far more dangerous to society, as he or she has more power and more capability for greater evil and destruction, than the evil person who is an ignorant one. (For instance, if Idi Amin of Uganda had had access to nuclear weapons, he probably would have proved a greater menace to world peace.) Consequently, therefore, it is good that the human being is an infinite mystery that is not easily understood so as to be utterly and tragically controlled like a puppet.

31. The questions of Destiny and those of Origin are usually inseparable in the human mind as they are by nature correlative. This is to say that human beings tend to think that the Destiny is determined by the Origin; cf. Chapter 1, notes 1, 4, 6 and 7. This is one of the main reasons why God should be shown to be at the beginning of the process in order to be its sustainer, transformer and ultimate fulfiller or completor at the end. Consequently, Rahner argues that unless God is at the beginning of the process, such as the philosophical proofs for God's existence, that he cannot be at the end; cf. Rahner, Foundations of Christian Faith, pp. 44-80; Spirit in the World, pp. 67-77; Hearers of the Word, Chs. 5-13; Soren Kierkegaard, Philosophical Fragments, Ch. III (pp. 46-60).

32. Cf. E. E. Evans-Pritchard, Theories of Primitive Religion (Oxford: Oxford University Press, 1965), pp. 1-9.

33. Ibid. See also Chapter I, notes 4-6.

34. See note 31 above.

35. And on the Sabbath he began to teach in the synagogue; and many who heard him were astonished, saying, "Where did this man get all this? What is the wisdom given to him? What mighty works are wrought by his hands! Is not this the carpenter, the son of Mary and brother of James and Joses and Judas and Simon, and are not his sisters here with us?" And they took offence at him." (Mark 6:2-3; cf. John 6:35-66.)

See also Kierkegaard's elaboration, namely, that Jesus' lowliness as God incognito in humanity, in the form of a "servant" who suffers, is a source of offense to the human intellect and that it can only be transcended by faith and not logic; Philosophical Fragments, trans. Howard V. Hong (Princeton: Princeton University Press, 1974), pp. 37-45; Training in Christianity, trans. Walter Lowrie (Princeton: Princeton University Press, 1972), pp. 25-26, 79-144.

36. Cf. Foundations of Christian Faith, p. 430:

> ... A Christian does indeed live a tangible and ecclesial life, but that the ultimately Christian thing about this life is identical with the mystery of human existence. And hence we can readily say that the ultimate and most specific thing about Christian existence consists in the fact a Christian alows himself to fall into the mystery which we call God; that he is convinced in faith and in hope that in falling into the incomprehensible and nameless mystery of God he is really falling into a blessed and forgiving mystery which divinizes us.

37. It is most probable that the lack of development in pre-colonial Africa was largely due to the lack of a dream or utopia to actualize, since the African concept of time was circular, with just a few months projected into the future. Life was otherwise lived in the present (Sasa), which is the remembered past (Zamani), the present and extends into the foreseeable future; cf. John Mbiti, African Religion and Philosophy, pp. 21-36. Since there was no extended future dimension and everything focused on the golden past (Zamani) rather than the unknown future, the Africans tended to live a static life oriented to the past. Consequently, there was no technological advancement and there were no permanent buildings built except in Egypt and the Zimbabwe stone city walls. Permanent buildings point to a long-term planning for the future, the very concept most African peoples lacked.

The Western linear concept of time has advantages, as it leads to a future-oriented modality of life, open to change, innovation and a conscious process towards the realization of the projected or perceived goals, dreams and utopias, hence leading to a forward movement in civilization or a creative advance, innovation and technological development that characterize the West. (But at the same time, note must be taken of the criticisms recently leveled against an over-emphasis on technological development.)

38. Cf. Karl Rahner, "The Concept of Mystery in Catholic Theology," Theological Investigations 4:37-73; Hearers of the Word, Chs. 5-13; Foundations of Christian Faith, pp. 44-89; Grace in Freedom, pp. 183-196. See also Chapter I, note 4.

39. Ibid.

40. Some of them are even trained to perform for television commercials and to star in a variety of movies, such as "Born Free," "Lassie Come Home," "Tarzan of the Apes," "Grizzly Ben" and "The Wild and the Free."

41. It can be argued that both apes and computers perform because they have been programmed to do so by human beings, and they can do nothing without this prior conditioning on the part of the apes and programming on the part of the computer. Most of

all, they have no personal freedom to act on their own or to pass on this culture to their own offspring as human beings do. So human instruction of the young cannot be compared to the programming of the computer or the training of the chimp. Human instruction of the young leads to both conditioning and understanding, whereas the training of the chimp is mainly conditioning it to behave or to react in a specific way in a given specific situation. Human education is, on the contrary, supposed to cultivate responsible and imaginative behavior or activity and originality.

42. Ibid. Human beings possess personal freedom, knowledge, intellect, language, religion and moral responsibility, in contrast to animals, who generally lack them or posess them at a very low level that is not significant enough to affect their way of life as animals.

43. See Chapter I, notes 1, 5 and 7.

44. See note 25 above. These repressed unhappy experiences end up causing mental diseases unless they are given positive release or another acceptable outlet.

45. Kierkegaard has most vividly described this state of _Angst_ in his books, _Fear and Trembling_ and _The Sickness Unto Death_. This is basically a human condition in which the subject is aware of his or her vulnerability and finitude. Kierkegaard's solution is the human acknowledgment of God as the Infinite Ground of finitude. This submission to God is not just a total surrender in worship, but also a "leap of faith" into this Mystery he perceives to be God and Savior; cf. _Philosophical Fragments_, Ch. II; _Training in Christianity_, pp. 122 ff., 144 ff.; _The Unscientific Postscript_, pp. 186 ff. This human surrender to God in the "leap of faith" is what Schleiermacher describes as the human awareness of "absolute dependence;" see _The Christian Faith_, ed. H. R. Mackintosh (Philadelphia: Fortress Press, 1977), pp. 12-19, 34, 40 and 125.

46. Cf. Ludwig Feuerbach, _The Essence of Christianity_, trans. George Elliot (New York: Harper and Row, 1957), pp. xxxvi, 50, 120-134, 270-336; _The Essence of Religion_, pp. 17-25, 140-285. Freud followed Feuerbach in his interpretation of religion as an illusory human projection.

47. Both Feuerbach and Freud are probably right in affirming that human needs, ideals and human projection are worked into most people's theology as crude idols, as anthropomorphism clearly illustrates. Rahner would argue, however, that this human failure to represent God adequately in both thought and language should be expected, since God is by definition incomprehensible, creative, transforming, infinitely Transcendent holy Mystery.

Consequently, idolatry and religious projections are not mere human illusions, as both Feuerbach and Freud claim; rather they are defective human religious ideas which originate from and essentially point (imperfectly) back to the Ultimate Reality enshrined in infinite Mystery. It is this incomprehensible Reality in which all other "realities" and beings are rooted is what we call God. This is the hidden God who out of his own free loving grace reveals himself to human beings in the beauty and the mysteries of the world, in reflection, through prophets and sages, and above all in Christ and in his teaching on unrestricted love and forgiveness.

48. Therefore it is necessary that the God of worship who must be the Creator should also be capable of loving his creation and powerful enough to save his people from evil and the threat of chaos and premature death. It is not surprising, therefore, that the Hebrew "Schema" (Deut. 6:4-5) is placed in the context of divine salvation history (Exod. 1-20), Divine redemption is the background, context and historical grounding for the Ten Commandments:

> And God spoke all these words saying, "I am the Lord thy God, who have brought thee out of the land of Egypt, out of the house of bondage. Thou shalt have no other gods before me... (Exod. 20:1-3, K.J.V.)

Therefore, God is God only if he is able both to create and, in loving grace, to save his creation from its own tendency to destroy itself, particularly, the free human being who is capable of both doing good as well as doing evil. Therefore, having the potential and capability for destruction in the same way he/she has the potential for creativity.

49. Sin is the human state of free resistance against or defection from or contradiction to his ultimate Destiny. Cf. Karl Rahner, Foundations of Christian Faith, pp. 44-137; Opportunities for Faith, pp. 79-108; Pannenberg, What Is Man?, pp. 54-67; Paul Tillich, Dynamics of Faith (New York: Harper & Row, 1957), pp. 1-29; Systematic Theology 3:11-110; Jurgen Moltman, Man, pp. 16-45, 105-119; Reinhold Niebuhr, The Nature and Destiny of Man 1:54 ff., 296 ff.

50. E.g., see Karl Rahner, Grace in Freedom, pp. 203-264; "The Theology of Freedom," Theological Investigations 6:178-196; "On the Dignity and Freedom of Man," ibid. 2:235-263. Consequently, Rahner asserts that the Christian should be the divine ambassador and harbinger of freedom in the world so as to enhance human rights and to encourage a more positive process of humanization of humankind and the world in which we live. He argues emphatically that the Lord's commandment that we love our neighbor as ourselves is the guiding principle and the basis of Christian community, freedom and socio-political activity in the world. Whitehead is therefore very insightful when he attributes Western civilization to be a growth in freedom due to Christianity, which teaches that love and persuasion are preferable to the use of force; cf. Adventures in Ideas, pp. 26-86. Similarly,

Whitehead views slavery as the worst social evil and case of inhumanity, as it deprives other people of their rights and freedoms which constitute them as human beings. Process Philosophy has consequently brought freshness to both philosophy and theology by its radical emphasis on complete freedom and self-determination or organisms and events; cf. Whitehead, Process and Reality, Part II, Chs. VII-X; Part III.

51. Rahner argues that inasmuch as human beings are free, moral and knowing creatures, they must also accept the concomitant consequences and responsibility for their freedom, knowledge and inevitable choice in their daily lives. Therefore, it is not responsible to drift through life in order either to avoid choosing for fear of consequences or to shrink back from responsibility for one's choice, be it good or bad. Therefore, one can hardly praise religious escapists such as the Balokole of Uganda, who blame all their wrongdoings and bad choices on the devil, thus escaping from the responsibility for their own personal choice. (If the devil was so bad as that, it would never tempt and entrap anybody except the very foolish ones!) Nevertheless, the human being is by nature a morally responsible being vis-à-vis animals, and therefore, authentic humanity is expected to manifest authentic human personal moral responsibility for one's actions that arise from personal free choice. See also note 17 above.

52. Cf. Anita Roper, The Anonymous Christian, pp. 126-137. See also Kierkegaard's pointed book, Either/Or, especially the last section; Karl Rahner, Faith Today (London: Sheed and Ward, 1967), pp. 9-18; Christian at the Crossroads, pp. 11-44; "The Order of Creation and the Order of Redemption," The Christian Commitment (London: Sheed and Ward, Ltd., 1963), pp. 44-55.

53. See Hearers of the Word, entire book, with special attention to Chs. 5-13; Foundations of Christian Faith, pp. 24-115; Hominisation, pp. 62-110. See also Chapter I, notes 6 and 7.

54. Karl Rahner, Foundations of Christian Faith, pp. 20-21.

55. Cf. Martin Heidegger, "Being and Time," Martin Heidegger: Basic Writings, ed. David Farrell Krell (New York: Harper & Row, 1977), pp. 41-89; "The End of Philosophy and the Task of Thinking," ibid., pp. 373-392. See also Karl Rahner, Foundations of Christian Faith, pp. 24-115; Hearers of the Word, entire book; Spirit in the World, pp. 57-230, 279-308, 387-408.

56. Ibid. There must be some kind of affinity between God and the human being that enables meaningful communication between them, love, fellowship and community. The writer of Genesis affirms this same basic truth when he states that God created man both male and female in his own image (Gen. 1:26-27). The Pentateuch says that God made a covenant between himself and Israel (cf. Exod. 6;4, 19:5, etc.), whereas the New Testament says that "God (Logos) became man" (John 1:1-14, 3:16, etc.) in the Incarnation by virtue of this "Hypostatic Union," it can be said that

"God became man" and likewise, "man has become God!" See Athanasius, On the Incarnation, 54:

> ...Immortality has reached to all, and that by the Word becoming man, the universal providence has been known, and its giver and artificer the very Word of God. For he was made man that we might be made God. (Cited in Christology of the Later Fathers, ed. Edward R. Hardy (Philadelphia: The Westminster Press, 1954), p. 107).

57. See notes 50, 51, 55 and 56 above.

58. Karl Rahner, Hearers of the Word, ending of Ch. 5; A Rahner Reader, ed. Gerald A. McCool (New York: The Seabury Press, 1975), pp. 20-21.

59. Ibid.

60. See St. Augustine's Confessions, I-X; Phil. 3:7-9; Romans 7:15-25. Things such as pleasure, romance, sex, food, drugs, wealth and success will probably not fill this emptiness or void felt at the very center of the human being. This kind of escapism eventually proves futile as this emptiness can become even more accentuated, sometimes leading to drug addiction and despair.

61. See Karl Rahner, Hearers of the Word, Ch. 3; Spirit in the World, pp. 379-408; Foundations of Christian Faith, pp. 51-70.

62. Cf. Karl Rahner, Foundations of Christian Faith, pp. 14-175; 311-321. See also Chapter I, notes 21, 22, 81 and 91.

63. The question of what is "Holy Scripture" as the authentic and normative Word of God, as opposed to other religious literature, is a central issue here. For instance, Martin Luther did not only look at the Old Testament (O.T.) and New Testament (N.T.) as the Holy Scripture, excluding the Apocrypha; he also, as it were, saw a special canon within this general canon. For instance, he preferred the Gospels, Romans and Galatians to the rest of the N.T. and the N.T. to the O.T. He also referred to James as the "Epistle of Straw"! See John Dillenberger and Claude Welch, Protestant Christianity: Interpreted through Its Development (New York: Charles Scribner's Sons, 1954), pp. 45-53; Gerhard Ebeling, Luther: An Introduction to His Thought (Philadelphia: Fortress Press, 1980), pp. 110-124; Paul Althaus, The Theology of Martin Luther, trans. Robert C. Schultz (Philadelphia: Fortress Press, 1979), pp. 72-104; Paul Tillich, A History of Christian Thought: From Its Judaic and Hellenistic Origins to Existentialism, ed. Carl E. Braaten (New York: Simon and Schuster, 1967), pp. 242 ff.; Karl Rahner, Grace in Freedom, pp. 95-112, and Revelation and Tradition, pp. 9-49.

Given this complex background, it should not be surprising, therefore, that for many Christians the Koran or the Hindu and

Buddhist scriptures cannot be accepted as part of the genre of literature termed "Scripture," or for that matter cannot even be respected as part of God's Word addressed to humanity. But for Rahner God is universal and similarly, his self-disclosure or revelation is also universal, and so is his love and salvific activity in gratuitous grace.

The implication would be that these sacred books, though containing God's Word, do not effectively convey the Divine Truth of God's Infinite Mystery, Love and Grace. In some instances, the Word is partially and defectively understood by the human beings to whom it was originally addressed by God, so that when they wrote it down as God's Word, they did so as they understood it. Hence, there is great need and urgency for Christian missionary activity to bring the Good News of a fuller divine revelation in the Incarnation and the manifestation of God's unconditional love, grace and forgiveness for everybody who responds in faith to this Gospel and tries to live accordingly as a responsible participant in this "New Being," as Tillich calls it, or the fullness of life which is given in Christ (cf. John 1:1-4, 9-14; 3:16; 10:10).

Therefore, the concept of "anonymous Christianity" and the availability of supernatural salvation outside the traditional, historical Christianity, and therefore outside the conventional, historical and institutional Church, does not mean the end or irrelevancy of Christian missionary activity to non-Christians such as Jews, Muslims, Hindus and Buddhists. It means instead a new and more culturally relevant, effective and more meaningful Christian missionary strategy and approach to these people, that is, following St. Paul's missionary example and Gospel presentation by finding local contextual links or fertile ground where to sow the Divine Word for effective rooting and maximum yield. For example, see Acts 17:22-23:

> Then Paul stood in the midst of Mars' Hill, and said, Ye men of Athens, I perceive that in all things ye are very religious. For as I passed by, and beheld your devotions, I found an altar with the inscription, TO THE UNKNOWN GOD. Whom, therefore, ye ignorantly worship, him declare I unto you. (K.J.V.)

Paul could have chosen to attack these people's idolatry (Acts 17:18) or un-Christian existentialist Stoic and Epicurean philosophies, but rather he chose a positive approach, since the positive approach leads to positive results, whereas the negative approach tends to put people on the defensive and consequently negates the very Good News of Christ, which is essentially positive (cf. John 3:16-17; 10:10; and Rom. 5).

64. For instance, each book in the Bible is written from a specific point of view, addressing certain issues; e.g., Amos addresses questions of justice, while Isaiah addresses issues of spirituality and how God will fulfill it in the <u>eschaton</u> through the "Suffering Servant" (cf. Isa. 7-11, 52-61). Similarly, each

book of the New Testament, including even the synoptic Gospels, have their own uniqueness due to the differences in the human writers, prevailing historical situation, perceived theological problems among the intended audience and the writer's own theological understanding of Jesus, both his person and ministry.

As regards the Epistles, they contain valuable evidence of the issues they were written to deal with, namely, divisions, heresy and discipline (cf. 1 Cor. 1:10-17, 5:1, 15:1-3 and 12-20; Gal. 1:6-9, 3:1-5; 2 Thess. 1:5-12, 3:6-15; 1 John 1:9-10, 2:18-27, etc.).

Similarly, it could be said that Muhammed recited the Word of God, which was later written down by his followers and collected together to form the Koran, as he perceived it for his situation and the situation of those nomadic Arab polytheist tribesmen. This strong monotheistic move from idolatry and polytheism to the worship of One Holy God, Merciful and Incomprehensible Creator and Righteous Judge, cannot be ultimately attributed to any other source of inspiration than God himself. This could also be said for other mystic prophets, such as Buddha or Nyakairima of Kigezi, Uganda. God's prophets, divine inspiration, revelation and salvation do exist outside Israel and therefore outside the O.T. and the N.T,.

Rahner's thesis would be that God has never ceased either to speak, to warn, to save his people and/or to punish evil-doers wherever they exist. Consequently, his Word of life, truth, love, judgment, hope and salvation exist wherever human beings exist, whether it is explicitly known and understood or not, and whether it is written or not. See also note 63 above.

65. See previous note above.

66See notes 56, 63 and 64 above.

67. Ibid.

68. Karl Barth, Church Dogmatics 1:1, especially p. 136. See also Klaas Runia, Karl Barth's Doctrine of Holy Scripture (Grand Rapids: Eerdman's Publishing Co., 1962), pp. 4 ff.

69. See notes 1, 3, 6, 31, 50 and 64 above.

70. See Karl Rahner, Foundations of Christian Faith, pp. 24-175; Grace in Freedom, pp. 69-94; Opportunities for Faith, pp. 7-122; Faith Today (entire book); Hearers of the Word, Chs. 5-13; Christian at the Crossroads, pp. 45-81; Prayers and Meditations, pp. 111 ff. The stage of life both human and supernatural, the life of both salvation or perdition, is the everyday life. The ordinary human life and existence is the stage and the means of human encounter with the divine or extraordinary, which is God both in self-communication in continuing creation and salvation. This is a universal phenomenon which accounts for religion wherever people have existed as human beings. See also note 32 above.

71. See Leo J. O'Donovan, ed., A World of Grace, p. viii;

notes 3, 6, 26, 55, 63 and 64 above. See also Chapter I, notes 4, 5 and 58.

72. Ibid. See also Karl Rahner, Foundations of Christian Faith, pp. 212-228; "Christology Today?", "Jesus Christ in the Non-Christian Religions," and "The Theological Dimension of the Question about Man," Theological Investigations 17:24-70; Emil Brunner, Man in Revolt, pp. 98 ff.; Karl Barth, Church Dogmatics 3:2; Pannenberg, Human Nature, Election, and History, pp. 13-61; Moltmann, Man, pp. 1-45, 105-119.

However, this is not a concept that is unique to Christianity. For instance, Mahatma Ghandi, the famous Hindu mystic who successfully mobilized the Indian peaceful mass nationalist (Satyagraha) protest against the British colonial occupation of India, affirmed that he experienced God in the midst of social and political as well as religious action, and that he saw God wherever his fellow human beings were and in whatever activities they were engaged as such. For instance, Ghandi wrote the following in his Harijan periodical:

> Man's ultimate aim is the realization of God, and all his activities, social, political and religious have to be guided by the ultimate aim of the vision of God. The immediate service of all human beings becomes a necessary part of the endeavour simply because the only way to find God is to see him in his creation and to be one with it [emphasis his own]. This can only be done by service to all. I am part and parcel of the whole and I cannot find him apart from the rest of humanity. My countrymen are my nearest neighbours. They have become helpless, so inert that I must concentrate on serving them ...I know I can not find him [God] apart from humanity. (Cited in William Johnston, The Inner Eye of Love (New York: Harper & Row, Publishers, 1978), p. 26).

It goes without argument that Ghandi is exercising unconditional love for the neighbor and that, according to Rahner's thesis, he has found the secret of authentic life as both fully humanized and divinized, whereas many explicit Christians have failed to find it. It is to such non-Christian devout and loving men and women that Rahner's term "anonymous Christian" correctly applies, and not to every non-Christian human being as Anita Roper suggests in her book, The Anonymous Christian, pp. 126 ff. See also notes 2, 6, 49-52 above.

73. E.g., see William C. Shepard, Man's Condition: God and the World Process (New York: Herder and Herder, 1969), pp. 31-96, 229-264; Karl Rahner, "The Order of Redemption within the Order of Creation," The Christian Commitment, pp. 38-74; "Nature and Grace," Nature and Grace, pp. 114-149; "Concerning the Relationship between Nature and Grace," Theological Investigations 1:297-317; "Some Implications of the Scholastic Concept of Uncreated

Grace," ibid., pp. 319-346; "The Theological Concept of Concupiscentia," ibid., pp. 347-382; "Reflections on the Experience of Grace," Theological Investigations 3:86-90; "Nature and Grace," Theological Investigations 4:165-188; "The 'Existential'," Sacramentum Mundi 2:304-307; "Grace," ibid., pp. 412-427; "Potentia Oboedientialis," Sacramentum Mundi 5: 65-67; "Salvation (Universal Salvific Will)," ibid., pp. 405-409. See also Regina Bechtle, "Rahner's Supernatural Existential," Thought 48 (1973), pp. 61-77; Kenneth D. Eberhard, "Karl Rahner and the Supernatural Existential,"Thought 46 (1971), pp. 537-561; J.P. Kenny, "Reflections on Human Nature and the Supernatural," Theological Studies 14 (1953), pp. 280-287; Thomas Motherway, "Supernatural Existential," Chicago Studies 4 (1965), pp. 79-103; Carl J. Peter, "The Position of Karl Rahner Regarding the Supernatural: A Comparative Study of Nature and Grace," Proceedings of the Catholic Theological Society of America 20 (1965), pp. 81-84.

74. Ibid. See also notes 17 and 50 above.

75. See notes 1, 2, 63, 64 and 72 above.

76. See Chapter I, notes 9, 21, 36, 80 and 91. See also note 73 above.

77. Cf. Calvin, Institutes, III; Karl Rahner, Foundations of Christian Faith, pp. 146 ff.; see also note 73 above.

78. Karl Rahner, Foundations of Christian Faith, pp. 146-147.

79. See notes 63, 64, 73 and 76 above. See also Karl Rahner, Foundations of Christian Faith, p. 228:

> Now God and the grace of Christ are present as the secret essence of every reality we can choose. Therefore, it is not so easy to opt for something without having to do with God and Christ either by accepting them or rejecting them, either by believing or not believing. Consequently, anyone who accepts his existence in patient silence (or, better, in faith, hope and love), accepts it as the mystery of eternal love and which bears life in the womb of death, is saying "yes" to Christ even if he does not know it.

CHAPTER III

THE AFRICAN[1] UNDERSTANDING OF HUMAN EXISTENCE AND SALVATION AS WELLBEING AND WHOLENESS (OBUSINGYE N'AMAGARA)

A. THE CONCEPT OF GOD

It has been recently proved by archaeology that East Africa is actually the origin of the homo sapiens, and as such, the origin of humankind.[2] Africa as the cradle of humanity and all the human civilization; the origin of Moses, the great prophet and lawgiver of Israel;[3] the refuge of the infant Jesus and his parents;[4] the producer of great philosophers and great Christian theologian bishops such as Cyprian and St. Augustine, and famous laymen such as Tertullian, Novatus and Donatus, has been given little attention by Western scholars in the past, largely because of racism and color-prejudice. Consequently, for many of these prejudiced Western White scholars, Africa has remained the "Dark Continent."[5]

This is especially true of Africa south of the Sahara, which became isolated by the almost insurmountable harsh barrier of the Sahara desert which stretches hundreds of miles between North Africa and the rest of Africa south beyond the desert. However, North Africa was always in trade and religious contacts with the region south of the Sahara.

As we know, there were well-established caravan routes between these two regions of Africa. Moreover, the Sahara desert itself was never so wide as it is now. The rock drawings and archaeological findings in the Sahara desert yield plenty of evidence that the present desert itself was once a fertile land with rivers and lakes greatly populated with aquatic creatures such as fish and hippos.[6] Consequently, the division between North Africa and the rest of Africa can be said to be rather superficial and, as such, untenable.[7]

However, whereas North Africa became internationally linked with the Mediterranean civilization, and subsequently became Christian during the Apostolic era, and later became Muslim in the seventh century as a result of Arab conquest and the African desire to be independent of the Roman imperialism, Africa south of the Sahara remained largely traditionalist or "pagan" until the last two decades of the nineteenth century. Nevertheless, prior to the arrival of Dini[8] (foreign religions), the Africans were very religious, loving, virtuous and Godfearing people. They had their own effectively functional religion, with a system of beliefs and practices or rituals, both individual/private and collective/public, that regulated life, both secular and religious.[9] They had a sound and deep religious understanding of humanity, human existence and vulnerability due to the omnipresent threat of evil forces in the guise of malevolent evil spirits, witchcraft, misfortune, illness, disasters, such as droughts, famines, accidents, floods, fires, injury, wars, etc., and the need for supernatural intervention to avert the evil and save the human beings from pain, harm and destruction.[10]

Therefore, the African Traditional Religion is the context for African philosophy, anthropology, and soteriology. The African metaphysics, world-view and ontology are contextually grounded in and determined by this all-pervasive African Traditional Religion, since it permeates all the departments of African life and orients the African to the divine presence of the Incomprehensible Mystery in whatever place and situation the person happens to find himself or herself. The Western observer or analyst might call this all-pervasive African religious attitude "primitive superstition," but the reality of its religious nature and significance is not thereby removed nor diminished by this kind of Western ethnocentric misrepresentation, ignorance, misunderstanding and insult of this religious phenomenon or denigrating it as "paganism," "superstition," "primitive," "magic," "Juju," "ancestor worship," "devilish," or animism."[11]

The Non-Explicit and Flexible Nature of the African Traditional Religion

The African religion, unlike Christianity, Islam, Hinduism and Buddhism, has no sacred books in the form of Scriptures, has no individual founder or reformer (with the exception of individual cults),[12] has no definitive creeds nor dogmas concerning beliefs or practice. Consequently, there is great flexibility and tolerance for pluralism in beliefs, practices and rituals, as there is no one dogmatic way of doing things. In African Traditional Religion there is neither orthodoxy nor heresy. Whatever ritual or belief functions best in a given community and is most convenient is adopted and others ignored until they are required to meet a specific need. As a result, in African traditional religion there are no heretics nor atheists.[13]

The African people generally believed that being religious was co-extensive with being human, and for that matter, they did not attempt any missionary activity among other people they came in contact with, whether African or foreigners, since they believed that each human being has some kind of religion. Nevertheless, there was the mutual borrowing and exchange of religious ideas and the abandonment of the old dysfunctional and ineffective cults and the spreading of new ones such as the Nyabingi cult in Kigezi, Ankole and Rwanda at the turn of this century.

However, the traditional African people never converted from their own traditional religion to another form of African traditional religion because religion was inseparable from their own culture and probably because they realized that all the African traditional religious cults and practices were basically different aspects of the same religion in its complex diversity and pluralism both in beliefs and practices. This phenomenon and complexity of the African religion is described by Aylward Shorter in reference to the debate among African scholars on the subject. He writes:

> More common, perhaps, is a third approach, followed by writers who explicitly declare their faith in the basic unity and comparability of African religious traditions. Their hypothesis is based usually upon impressions gained from wide reading, travel or discussion, but it is not systematically elaborated or tested out. For Professor Abraham there is a basic 'paradigm' which justifies his study of the Akan religious system as representative of all other African religions. For Professor Mbiti African religions are many, but they all derive from, and subscribe to, a basic religious philosophy. For Canon Taylor there is, in Africa south of the Sahara, 'a basic world-view which fundamentally is everywhere the same,' while for Professor Idowu there is a 'common factor' or 'common Africanness' behind African religion. Faith in, or intuition of, this common unity then allows these authors to enumerate instances on grounds of similarity.[14]

In support of Idowu, it can be pointed out, for instance, that the Africans consider the African traditional religion an *a priori* in one's given community and ethnic group. Mbiti, on his part, also realizes this fact that, for instance, one is born a Mukiga or a Munyankole and is consequently brought up as such in the religious tradition of the society into which the individual is born, through the usual normal process of socialization and humanization of the young into morally responsible human beings (Abantu). Like Judaism or Hinduism, one has to be an African in order to belong to the African Traditional Religion, as it is by nature the main element for the grounding of Africanness as such. It does not only determine and orient us to the omnipresence of the awe-inspiring Supernatural, Holy Infinite, Incomprehensible Mystery that encompasses us as the ocean water encompasses the fish; it also acts as the filter for our knowledge, being the main grounding principle of the African worldview and metaphysics, since for the African, God's universe is basically a religious universe.[15]

Consequently, Africans, regardless of whether they are well educated, Muslim or Christian, tend to fear evil spirits, witchcraft and sorcery, and also tend to attribute natural disasters such as lightning, drought and floods to these malignant evil spirits, hatred and witchcraft, mainly due to the implicit conditioning received from the African Traditional Religion. As a result, many well-educated Christians consciously or unconsciously still live in two worlds, one western and Christian or Islamic and the other African, determined and regulated by African Traditional Religion.[16]

Subsequently, many African Christians go to church on Sunday morning, and African Muslims go to the mosque on Friday afternoons, and the rest of the week's six days and a half are lived in the guidance and practice of the African Traditional Religion! Christians still visit the diviners and the "Bafumu" ("medicinemen" and "witch-doctors") for the purpose of divination, diagnosis and healing or obtaining protective medicine against witchcraft and misfortune.[17]

This means that the African Traditional Religion, which has been identified as the grounding of our Africanness, has withstood the pressure of foreign invading religions from turning the African into either a "Black European" or a "Black Arab." Therefore, it can be said that the African Traditional Religion has in some cases accommodated both Christianity and Islam without being overwhelmed or abandoned by the apparent African conversion to these foreign religions. However, with time and the gradual westernization of Africa and the current rapid change due to secular education, modern economy and international politics, one is bound to predict an eventual extinction of the African Traditional Religion in its traditional form, but it would probably survive in the "respectable guise" of an African version of Christianity and an Africanized Islam.[18]

It has been pointed out that the African Traditional Religion was so much all-pervasive and so identical to African life itself that it was hardly conscious of itself as a religion! The term or word "Dini" which is an Arab-Swahili word adopted in East Africa for religion, denotes only the foreign religions (Islam and Christianity), mainly because the Africans in this area never referred to their own traditional religious practices as constituting a religion. It was regarded and accepted as a given way of life that enhanced the vitality of life itself.[19] However, there were several additional religious cults which individuals could elect to belong to, in addition to their own basic African Traditional Religion which was usually co-extensive and sometimes identical with the tribal way of life.[20]

These cults were given names such as Emandwa, Nyabingi, Kasente and Ryangombe in Ankole and Kigezi. As these cults were optional, no one was ever forced to be initiated into them although the Ryangombe cult probably tried to coerce people indirectly to join it by preaching that those who were not initiated into it by the time of their death would be judged, when they died, by Ryangombe as disobedient sinners and as rebels against him, to be thrown into the fires of the Birunga Volcanic Mountains, while the initiates enjoyed bliss in fellowship with the Imaana (God) and Ryangombe as Lord in the more beautiful and cooler ranges of the Birunga Mountains.[21]

It is these very same religious people who even believe in Ruhanga/Katonda as the omniscient and omnipotent creator <u>ex nihilo</u> and who are also described by Professor Mbiti as "incurably religious," who if asked the question, "What is your religion?" then reply, "I have no religion," unless they have been converted to either Islam or Christianity.[22] Others will even claim that they are "Bakafiri" (Kaffir), an Arabic derogatory word meaning an infidel (or pagan) because they have been made to believe that that is what their religious state is![23] This kind of imperialistic missionary attitude and the denigration of the African traditional religion was sometimes also prompted by the fact that these "African people had no religion" that the foreigners could readily recognize as a religion, since it was on the whole unorganized, with no imposing features such as temples, books, creeds, hierarchy, and regular worship meetings.

Whereas the travelers and explorers often wrote about the bizarre religious practices of the "primitive peoples" they encountered on their adventures in Africa, Professor E. E. Evans-Pritchard cautions us:

> What travelers liked to put on paper was what struck them as curious, crude, and sensational. Magic, barbaric religious rites, superstitious beliefs, took precedence over daily empirical, humdrum routines which comprise nine-tenths of the life of the primitive man and his chief interest and concern...[24]

Having discredited these sources as ethnocentric, prejudiced and unreliable, Evans-Pritchard goes on to evaluate western missionary literature on African religion in the same way, though he admits that this category of literature is more reliable and less distorted in favor of the sensational than the first category. However, he makes the following apt remark concerning all the literature on the African Traditional Religion:

> Statements about a people's religious beliefs must always be treated with the greatest caution, for we are then dealing with what neither European nor native can directly observe, with conceptions, images, words, which require for understanding a thorough knowledge of a people's language and also an awareness of the entire system of ideas of which any particular belief is part, for it may be meaningless when divorced from the set of beliefs and practices to which they belong.[25]

Professor Evans-Pritchard's evaluation and critique of the western religious anthropological literature and <u>Theories of Primitive Religion</u> have been a positive influence on the study of African Traditional Religion, as it happens to be one of the major types of the so-called "primitive religion," being without sacred books, creeds, literature and dogmas to be studied by the scholars, and also being the religion of a non-technological people who still live a simple rural life in their natural "habitat"! Evans-Pritchard rejects the theories of religion that degrade "primitive religion" as either totemism, magic, or the psychological theories that try to discredit it as superstition arising out of the fear of the unpredictable environment and vulnerability or as a mental aberration, and as such an illusion.[26]

Evans-Pritchard's main argument against these views is that the source of the "higher religions," the universal religions such as Christianity, is the same source for other religions, be it Judaism, Islam, Buddhism, Hinduism, and so-called primitive religions such as the African Traditional Religion. If one is attributed to mental aberration and, as such, an illusion, then all of them could be explained away in the same fashion, and if one of them is to be attributed to divine revelation, then all of them are similarly to be attributed to the same revelatory source to a certain extent. Professor Evans-Pritchard puts it very vividly as follows:

> I am of course aware that theologians, classical historians, Semitic scholars, and other students of religion often ignore primitive religions as being of little account, but I take comfort in the reflection that less than a hundred years ago Max Muller was battling against the same complacently entrenched forces for the recognition of the languages and religions of India and China as important for an understanding of language and religion in general, a fight which it is true has yet to be won... but in which some advance has been made.

He goes on to elaborate the point more emphatically:

> Indeed I would go further and say that, to understand fully the nature of so-called natural religion, for nothing could have been revealed about anything if men had not already had an idea about that thing... The dichotomy between natural and revealed is false and makes for obscurity, for there is a good sense in which it may be said that all religions are religions of revelation: the world around them and their reason have everywhere revealed to men something of the divine and of their own nature and destiny. We might ponder the words of St. Augustine: 'What is now called Christian religion, has existed among the ancients, and was not absent from the beginning of the human race, until Christ came in flesh: from which time the true religion, which existed already, began to be called Christian.'[27]

The Hierarchy of Being

The interlacustrine Bantu people of Uganda are famous in pre-colonial history of East Africa and African history in general for their well-organized successive kingdoms, the best known being Bunyoro-Kitara Empire, which is supposed at one time to have covered most of Uganda, Rwanda and Burundi, parts of Tanzania, Kenya and Ethiopia, followed by Buganda, which by Kinyoro Bito tradition is said to be an offshoot dynasty from Bunyoro in the same way Ankole, Rwanda, Burundi, Mpororo, Igala, Koki and Toro Kingdoms were all supposed to have had their origin directly or indirectly from the Babito Empire of Bunyoro Kitara.[28]

The significance of this fact is that since all these people were in contact with Bunyoro, and since Bunyoro had advanced religious ideas such as the one supreme divine omniscience, divine omnipotence, creation <u>ex nihilo</u> and divine kingship, these ideas did spread to these areas if they did not exist there before.

Since many people tend to correlate their political concepts with their main religious views, inasmuch as they aspire to be like the God they worship, and on the other hand, also tend to conceive God anthropomorphically as King or the chief "Ancestral spirit," depending on the cultural ideals of a given society, it would therefore appear that the people of Bunyoro, Buganda, Toro, Ankole, Kigezi and Rwanda probably understand God Ruhanga/Katonda to be like a great king. Possibly, this is the origin of the local conception of God as a king who often opts to conduct business with mundane creatures through a chain of mediators such as kings, priests, diviners, healers and elders, except in some desperate cases of emergency, despair, disaster or conflict within the society or within the chain of mediation itself, when the individual is considered free to approach God directly.

On the top of the African "chain of being," such as in the Bakiga-Banyankole (Bantu) metaphysical hierarchy, is God (Ruhanga) as the transcendent, infinite creative Mystery, followed by spiritual beings such as divinities and the good ancestral spirits (or other good spirits). Thirdly, come the Bantu (human beings); next are evil spirits (rejected by God and the good spirits because of their wicked lives while on earth); then animals, followed by the plants, then inanimate objects, and finally at the bottom of the hierarchy comes the category of space and time.

This hierarchy has an implicit valuation of these categories. For instance, time being put as the least important of these categories would tend to support Professor Mbiti's observations regarding the African understanding of life. It would probably also explain why most Africans tend to be late or appear not to be mindful of time. Furthermore, Professor Mbiti argues that for traditional Africans future time has no being or reality as it is only potentiality of being to be realized and actualized in the present, and therefore becoming a concrete reality in the active present or in the sedimenting reality of the past in history.[29]

This hierarchical chain of being correlatively indicates the intrinsic value placed on each category of being by the "Muntu" (human being), who regards himself/herself as "the center of the created universe."[30] Nevertheless, value is measured in connection with God, who is Creator and pure perfection. Therefore, the further away the category is placed from God, who is the absolute reality, origin (as creator ex nihilo), sustainer and perfector of everything, the less perfection and value the category has.[31] God reigns supreme at the top as the emanating Source of the hierarchy, followed by spiritual beings, then human beings, animals, plants, inamate beings (things/ebintu) and at the bottom, lies the categories of time and space.

It is also widely believed that these categories of being and modalities of existence, inasmuch as they have being (NTU) in themselves, to some varying degree, they correspondingly participate in the universal divine "NTU" (BEING), which is the source and ground of all forms of being or existence.[32] Those beings that are most close to God are consequently thought to have more perfection in -"NTU". This perfection is thought to manifest itself in terms of greater access to the divine infinite knowledge, a "spiritual body" that transcends the limitations of both time and space, wealth, power, beauty, great strengths, ability to heal, and greater capacity for unconditional love and uprightness.

"Omuntu," inasmuch as he or she acquired human perfection by practicing "Buntu" (humaneness/humanness), he/she can be regarded as the categorial self-revelatory expression of divine being itself "NTU" in this concrete world of things (ebi-ntu) and of space (ha-ntu). "NTU" in this sense is not the equivalent of Aristotle's substance that constitutes actuality, but rather it is more like Heidegger's "Being" that expresses itself in beings and Dasein (the human being) in particular.[33] However, "NTU" as being is to be distinguished from becoming, which is denoted by the Runyankole-Rukiga verb "Ku-ba" (to be). The "Ku-ba" indicates a process of becoming and implies improvement or an increase in both perfection and value.

In addition, "Ku-ba" can also mean that an event is coming into being or taking place, whereas "NTU" generally indicates a static form of being. Consequently, God as both the source and this "NTU" (Being) itself, is also generally thought of by these people in a static manner. For instance, Ruhanga is generally conceived of as being all perfect, (Just like in St. Thomas' works), and as such, requiring no further growth or increase in perfection.[34]

God (Ruhanga) as Creator and Transcendent Mystery

The people of Kigezi, Ankole, Toro, Bunyoro and Buganda, among other African people, are monotheistic, inasmuch as they recognize only Ruhanga or Katonda in Buganda as God the Creator (creating ex nihilo) and Sustainer of everything that has being or existence.[35]

The name Ruhanga/Katonda literally means "Creator." It is derived from the verb "kuhanga/kutonda" (to create). The term "kuhanga/kutonda" means to create *ex nihilo*. This Bantu idea is similar to that found in the book of *Genesis*, where God calls or brings into existence the world and its various categories of beings that had no prior existence, unlike Plato's Demiurge in the *Timaeus* that creates or fashions the world from pre-existent matter, following the *a priori* eternal "ideas" or "forms" as patterns like a carpenter or architect.[36] For the Bakiga, Banyankole, Baganda, Banyoro, Batoro, and Banyarwanda and others in this area, God is only God as he is Creator *ex nihilo*. In other words, whatever Being or Power that is the Creator (Ruhanga/Katonda) is according to their philosophy and religion God.[37]

Consequently, among the Bantu people God is conceived of as being an Incomprehensible Creative Mystery that has no proper name, since a name for them is considered to be expressive of the essential inner nature of its bearer.[38] Therefore, the so-called names for God in this area should be more appropriately termed divine attributes and descriptions rather than God's names.[39] For instance, in both Kigezi and Ankole God is referred to in the following terms:

"Ruhanga"	Omnipotent Creator (i.e., creating *ex nihilo* by his infinite divine power).
"Omuhangi/Nyamuhanga"	Creator, Ultimate Origin of everything.
"Kazooba"	Light/Sun and Seer of everything on earth at the same time or the Omniscient; He who makes the sun to rise or set; the Eternal One, i.e., he who has seen many sunrises and sunsets.
"Rugaba"	The Great Giver of everything on earth (and similarly, the one who takes it away); the Supernatural Provider.
"Mukama(we)Iguru"	The Heavenly King, Lord over the sky or heaven.
"Nyineiguru"	The Owner/Lord of Heaven/sky.
"Biheeko"	The Great Being that carries everything and everyone on its back, i.e., the Omnipotent, and unconditional Sustainer of everything that has existence. An analogy is a ship on the sea with its assorted cargo or the planet earth that carries everything on it without ever getting tired or overweight.
"Mukama"	King, Master, Lord.

In Buganda God is referred to as:

"Katonda"	Creator of all things.
"Kigingo"	Creator, Master and Giver of life.
"Mukama"	Master/Lord; God; Owner
"Ssewanaku"	The Eternal One.
"Ddunda"	Supernatural Shepherd/Pastor.
"Lugaba"	The Ultimate Divine Giver of all things.
"Ssebintu"	The Owner and Master/Lord of all things.
"Lisoddene"	The Great Eye that sees all things; the Omniscient.
"Nnyinigguru"	Owner/Lord of the sky/heaven.
"Namuginga"	The One who shapes, fashions or creates; the Great Architect.
"Ssewannaku"	He who has pity on the poor, the destitute and the suffering.
"Gguluddene"	The Great One; the One who fills the sky/heaven.
"Namugereka"	He who creates or arranges things and distributes them freely according to his discretion.

This catalogue of the titles and "names" or attributes of God indicates a profound understanding of God as primarily being an Omniscient and Omnipotent Creator who creates <u>ex nihilo</u> (Ruhanga/Katonda), Transcendent King/Lord, the Giver/Provider and Protector of the weak, the needy and the poor; i.e., Ssewannaku. Nevertheless, this list shows consistently that according to these African people God is essentially an intelligent, Supreme, Eternal, Omnipotent, Infinite, Creator, Holy, Primordial Ancestor, Giver/Provider, Creative Transcendence and Incomprehensible Mystery.

Most of these people (both Christian and non-Christian) generally agree that God is such a mystery that, apart from his works manifested in the historical processes of the world, particularly in creation and its delicate processes, wonders and mysteries, God remains an incomprehensible transcendent mystery to be worshipped in awe, reverence and faith rather than being the subject of study, analysis and speculation.[40] Furthermore, some of them believe that such a philosophical or theological inquiry would end up in frustration, skepticism, or even in atheism itself.[41]

Some Pre-Christian Understanding of God in Southern and Western Uganda

On my recent research trip to Uganda, during an interview with Mr. Antyeri Bintukwanga, an outstanding old man in Ankole, I became aware for the first time that in the traditional speculation about God (Ruhanga) there existed a trinitarian understanding of God that is almost similar to the Christian one. However, it existed in both Ankole and Kigezi before the arrival of Christianity in these areas, and therefore, could not have borrowed from it, since this local trinitarian understanding of God predates the arrival of Christianity itself. Mr. Bintukwanga testified that:

> Before the Europeans came to Uganda and before the white Christian missionaries came to our land of Ankole or to your homeland of Kigezi, we had our own religion and we knew God well. We knew God so well at the missionaries added to us little...worship of the Blessed Mary the Virgin Mother of Jesus...We even knew God to be some kind of externally existing triplets: _Nyamuhanga_ being the first one and being also the creator of everything, _Kazooba Nyamuhanga_ being his second brother who gives light to all human beings so that they should not stumble either on the path or even in their lives....

Mr. Bintukwanga went on to describe Kozooba in terms usually associated with the Logos in Western reliogious and philosophical thought:

> _Kazooba's_ light penetrates the hearts of people and God sees the contents of the human hearts by _Kazooba's_ eternal light...The third brother in the group is _Rugaba Rwa Nyamuhanga_, who takes what _Nyamuhanga_ has created and gives it to people as he wishes...You see! We had it all before the white missionaries came, and all they could teach us was that _Nyamuhanga_ is God the Father, _Kazooba_ Jesus Christ his son and not his brother as we thought, and that _Rugaba_ as the divine giver is the Holy Spirit.[42]

Since this was the first time that I had ever come across this claim, namely, that the Banyankole and the Bakiga people had a trinitarian concept of God prior to the arrival of Christianity, and it had been so well and clearly stated and compared to the Christian trinitarian doctrine, I decided to check it out for authenticity. Surprisingly, I found reliable written evidence recorded by Father F. Geraud, a Roman Catholic pioneer missionary in Kigezi and an amateur historian and ethnographer, to support it. Father F. Geraud writes concerning the "Idea of God" in pre-colonial and pre-Christian Kigezi as follows:

> To analyse the idea of God, here is a testimony about an ancient cult which provides a clue about the understanding of the divinity: They [the Bakiga] were offering sacrifices, and after roasting the meat they would gather some of it, put it on leaves (kiko) and bring it to the hut dedicated to the Mandwa. Then they would say: 'eat, be satisfied, give to the one who gives to you, and recognize the one who gives to you, and recognize the one who refuses you. Come to me, your ears and eyes, and return to your dwelling; open my eyes to see...

Then Father Geraud goes on to describe the African sacremental ritual in the following graphic terms:

> 'They would then gather some meat, not offered to the Mandwa and divide it into three parts. A man would throw up one piece saying: "This is for you 'Ruhanga/Nyamuhanga' (God Creator) who created me." Then he would take another piece and say: "This is for 'Rugaba' (the Giver) who gives me life." With the third piece of meat he would say "This is for 'Kazooba'" (Sun/Light) who shows me the way." Sometimes they would take the three pieces of meat together and throw them up [all at once] saying: "These are yours.... Banyinabutaka (Landlords) 'Nyamuhanga,' 'Kazooba,' and 'Rugaba' (Creator, Light/Sun, Giver)." Then after the meal they would say: "Landlords eat from there, make me see, travel and return, take away from me all my enemies."[43]

It is very clear from Father Geraud's account that the Bakiga and the Banyankole worshipped God (Ruhanga) as One God who is who he is by essential nature of creativity (Kuhanga) an "Eternal Tribune of Divine Brothers": Nyamuhanga being their senior as Creator of everything, followed by Kazooba who, being the Divine Light, illumines the world and enlightens the lives, minds and hearts of human beings,[44] and Rugaba, who is the Giver of life to all living things and the free Distributor of talents, wealth and all the other things according to free personal discretion. As in Christian theology, this trinity is always inseparably bound together working jointly as a team (Ruhanga/-Godhead) complementing each other's work, and it could also be misunderstood in a "Sabelian modalistic" manner.

Extreme Divine Transcendence and the Human Need for Mediation

The "names" and titles of God as found among the African people of Uganda and Rwanda, under discussion, focus on the radical transcendence of God as the wholly other, distinct and independent of all human beings, who unlike contingent creation is self-subsisting. Creation then simply exists by his will and is utterly dependent upon him for its existence. However, the human being, though dependent on God, feels (at times) that his/her life is radically threatened by forces of chaos and "non-being" or annihilation. For instance, the human being is aware of personal finitude, utter dependence and vulnerability.

Human life, unlike that of other animals, is generally lived consciously and deliberately. It is usually willed, planned and experienced. It is in this conscious human process of self-reflection, self-examination and self-determination, both individually and collectively as a community, that limitations and frustrations are also usually experienced.

For instance, the human being discovers his/her own finitude and powerlessness in the presence of evil in the world as it manifests itself, particularly, in disease, pain, evil spirits, poverty, ignorance, wars, human irresponsibility, malice, wickedness, envy, witchcraft, hatred, murder, and natural evils and disasters such as floods, lightning, drought, famine, misfortune and accidents. According to Tempels, it is when the Bantu are faced with this predicament that they are meaningfully oriented to God the Creator as the source of life, strength, well-being, protection, guidance and safe-keeping, and therefore, divine salvation.[45]

However, the problem of divine radical transcendence presents the poblem of dialogue between God and the Abantu (human beings) in both prayer and contemplation. Consequently, need of intermediaries between God and the human beings. This religious intermediary chain was subsequently modelled according to the prevailing social and religious culturally established procedure of observing the seniority of the well established traditional socio-political hierarchical chain of communication. This system of religious intermediaries was developed so as to bridge the great gap between the transcendent God "Omwiguru" (in heaven or up in the sky) and the human beings below "omunsi" (here on earth).

Therefore, the Mandwa, the Chwezi, Nyabingi, Kasente, Mukasa, and Ryangombe cults were either "invented" or evolved to serve this religious need for human mediation.[46] The ancestral spirits, being concerned for the well-being of their offspring, were instituted as the category in this chain of mediators, as they were considered the most concerned and capable of understanding, since they had previously lived exemplary lives themselves and were now in direct communication with God, unlike the Abantu, who still need mediation.

This chain of mediators was initially developed so that the finite human beings could be able to reach the transcendent God in heaven so as to be heard. Consequently, most of the traditional African prayers and petitions for protection from threats of evil and chaos, pain and a premature death, and for blessings in the form of material wealth, many children, peace, good health and general well-being, are usually relayed to God through these intermediaries.[47]

The intermediaries between the human beings and God are usually very many, and vary depending on occasion, time and place. Nevertheless, in Kigezi, Ankole, Buganda, Bunyoro and Toro, the intermediaries will often include an elder or the head of the household, a medium or a diviner, a priest, an ancestral spirit and a deity (such as Nyabingi, Kasente, and deified heroes like Mukasa or Kibuka in the case of Buganda).[48]

Nevertheless, if this mediation did not produce the desired results, then the worshippers and petitioners often petition God directly themselves, pleading their own case as best they can in order to persuade him to hear their pleas and petitions, and to respond favorably. For them God is free to act as he wills and even to change his own mind and reverse his earlier decrees, the same way that their own earthly kings did.[49]

The fact that the African peoples have been found to have many gods and a host of religious intermediaries has led to some denunciations of the African Religion as pagan, polytheistic and devilish.[50] However, none of these same writers would probably describe Roman Catholicism in the same way, even when it also has such a comparable system of intermediaries in the form of Jesus, "the ascended Blessed Virgin Mary," angels and the whole host of saints and priests.

Therefore, the African long chain of intermediaries and the deification of the departed heroes and the ancestral spirits is to be viewed positively as both the empowering and the enabling of these agents to become more capable human representatives, priestly advocates or mediators and ambassadors to the transcendent God, who is thought to dwell in celestial remoteness, leaving the finite human being insecure on earth, since it is thought divine presence and good-will are necessary for a happy life, protection and guidance (enlightenment) and blessings in the form of general well-being.

However, this divine presence is believed to be sometimes effectively mediated to human beings through these intermediaries. This essential and efficacious divine presence is thought to express itself in healing, good health, general prosperity, fertility of people, farm animals and of the fields; peace and harmony within the individual and the community.[51]

Radical Divine Transcendence and Anthropocentricity

Since according to the African people under discussion, God is conceived to be so transcendent, remote and removed from the ordinary people and their detailed affairs of existence from day to day, the human being finds himself or herself free to do as he or she likes, and this consequential freedom frightens him or her, as it also bears responsibility for one's decision, actions and their consequences. This seemingly unlimited human freedom is attributed by these Bantu Africans to the apparent "absence of God" brought about by the divine radical transcendence.

Unlimited human freedom tends to threaten the human being and the society, largely due to the uncertainty and unpredictable results, and consequences of such unlimited human causal and definitive freedom. Consequently, the African society has taken steps to limit this human freedom so as to ensure social stability, harmony and peace between individuals, families, clans, and tribes, hence safeguarding peace and general well-being within the whole community.

This is normally done within the context of culture and the "socialization" of the younger to observe appropriate customs, norms, taboos, and religious laws and prohibitions. By the end of this process, human freedom in these African traditional societies is so cropped that usually there is a kind of conformity to be observed about the various ethnic groups in their behavior and general mode of life.

Therefore, deviation from the communal consensus or culturally established ways of doing things is generally strongly discouraged, as it is considered a possible source of tension or disruption within the community and therefore a potential threat to communal harmony and as such, to be crushed at its earliest manifestation.[52] This is mainly because it is believed that the greatest societal value is order, peace and harmony within the community.

Subsequently, whatever enhances this peaceful harmony is esteemed as good and encouraged, whereas whatever creates tension, disharmony and disruption within the community, especially at the family level, which constitutes the primary unit of the society, is considered to be evil (or sin) and to be resisted or uprooted altogether.[53] Consequently, among these Bantu people the society and the ancestors are regarded as the main custodians of moral law, its police and magistrates, rather than God, who is considered too remote to be bothered with the details of human daily life far away on earth, except in very serious cases of moral failure or breach in divine law, such as committing murder, incest or bestiality.

Subsequently, the human being is regarded as the center of the world (Ensi), since God is centered in heaven (Eiguru) far away "above" the world.[54] For instance, according to the Kiganda tradition of both creation and "The Fall," Kintu, the first human being, was created by God in heaven and then dropped down on the lonely earth with a cow, which supplied him with milk but failed to give him a satisfying companionship. Then God saw the misery and loneliness of Kintu and had compassion on him and gave him Nnambi for a wife.

Nnambi came down to Kintu on earth from heaven bringing some chickens along with her to farm for food. But she had to return to heaven to get the chicken feed, which she had forgotten, thus disobeying God's command that, once she left heaven for her new home on earth, she should never return to heaven if she wanted to live in eternal peace and happiness with Kintu, her husband, and the children that would be born to them. When Nnambi had returned to heaven in disobedience to God's advice, "Walumbe" (death) had followed her back to the earth, subsequently, causing death on the earth to Nnambi herself, her husband Kintu, their descendants, and all the other living things.[55]

This myth or tradition illustrates the African anthropocentric religious ontology, as it indicates that Kintu and Nnambi were created in heaven and put on the earth (or world/Omunsi) to be its masters and to try to make it as comfortable as possible for themselves as their eternal home. It is made very clear that everything on earth is created for the sake of the human being (either as food, as the case of Kintu's cow and Nnambi's chickens[56] clearly illustrates, or as a companion and sexual partner, as in the case of Nnambi in relation to Kintu, the first man). In other words, the human being becomes the center of the world and its terrestrial things in the same way God is the center of heaven and everything in it.

For these African people, therefore, the human being becomes the measure of all things on earth.[57] Whatever is of use to the "Abantu" becomes valuable and its worth becomes equivalent to its potential utility for the human being. This African utility principle is applicable to everything, including the value of the divinities, and religious cults which are themselves measured by their functional utility.[58] For instance, if a given divinity delivers to these people the needed security and protection against evil in the form of disease, witchcraft, theft and misfortune, it is esteemed and retained, whereas it is usually abandoned if it fails to deliver these services and is replaced with another that will at least appear to be rendering this very much needed supernatural salvific activity.

As a result, in Buganda, Ankole, Kigezi, Toro and Bunyoro there is a constant heavy traffic in religious sales of new religious objects and the acquisition or adaptations of new gods to replace the old ones that have either malfunctioned or have become completely dysfunctional.

This religious cultural trend, partly explains why a great number of Africans have recently become converted to either Christianity or Islam without abandoning a large portion of the African Traditional Religion, which they know from experience to function well. Very often there is deliberate synchretism so as to produce a better, and a more efficient functioning religion in order to meet the challenges and stresses of this modern age, which the African Traditional Religion alone is unable to meet most effectively, due to its being largely tribal, culturally bound, static and rural community oriented in nature, whereas modern times are characterized by rapid social change, urbanization, technological development, westernization and globalization or "universalization."

The African Concept of Time as Ground for African Metaphysics and Ontology

Having done a detailed study in East Africa, Professor John Mbiti strongly believes that the African concept of time is the key to the understanding and interpretation of African religion and philosophy. He writes:

> The concept of time may help to explain beliefs, attitudes, practices and general way of life of African peoples not only in the traditional set up but also in the modern situation (whether political, economic, educational or Church life). On this subject there is, unfortunately, no literature... The question of time is of little or of no academic concern to African peoples in their traditional life.

Mbiti goes on to make the following fundamental statement which underlies most of his understanding of African metaphysics and ontology:

> For them [Africans] time is simply a composition of events which have occurred, those which are taking place now and those which are immediately to occur. What has not taken place or what has no likelihood of an immediate occurence falls in the category of "no time." What is certain to occur, or what falls within the rhythm of natural phenomena, is in the category of inevitable or <u>potential time</u>.
>
> The most significant consequence of this is that, according to traditional concepts, time is a two dimensional phenomenon, with a long <u>past</u>, a <u>present</u> and virtually <u>no future</u>. The linear concept of time in Western thought, with an indefinite past, present and infinite future, is practically foreign to African thinking.[59]

Mbiti's insightful exposition of the African concept of time helps us to understand and explain the constant conflict and tension between the Western missionaries and expatriates working in Africa and their African colleagues and subordinates. Some Westerners have accused East Africans of being "rather lazy," not time-conscious and ever coming late to the office, meetings and appointments.[60] This conflict is mainly rooted in the difference between the African circular concept of time and the Western linear concept of time.

The African concept of time is also both event-centered and human-centered time (kairos) in opposition to the Western linear time (chronos). For the traditional African, as Professor Mbiti correctly observes, time is made by the human being and other happenings or events, such as the falling down of a big tree near or on the house, morning, noon, evening, night, rain, drought, planting or harvesting, and the like. Time is measured in days and nights according to sunrise and sunset. It is also measured in lunar months, seasons, years and generations extending backwards in time.

In traditional African life, daily routine is eternally self-repetitive. Life tended to be the same for each day, depending on the seasonal changes, except in Kigezi, where the Kasente cult demanded that one day in a week, namely, Thursday, should be set aside as a religious holy rest day dedicated for the worship of God and Kasente as the intermediary. Where the people had no cattle, this daily routine was adapted and based on an agricultural routine, such as going to the garden (8:00 a.m.), resting for lunch (12:00 noon), "Okuhinguka" (returning from the garden, 5:00 p.m.), and chickens or goats coming home (7:00 p.m.), and the rest being the same.[61]

The daily routine of the cattle-keepers tended to remain exactly the same from one day to the next, whereas it varied for those people engaged in agriculture, depending on the seasons. For instance, in the rainy months the people planted their seeds in the previously prepared fields, then later weeded their crops and harvested them when they were ready.

Then there followed a dry season in which these people, having now plenty of newly harvested food, usually feasted on it. A family would usually invite neighbors and relatives to join in communal festivities, eating, drinking, dancing and making merry. This season would also be the annual time when the people of the community would gather together for communal activities such as games, hunting, feasting, weddings, and probably most important of all, communal religious cultic worship activities such as "Kubandwa" and ceremonies such as the initiations of the young people into the mystery and secrecy of the Mandwa cult and "Kubandwa."

The training of the young adults and their initiation process into the "Mandwa" cult in both Kigezi and Ankole was usually done in such a way as to impress on the initiates the fact that the human being exists in a state of finitude, and as such, he or she is limited in strength and knowledge and that he/she is vulnerable, subject to evil, pain and death. Consequently, the candidates for initiation were, generally, subjected to painful experiences so as to impress on them the need for bravery and endurance as they face the uncertainties of life in its unforeseen future.[62] It was impressed upon them that life in its capricious nature can be faced courageously together with their fellow human beings, particularly their kinsfolk and their neighbors, in the community.

What this training process teaches, then, is that the future is unpredictable, consequently requiring collective solidarity and mutual support in case of any eventualities such as misfortune, accidents, hard times, and most of all, death. Humanity and harmonious, reliable, supportive human relationships are considered to be the highest value in the community[63] and as such, they are valued more than time, whose value is in turn measured by its potential utility for enhancing these human relationships.

For instance, a full traditional greeting in Buganda lasts

for about twenty minutes! Should a Muganda office worker meet his visiting mother-in-law or father-in-law on his way to the office, he will be understandably late on that day, and his fellow Baganda colleagues in the office would probably understand and excuse him. But, what about his Western colleagues? Will they too do the same? They might have a different impression, and might even take serious offense at him if they had an appointment with him for that morning. Nevertheless, for the African, he or she would rather be late or even not go at all rather than cause a breach in this close relationship.[64]

Furthermore, for the African, what is important is this humane treatment of one's relatives, since this is regarded as the quintessence of a good life (as far as the African traditional society is concerned). For instance, an individual is known as good or bad for his/her manner of treating other human beings. If it is kind, patient, considerate and generous, he or she is considered good, whereas if it is hurried or too orderly planned to allow casualness and flexibility, the individual is usually disliked as proud, anti-social and inconsiderate. This is because in the African traditional society people generally make no appointments to see or to visit others. They just go and may even expect more hospitality due to the added element of surprise and the joy it is supposed to create![65]

For the African, the time to enjoy oneself or to be kind, generous and loving is the present. According to Professor Mbiti, for the African, the future has no existence, as it has not yet acquired any actuality or concreteness as reality, which it can only acquire by becoming part of human history. He argues that for the African the future dimension has such a short span that it only covers the immediate predictable future. It is the "extended present" into the realm of "potential being" which is still in the process of becoming "actual time" in the concrete present (Sasa/Hati) as it gradually passes on into the realm of the "accumulated sedimenting and sedimented past" (Zamani/Ebya-Ira). Mbiti elaborates on this African orientation to both the present (Sasa), and to the past (Zamani), as the only reality and actuality that counts. He puts it as follows:

> The future is virtually absent because events which lie in it have not taken place, they have not been realized and cannot, therefore, constitute time. If, however, future events are certain to occur, or if they fall within the inevitable rhythm of nature, they at best constitute only potential time. What is taking place now no doubt unfolds the future, but once an event has taken place, it is no longer in the future but in the present and the past. Actual time is therefore what is present and what is past. It moves "backward" rather than "forward;" and people set their minds not on future things, but chiefly on what has taken place.[66]

As a result of this African orientation to Zamani (past), which is regarded in creation traditions (or myths) as the golden time of direct human interaction with God, the beatific vision and eternal life are consequently located in this Zamani period before human disobedience to God and the consequent entry of death into the world,[67] according to the "Creation and Fall Myths" (accounts or traditions) found in Buganda, Ankole, Kigezi and Rwanda.[68] Because of this disobedience (in all cases by the woman) against God, death is said to have come into the world as punishment for this human sin. Consequently, death had become an irrevocable constitutive part of the natural order, causing the familiar conditions of pain, loss, chaos and decay in the world.[69]

According to the Bakiga and the Banyankole traditions, in the beginning human beings had the supernatural gifts of resurrection and rejuvenation freely given to them by God, but these gifts had become lost because of human social discord and hatred. This loss is symbolized by the Musingo Woman tradition, which states that a Musingo woman hated her mother-in-law so much that when her mother-in-law died the Musingo woman was determined to stop her from resurrecting. Consequently, she waited by the graveside and when the grave began to heave, trying to let out the newly resurrected and rejuvenated mother-in-law, she pounded it with a big stick (omuhini) saying, "Abafa tibazooka" (those who die should never resurrect to life again).

It is said that as a result of this incident, the mother-in-law died again, and subsequently, no human being ever resurrects, because God punished all humanity due to this woman's hatred and cruelty to her mother-in-law. For these people, therefore, both creation, resurrection or eternal life lie in the golden past (Zamani); consequently, as far as they are concerned, there is nothing to look for (or to hope for) in the distant future (eschaton) apart from posterity, old age and death, which for them marks the end of all meaningful human existence as "Abantu" (human beings) vis-à-vis "Bafu" (the dead).[70]

Unlike Christianity, in African Traditional Religion there is no concept of future fulfillment in heaven or punishment in hell after one's death. The Africans generally believe that the best and most fulfilling life for human beings is to be found here on earth and not anywhere else. Consequently, the present is the arena of life in its fullness and, as such, to be celebrated now. Self-enjoyment, generous living and loving are to be expressed here and now in the course of day-to-day ordinary living and not to be deferred to the unknown and unforeseeable future.

This emphasis on the celebration of life now very often leads to the hedonistic philosophy of "Eat, drink and be merry now, for tomorrow we die."[71] It also accounts for much of Africa's poverty, mismanagement, corruption and poor planning both in Church and State, and subsequently, the serious prevailing unrest in much of Africa today.

Since for the African, the fullness of life lies on earth in the present, (despite the threat of evil, disease, pain, chaos and death), the society, acting on behalf of God, is expected to reward the good people (with approval, praises them as "good") and expects God, too, to reward them here on earth (with prosperity, good health and general well-being). Conversely, the evil people are castigated as "wicked," ostracized and occasionally beaten, mutilated or even sentenced to humiliating public execution as a deterrent and warning to others.

The community generally deals harshly with serious crimes, such as murder, witchcraft, disobedience to the elders, sex-related offenses, and particularly incest. Punishment for this kind of wickedness was usually very severe because it was believed that there was no other punishment to be meted out by God in the distant future for these crimes and offenses.

Nevertheless, it is speculated that when the wicked people die, their spirits turn into malignant evil spirits or ghosts (emizimu), the very evil beings ostracized by God and feared by the living, who would ordinarily honor them as the "living dead."72 Conversely, the spirits of the good people are thought to be acceptable in the "sight of God" and to the community. It is these good spirits that are generally categorized as "the ancestors" (Bai-shenkuru-itwe),73 despite the fact that they include the spirits of those people who were not genitors themselves.

The spirits of non-genitors are elevated and honored as those of genitors (ancestors) because of their good social service by their good acts and general good behavior while alive on earth. They are also esteemed as exemplary parents and hence ancestors. In this sense, God would qualify to be called the "Chief Ancestor," both literally as the ultimate origin of humanity, and also, as the example of perfection.74 People, like God, are measured, known and categorized by their actions, whether good or bad. People are thought to be what they do, as action is thought to be the personal self-expression and self-externalization of the hidden inner being of the doer.

In African thought the world is eternal. The wheels of time keep on rotating endlessly. Days, months and seasons come and go with their related activities, such as planting and harvesting. They appear to be rotating endlessly in self-repeating cycles. Furthermore, the geographical area being tropical, provides no sharp break in the life cycle (such as winter in the temperate climates, which creates an impression of death and spring, a return of new life analogous to a resurrection, so as to bring to the African mind the possibility of an overall human, definitive, eschatological resurrection).

Consequently, these African people, being Zamani-oriented and having no "mythical utopias" in their religious tradition to be actualized in the future nor a concept and hope of a "kingdom to come" or messianic expectations, and being primarily oriented to God's activities in Zamani or the past, as a result have no interest either in speculative eschatology. Nevertheless, they have great interest in the personal and collective continuity of life in their own offspring as the kind of immortality that matters *vis-à-vis* the change into a free spiritual being at death. The disembodied life as a spirit is generally distasteful to these people, even if one had to be elevated as an ancestral spirit or even to be deified, as in the cases of Ryangombe, Mukasa, Kibuka and Khabengu.75

Nevertheless, whereas for these Bantu people the human

being lives only in the present (Sasa) as the real arena of human life and meaningful existence, being in reference and continuity with the past (Zamani), and whereas the indefinite future is so meaningless that there is no word to denote it,[76] God Ruhanga/ Katonda is thought to be above time as its creator and as its controller. God is also thought to be, simultaneously, omnipresent to all these three dimensions of time (i.e., past, present and future), so that to him all the three dimensions of time form a single eternal "now" before him.[77]

B. THE CONCEPT OF "OMUNTU"/HUMAN BEING

"Omuntu" is regarded as the center of the world (Ensi), and the main concern of the Creator (Ruhanga) is all creation.[78] The "Omuntu" is not only the representative of God in creation, but also shares in divine being (NTU). This special kinship between "Omuntu" and Ruhanga (God/Creator) is demonstrated in the fact that "Omuntu" participates in Ruhanga's divine intelligence and skill of creativity (Kuhanga-hanga).[79]

Consequently, the human being is marked off as God's special creature by the possession of these divine qualities, primarily intelligence and creativity, which are thought as the quintessence of God's own nature as Ruhanga (or Creator). God is thought to have mercifully and gratuitously given these divine qualities as gifts to the human beings (Abantu) so that they, too, would participate in his divine nature and become his intelligent creative assistants, and responsible representatives in the world (Ensi) which depends on the human being for brain, thought and priestly intercession to God for rain and fertility.[80] In return, the human being (Omuntu) depends on the earth for livelihood, specifically for food, shelter, possessions, wealth and recreation. Furthermore, the human being is also dependent on the world for the mediation of divine mystery and revelation.

Subsequently, "Omuntu" is by essential constitution unique and God's (Ruhanga's) special creature in creation. Although "Omuntu" shares in divine qualities of spirit, intelligence, creativity and loving, he simultaneously also shares in the animal characteristics, such as the possession of a body and its physical needs for food, shelter, security and reproduction. In addition, the human being even sometimes participates in animality itself by expressions of aggressiveness, selfishness and brutality.

According to the Bantu people under discussion, "Omuntu" (the human being) _qua_ unique human being (Omuntu) is composed of the following essential elements:

1. "Omubiri" (body, form, flesh)

2. "Omwisyo/Amagara" (breath, air, life)

3. "Ekicucu" (shadow, spirit, soul or the double)

4. "Amaani" (vitality, strength, force, energy)

5. "Omutima" (heart as the seat of emotions)

6. "Omutwe/Obwengye" (head or brain/intellect)

7. "Orurimi" (language or tongue, speaking)

8. "Obuntu" (humaneness, humanness or _huminitus_ _vis-à-vis_

humanitus).[81]

The first four elements, "Omubiri" (body), "Ekicucu" (shadow or soul), the "Amagara/Omwisyo" (life, breath), and "Amaani" (force, strength or energy), are shared by all living things as necessary basic ingredients for biological life on earth. The remaining four elements, "Omutima" (heart, humane emotions), "Omutwe" (intellect, head or thinking), "Orurimi" (speaking/language) and "Obuntu" (humaneness/humanness), are specific qualities that make "Omuntu" *qua* "Omuntu" (the authentic human being), the very special creature of God in the world who is center of creation.[82] Furthermore, these four abstract elements are supposed to survive death, at which time they get embodied in the "Ekicucu" (shadow/spirit) as their new spiritual embodiment.

However, these eight qualities have to fully present for the creature or being in which they manifest themselves to be recognized as a human being (Omuntu) *vis-à-vis* "Ekintu" (a thing). The "Kintu" (thing) category, in *contrast* to the "Muntu" category, is composed of all other objects, creatures and beings in the world which are not either divine or human.

However, the "Muntu" category only includes people who are *whole* in respect to these eight constitutive elements; otherwise they get categorized as "Kintu." For instance, most Bakiga and Banyankole categorize the seriously physically or mentally handicapped people as "Ekintu" (a thing or "it").

These "Birema" (deformed/handicapped people) are not recognized as "fully Bantu" (human beings). They are regarded as incomplete, and therefore, categorized as "Kintu" (things). This also applies to those people who are sexually impotent. They are referred to as "Ebifeera" (those who are dead).[83] Although they are physically alive, they are regarded as socially and religiously dead, mainly because life, its continuity and personal immortality, according to these people, depend on the stability, viability and continuity of the family through the offspring.

Consequently, the traditional African society valued the ability of each individual member of the society to marry and have a big family composed of many wives and children, so as to be able to work the agricultural fields more easily with this large free labor force, and perhaps, most important of all, to preserve more effectively the memory and names of the departed ancestors and relatives, since it is believed that with more numbers there is "corresponding increase" in ability and potential for immortality of family members through their posterity.[84]

The African society is strongly oriented to practical communal action, and requires participation by all its members, including even children at their own level. Therefore, anybody who is too handicapped to participate will also be unable to maintain relationships and the required obligations to join in these family and communal activities, which are considered as constituting the authentic life of "Omuntu," who is basically to be a considerate, loving and able-bodied participatory member of the community. Consequently, the term "Omuntu" only refers to the normal people and not to the "Birema" (deformed people), "Empumi" (the blind), "Biteeta" (the dumb) and the like, because these handicapped individuals are regarded as incomplete, and even more important, perhaps, they are unable to participate fully in the activities of the community. For that matter, those who were born very abnormal (ebihiindi) were usually quietly killed at birth.[85]

For these Bantu people of Uganda, language or speaking is considered to be a uniquely human characteristic to the extent that whatever speaks would be regarded as a form of "Omuntu" and that people are identified with their own language. Therefore, for anybody to be dumb or deaf is regarded as a terrible misfortune that deprives that individual of the opportunity of ever becoming fully human, since to be human is not only to be humane (Obuntu), but also to be linguistic and dialogical. Subsequently, among these predominantly illiterate African people, language in its flowery verbal form is greatly esteemed as indicative of "Omutwe" (intellect), "Orurimi" (language/speaking) and being expressive of the "Omutima" (the heart) and, perhaps most important of all, it is the medium for "Omuntu's" expression of "Obuntu," or human essence (through acts of love), which is considered to constitute authentic human existence and "Bantu" (human) _raison d'être_.[86]

"Obuntu" as the Quintessence of Authentic Humanity That Expresses Itself in Unconditional Love for the Neighbor

Among the people of Ankole, Kigezi, Toro, Bunyoro and Buganda, the "Buntu" is considered to be the most important quality of "Omuntu", being the quintessence of authentic human existence. The person possessing the greater degree of "Buntu" is greatly praised as good, humane, thoughtful, caring, considerate, kind, wise, godly (religious), loving, generous, polite, hospitable, mature, virtuous and blessed. "Obuntu" indicates an inner state of complete humanization as attested by loving, humanness, humility and understanding.

Since "Obuntu" is regarded as the quintessence of authentic humanity and being, the essence of the "Omuntu," it is possible then to be a good person or an authentic "Muntu" without the "Buntu" as the main element that constitutes the human being, as such.[87] "Obuntu" is then a free divine gift as well as positive training and regular practising of virtue by doing good deeds and treating other people appropriately and treating them with respect and dignity as "Abantu" (human beings) _vis-à-vis_ "Ebintu" (things/"its") or treating them impersonally as the nameless and faceless "they."

Therefore, society tries to train the young in virtue so as to condition them into a permanent state of virtue that is grounded in the "Obuntu." In the final analysis, it is this state of virtue as free human existential personal condition of the degree of humanization, that is self-expressed externally in free personal deeds or acts and attitudes that reveal the state of the inner quality at the core of one's humanity. The positive expression of humanity in humane acts of love is what is generally termed "Obuntu" and applauded as human perfection, whereas its absence is condemned as evil, wickedness and animality. The underlying philosophical basis of value judgement being the assumption that HUMAN BEINGS ARE WHAT THEY DO.

To put it differently, "Obuntu" is the divine means for the humanization of the "Abantu" and as such, God's gratuitous proffer of salvation and perfection. The person with full "Obuntu" is consequently esteemed as the ideal, authentic, complete, blessed, good, loving, godly and "perfect human being." Africans, being action-oriented, tend to think that a person is what he/she does. Therefore, good deeds are considered not only to come from a good person, but also to make the doer good. Conversely, wicked deeds come from a wicked person and make him/her even more so for the public to see. As a result, the greatest compliment a person or the society can pay to an individual is to call him or her "GOOD" (Omuntu Murungi). This is the kind of person usually thought to possess a greater degree of the actualized "Obuntu" in one's life and actions, particularly, the capability to love and share one's goods with the concrete neighbor and relatives.

Consequently, human wickedness and moral evil are mainly attributed to failure in unconditional love (Rukundo) for the relatives, neighbors and other members of the community and the consequent deficiency in "Obuntu" or humanity.[88] For instance, most of those people accused of witchcraft are usually those people who are antisocial or those expressing hatred for their neighbors and relatives! Therefore, the "Obuntu" helps in the building of good interpersonal relationships and leads to the increase of human value, dignity and trust, therefore, enhancing harmony and cohesion.

Conversely, its absence leads to tension, conflicts, frustration and the disintegration of these basic human relationships and the community, since "Buntu bulamu" is not just human positive qualities but the very human essence itself, which "lures" and enables human beings to become "Abantu" or humanized beings living in daily self-expressive works of love and attempts to create harmonious interpersonal relationships in their community and the world beyond.

The Community as the Context for "Omuntu" and "Obuntu"[89]

In African thinking and cultural practices, the community is the context and focus of all human activities, as it is thought to be the arena and grounding of human existence, particularly at the family level in its indefinitely extended broad scope.[90] This primacy of the community over the individual is probably best summed up in Professor Mbiti's words, "I am, because we are: and since we are, therefore I am."[91] The Africans usually put the community before the individual because, without the prior existence of the community, no individuals would be born. Individuals are born out of and into the human community, by which they are socialized into becoming responsible human(e) beings (Abantu) endowed with Obuntu (humanness), which exists prior to the individual as an *a priori* within the human community in which the individuals are born.

Therefore, the community, on behalf of the wider human society, undertakes the duty of turning the infant into a viable, responsible, well-humanized individual (Omuntu) member of the community and the human race (Abantu) in general.[92] This means the acquisition of the art of speaking and language (Orurimi), the mental development and the acquisition of basic skills (Omutwe/Obwengye), sound grounding in the culture and history of the family and the community (tribe and nation). It also means the acquisition of humane normative principles for responsible decision-making and action (Obuntu) in the context of the felt common good and the total community (without disrupting the harmony and communal cohesion and well-being, but rather enhancing them); and learning to master one's emotions and not letting them dominate him/her so that he/she fails to manifest responsible mature reactions (Omutima) during situations of stress or danger, such as showing pity and grief during bereavement, whereas manifesting bravery in the case of trouble or danger, rather than the despised cowardice.

These elements were generally covered in the training and initiation into the "Emandwa" cult in both Kigezi and Ankole. To dramatize it, all the initiation candidates were stripped naked before the community, to impress on them that they were born naked and open to the community, and therefore, the need for them to remain humble, open and receptive to the guidance and customs of the community that seeks to clothe, nurture, nourish and enlighten them as members into the hidden mysteries of God and the community that are required for authentic existence and happiness.[93]

In addition, the community being primary over the individual, imposes over the individual a system of norms, codes of behavior and obligations. Kinship is one of these systems that is central to the life of the community. Mbiti describes vividly the central role kinship plays in the life of the community as follows:

> The deep sense of kinship, with all it implies, has

> one of the strongest forces in traditional African life. Kinship is reckoned through blood and betrothal (engagement and marriage). It is kinship which controls social relationships between people in a given community: it governs marital customs and regulations, it determines the behaviour of one individual towards another. Indeed, this sense of kinship binds together the entire life of the "tribe," and is even extended to cover animals, plants, and non-living objects through the "totemic" system.

Mbiti goes on very insightfully to write:

> Almost all the concepts of connected human relationship can be understood and interpreted through the kinship system. This it is which largely governs the behaviour, thinking and whole life of the individual in the society of which he is a member.[94]

Mbiti is probably justified to stress that kinship governs and regulates African life, but he is wrong in claiming that it governs the <u>whole</u> life of an individual, because being regarded as a moral creature cannot be entirely regulated by custom. This is where the importance of the "Obuntu" as the permanent conditioned or habitual state of human moral goodness, uprightness and humaneness comes into the picture to explain why some individuals fulfill their expected roles, whereas others rebel. The community acts as the divinely appointed custodian, police and court for human ethics and morality.

Therefore, the community regulates human behavior and punishes evil because it believes that it has the divine approval and the mandate of God to do so. The community in a sense thinks of itself as the proper divine representative on earth, rather than any individual finite component member of this human community, which is generally thought to be itself infinite, and the immortal embodiment and source of humanity and as its definitive guardian and source of history, culture and civilization, norms, humanness (Obuntu), religion, language, and personal identity.[95]

However, the limitations of kinship were realized and corrective measures were made within the same context of kinship, in the manner of the establishments of "Omukago" (blood-brotherhoods) that adopted people of different "tribes," "races" and "colors" as conventional brothers and sisters deserving humane treatment, love and protection under the kinship system as real consanguinous brothers and sisters. This was an extension of kinship and universalization of "brotherhood" under the "Omukago" procedure, the customary practice of polygamy and the imperative even more meaningful, for it made intermarriage necessary, thus creating an actual natural kinship and political alliances which were valued for the stability of the African neighboring "tribes" or other people who otherwise would have constituted a threat and danger of war.

Furthermore, polygamy was valued as a practice, as it gave the African men more prestige as owners of large households, indicating more capacity for cheap labor and more prosperity, as there were more hands to work in the fields within a polygamous extended family than in a monogamous family, which was equated with youth and poverty. In addition, there were more children born in a polygamous family, which was thought to be indicative of more divine blessing and better prospects for the future personal immortality of the genitors through their offspring and their descendents. Wives and children also generally felt more secure and proud to be members of a large household overflowing with prosperity, fame and honor in the local community.

Therefore, in the final analysis, for the traditional African people, such as, the Bantu groups of Zaire, Rwanda, Uganda, Kenya, and Tanzania human community is not only the context for the humanization of the "Abantu" (human being), particularly the young. In addition, also the context for interpersonal dynamic human relationships ("I-thou" vis-à-vis "I-it"). It is also the context for personal identity as a human being (Omuntu).

Subsequently, the community is inevitably also the arena for serious personal and group challenges, tension, conflicts and sin. This being the case, the community is also the context for the human quest for forgiveness and the expiation of the torment of guilt and broken relationships. Since this forgiveness is obtained through priestly mediators, it is also the categorial, historical context for divine mercy (grace), forgiveness and gratuitous supernatural salvation, anonymously as well-being, wholeness,[96] harmony and peace (Obusingye n'amagara).[97]

NOTES

1. The main focus being on the central, western and southern Bantu ethnic groups of East Africa, particularly, the Baganda, Banyankole, Banyoro, Batoro and the Banyakigezi (Bakiga, Bahororo, and Banyarwanda). The Bantu people form a great percentage of the total population of Africa. Professor John S. Mbiti, being the main authority in East Africa on African Traditional Religion, will be tentatively regarded as its main authoritative exponent.

2. In September, 1982, Dr. Leakey, the famous archaeologist, discovered yet another proto-human fossil at the Oldvern George Valley in Tanzania. With this new discovery, Dr. Leakey is convinced that at last he has now discovered the so-called missing link in the evolutionary ascent between us as the _homo sapiens_ and "our distant cousins, the apes." The University of Oxford in a BBC Science Magazine aired in April 1986 provided further evidence and proof of this African origin of all humanity.

3. Cf. Exod. Ch. 2. Egypt and the rest of North Africa is regarded as African. In this respect, therefore, Egyptian and North African civilizations and Christianity will be claimed as African. See: John S. Mbiti, _African Religions and Philosophy_, pp. 300 ff.; Richard A. Wright, ed., _African Philosophy: An Introduction_ (Washington, D.C.: University of America, 1980), pp. 55-70, 201 ff.

4. Cf. Matt. 2:13-23.

5. And supposedly remained so until the 19th century colonial conquest and occupation of Africa, when written records were made by the various groups interested and working in Africa, particularly, the explorers and the missionaries. Until recently most universities rarely offered courses in African pre-colonial history, traditional religion and philosophy, because it was generally believed that where there are no written sources for analysis, there was no objective knowledge. It is probably more difficult to get at objective sources without written texts, but even written texts themselves, like oral tradition, are often lacking in objectivity due to the personal biases and idiosyncrasies of their authors.

6. See Henri Lhote, "The Fertile Sahara: Men, Animals and Art of a Lost World," _Vanished Civilizations of the Ancient World_, ed. Edward Bacon (New York: McGraw-Hill Book Co., Inc., 1963), pp. 11-32, 55-78.

7. The fact that the Organization of African Unity (O.A.U.) includes these African states north of the Sahara, such as Egypt, Libya and Morocco, is another form of evidence to indicate the essential unity of these two regions despite the apparent differ-

ences of color, language and history. The fact that Egypt and the Sudan are currently working on a merger plan illustrates this point even further.

8. "Dini" is an Arab-Swahili word which was adopted in East Africa to mean religion. This was necessitated by the fact that there was generally an absence of the word "religion" or its equivalent in the local languages. Due to foreign missionary influence, the word "Dini" was then locally understood to mean only the foreign religions, which in Uganda are generally known as the following three:

"Abakristayo" (Protestantism/Anglican, ca. 42%)
"Abakiristo" (Roman Catholics, ca. 43%)
"Abasalaamu" (Muslims, ca. 8%)

The pioneer Anglican and Catholic missionaries in Uganda were so violently opposed to each other that their local converts were led to misconstrue Anglicanism and Catholicism as two religions rather than two denominations or branches of the same religion, namely, Christianity. However, these original religious hostilities and intolerance still pervade and disrupt the religious and political life in modern Uganda that is currently divided and ravaged by war, hatred and repression, which are mainly attributed to these religious misconceptions, bigotry and intolerance in personal ambition and excessive tribalism.

9. Cf. John S. Mbiti, <u>African Religions and Philosophy</u>, p. 1:

> Africans are notoriously religious, and each people has its own religious system with a set of beliefs and practices. Religion permeates into all the departments of life so fully, that it is not easy or possible to isolate it.

This total religious permeation into the spheres of life probably explains why in these African languages there is no single word for religion, because there is no such thing as religion in traditional African life, as the whole entire sphere of life itself is by nature essentially religious. In other words, the entire life of an African is conceived to be lived in a religious arena before God (Ruhanga) as Kazoba (Light or Sun), who sees and reviews every human act in light of humanity and the context of the community. See also Newell S. Booth, ed., <u>African Religions: A Symposium</u> (New York: NOK Publishers, Ltd., 1977), pp. 3-10, 22-68.

10. God (Ruhanga) as Nyamuhanga is Creator, but as Kazooba (Light/Guide) and as Rugaba (Giver/Provider) he is also considered Redeemer or Savior. He saves every moment of human existence, since every moment is regarded as lived by divine protection and sustenance against the equally pervasive forces of evil in terms of threats of disease, poverty, witchcraft, misfortune, distorted relationships, pain and most of all death, and the irrevocable loss and heartbreaking agony it brings to those left

behind. Cf. Noel King, Religions of Africa (New York/London: Harper & Row, 1970), pp. 32-61; Placide Tempels, Bantu Philosophy (Paris: Presence Africaine, 1969), pp. 17-114, 167-189.

11. Cf. John S. Mbiti, op cit., pp. 11-12, and E. Bolaji Idowu, African Traditional Religion: A Definition (New York: Maryknoll, and London: SCM Press, 1973), pp. 108-135; P. Tempels, op. cit., pp. 10-15, 167-189. See also note 9 above.

12. Such as Nyabingi, Ryangombe and Bachwezi in Ankole and Kigezi, Mukasa and Kibuka in Buganda, Khabengu among the Sonjo of Tanzania. These cults are founded by people and get reformed while the African traditional religion in itself generally remains static and the same or unaffected; cf. Aylward Shorter, "Symbolism, Ritual and History: An Examination of the Work of Victor Turner," ed. Rauger and Kimambo (Berkeley and Los Angeles: University of California Press, 1972), pp. 137-150.

13. Both concepts of "heresy" and "atheism" are foreign to traditional Africa and they are being introduced by foreign religions. It can also be said that missionary Christianity has done harm in Africa by rejecting and repudiating the African culture as "pagan" and introducing Western secularism that is responsible for turning some educated Africans into agnostics and even atheists! When these Christian missionaries rejected the well-entrenched African traditional religion as a viable religion, they subsequently created ground in the African mind for doubting all other religions, including Christianity itself. For instance, on what basis was Western Christianity to be accepted as true and the African traditional religion, that had faithfully served the African people for centuries immemorial, to be judged and be repudiated as false?

Consequently, at first, many Africans adopted Christianity or Islam as long as there were demonstrated material advantages to be realized. The Africans also tended to view Western superior technological development and Western Christianity as correlatives, in the same way African traditional religion and the African modality of human existence were so intertwined that it was impossible to separate them. Cf. note 9 above; Mbiti, op. cit., pp. 302 ff., "There is no Roman Catholic priest and a European -- both are the same!" (p. 302). See also Asavia Wandira, Early Missionary Education in Uganda (Kampala: Makerere University, 1972), pp. 2 ff.; Ranger and Kimambo, ed., The Historical Study of African Religion, pp. 219-276.

14. Aylward Shorter, Prayer in the Religious Traditions of Africa (New York/Nairobi: Oxford University Press, 1975), p. 6; see also P. Tempels, Bantu Philosophy, p. 38 and note 1.

15. See, e.g., John S. Mbiti, op. cit., 1-7, 19-21, 341ff.

> ... In their traditional life African peoples are deeply religious. It is religion, more than anything else, which colours their understanding of

> the universe, and their empirical participation in that universe making life a profoundly religious phenomenon. To be is to be religious in a religious universe. That is the philosophical understanding behind African myths, customs, traditions, morals, actions, and social relationships. (p. 341).

See also Newell S. Booth, ed., African Religions: A Symposium, pp. 1-10, 32-62; Noel King, Relgions of Africa, pp. 20 ff., P. Tempels, Bantu Philosophy, pp. 17-70, 167-189.

16. Personal experience and confidential pastoral encounters with this category of people during my role as an ordained Anglican Assisting Chaplain at Makerere University, 1970-73, and as Anglican Chaplain and Lecturer in Religious Studies at the National Teachers' College, 1974-77. See also Mbiti, op. cit., pp. 342 ff.; Fred Wellman, The East African Christian (Nairobi: Oxford University, 1960), passim; Placide Tempels, Bantu Philosophy, pp. 18-69, 95-166.

17. Cf. Noel King, Religions of Africa, pp. 32-61.

18. Cf. John S. Mbiti, op. cit., pp. 299-363. If African traditional religion, which is mainly static and rural-oriented, has to survive it has to adopt a measure of modern outlook from Christianity or from Islam, and in this process it can easily survive either as an "African Islam" or an "African Independent Christianity" that allows the practice of basic African traditional elements such as polygamy, spirit possession, divination (or prophecy) and an emphasis on charismatic healing by prayer, ointment and laying on of the hands. Cf. Adrian Hastings, African Christianity (New York: The Seabury Press, 1976), pp. 60-76; David Barrett, Schism and Renewal in Africa (most of the book) and African Initiatives in Religion (Nairobi: East African Publishing House, 1971); J. S. Trimmingham, Islam in East Africa (London: Cambridge University Press, 1964).

19. See Tempels, op. cit., pp. 55-57.

20. See notes 8 and 16 above.

21. Cf., e.g., Anthony Munyazangabo, "The Function of Religion in Bufumbira History," in A History of Kigezi, ed.. Donald Denoon, pp. 258-263. The presence of an active volcano in these mountain ranges, that some time back erupted disastrously, burning the people around, probably gave the local people a unique concept of future punishment in this volcano for the disobedient non-believers, i.e. non-initiates. This concept is almost similar to that of "hell/Gehenna" in the New Testament. However, this concept and that of the Sonjo of Tanzania and Shilluk of Sudan, which expect future judgement and punishment of the evil-doers and the rewarding of those found good and faithful, is unique in traditional Africa. Generally, there is an absence of such eschatological concepts in the African traditional religion. Cf. Mbi-

ti, op. cit., p. 6:

> There is neither paradise to be hoped for nor hell to be feared in the hereafter. The soul of man does not long for spiritual redemption, or for close contact with God in the next world. This is an important element in traditional religions, and which will help us to understand the concentration of African religiosity on earthly matters, with man at the centre of this religiosity.

22. And for that matter, the Portuguese voyagers and explorers reported that they had found people in Africa who were atheists, i.e. having no religion; cf. Newell S. Booth, op. cit., pp. 1, 10.

23. By both Christian missionaries and Muslims, both as a rejection of the African traditional religion as a valid religion and probably missionary strategy to scare the people so as to yield more easily to the new religion. As a missionary strategy it was ineffective, since conversion out of fear is not meaningful nor as endearing for the convert as conversion out of conviction and love. Conversion out of conviction and love endures, as the case of the Ugandan martyrs clearly illustrates, whereas conversion out of fear only lasts as the fear of damnation itself lasts.

24. E. E. Evans-Pritchard, _The Theories of Primitive Religion_ (London: Oxford University Press, 1965), p. 8.

25. Ibid., p. 7; see also Placide Tempels, _Bantu Philosophy_, pp. 17-38, 167-189.

26. Evans-Pritchard, op. cit., pp. 20-47.

27. Ibid., pp. 2 ff. Evans-Pritchard makes a lot of sense to people like me in that text. The main reason for that is that unless we already had God's preparatory grace, we could not have responded to the missionary preaching of the Gospel in Africa. But since we did, it indicates that God was already present at work prior to the arrival of the Gospel in this part of Africa, and this divine work we can assume, in light of Rahner , to have consisted of God's self-communication in gratuitous grace for supernatural salvation to these pre-Christian Africans.

Consequently, the African Traditional Religion can be considered for these people to be revelatory, salvific, and a preparation for a fuller divine revelation in Christ Jesus. That is in the Incarnation which is God's becoming manifest to the categorial world in humanity itself for better and more effective personal self-revelation (or disclosure) and communication with the humankind at their fundamental level as human beings, so as to persuade them more effectively by example, to be more human(e), loving and forgiving, in order to attain their maximum humanization or divinizaion, since the authentic humanity is in itself a divine quality attained through unconditional love for the neighbor. Cf. 1 John 4:7-21. See also Tempels, op. cit., pp. 17-84, 115-189; Kwasi Wiredu, Philosophy and African Culture (London/New York: Cambridge University Press, 1980), pp. 6-23.

28. E.g. see M. S. Kiwanuka, The Empire of Bunyoro Kitara: Myth or Reality?, Makerere History Paper No 1. (Kampala: Longman, 1968); A. R. Dunbar, History of Bunyoro-Kitara (Nairobi: Oxford University Press, 1969); The Bakitara (London: Cambridge University Press, 1923); J. W. Nyakatura, Abakama ba Bunyoro-Kitara (Quebec: St. Justin, 1947); K. W., "Abakama ba Bunyoro-Kitara, the Kings of Bunyoro-Kitara," Uganda Journal 3(1935) 149-160, 4 (1936-1937): 65-83, 5 (1937): 53-84; M. C. Fallers, The Eastern Lacustrine Bantu (London: Oxford University Press, 1960); John Roscoe, The Baganda (London: Cambridge University Press, 1911); John Roscoe, The Banyankole (London: Cambridge University Press, 1923); Apollo Kagwa, Basekabaka ba Buganda (London: Cambridge University Press, 1953); S. M. Kiwanuka, The Kingdom of Buganda: From Foundation to 1900 (Nairobi/Kampala: Longmans Publishing House, 1970); H. F. Morris, A History of Ankole (Kampala: EALB, 1962); and Donald Denoon, ed., The History of Kigezi.

29. Cf. John S. Mbiti, New Testament Eschatology in African Background, pp. 24-62; African Religions and Philosophy, pp. 15-27; Tempels, op. cit., pp. 61 ff.

30. Cf. Tempels, op. cit., pp. 61-64; Mbiti, African Religions and Philosophy, p. 6.

31. Cf. Placide Tempels, Bantu Philosophy, pp. 18-70, 95-114.

32. For a full discussion of this subject, see: Alexis Kagame's good treatment in the second half of his book, La Philosophie Bantu-Rwandaise de l'Être, and Janheinz Jahn, Muntu: An Outline of the New African Culture (New York: Grove Press, 1961), chapter on African philosophy; Placide Tempels, op. cit., pp. 39-114. Jahn, like Tempels, sees NTU as a divine universal "vital force" underlying all things, whereas Kagame views it primarily in Aristotelian terms as the primary substance that grounds and constitutes all actualities including God and the Soul, who are grouped together with all the intelligent beings in the one category of "Muntu," who preside over the category of "Kintu" as non-intelligent force, the third category being "Hantu," covering space and time, and finally inventing the word "Kuntu" as the fourth category, which he describes as "mode." This category covers human moods as well as general aesthetics.

However, the trouble with this grouping is that God becomes hypostasized into another being besides other beings as a kind of *primus inter pares*! This is therefore unacceptable as a method of categorization of Being (NTU) and beings (Bintu). Furthermore, it would seem that if God (Ruhanga/Imaane/Katonda) is categorized together with human beings as MUNTU, sharing in the universal force NTU, this NTU is the actual God, being the most inclusive and the origin of everything, as Being or NTU. "Omuntu" can also mean native to or an insider to "UTU," i.e., being more expressive of being, whereas "Eki-ntu" can also mean on the external or the periphery of NTU, and as such having less "NTU" than the "Omuntu" who, being more on the inside (Omu-NTU), has more "NTU" and is the most akin to "NTU" as God in the whole of creation, and therefore, "NTU's" image and categorial expression in all creation; cf. Tempels, op. cit., pp. 49-55.

33. Cf. Martin Heidegger, Being and Time, trans. John Maquarrie & Edward Robinson (London: SCM Press, Ltd., 1962), H. 15, H. 41-126, H. 212-246, H. 334-392; see also Tempels, op. cit., pp. 44-114; Kagame, op. cit., pp. 109-123.

34. Cf. Thomas Aquinas, Summa Theologiae, I:qq. 1-13. However, the African philosophical understanding of God in this area has not yet been well researched into. Nevertheless, Kagame's work, though primarily on Rwanda, can be cited to support this claim; cf. La Philosophie Bantu-Rwandaise de l'Être, pp. 240 ff.; Tempels, op. cit., pp. 44-114; Richard A. Wright, ed., African Philosophy: An Introduction (Washington, D.C.: University of America, Inc., 1979), pp. 149-156; Kwasi Wiredu, Philosophy and African Culture, pp. 37-50.

35. Cf. Tempels, op. cit., pp. 39-114; Noel King, Religions of Africa, pp. 32-61.

36. See Plato's Timaeus.

37. Cf. Tempels, op. cit., pp. 44-94.

38. The exception being the Banyarwanda, who call God "Imaana" as a proper name in addition to the usual descriptive terms for God, which in this case hinge around the name "Imaana," e.g. "Hategikimana" (Imaana/God reigns), "Bizimana" (God knows all things), "Hashakimana" (God only plans). These divine attributes also form names of people to express total human dependency on God and their humble acknowledgment and gratitude. Cf. Alex Kagame, La Philosophie Bantu-Rwandaise de l'Être, pp. 280-300.

39. For a comprehensive catalogue of these divine terminologies and names, see John S. Mbiti, Concepts of God in Africa, pp. 327-336.

40. Most people that I interviewed in the villages who were not enlightened by Christian teaching did not know much about Ruhanga, whereas they were very familiar with individual religious cults and knew a great deal more about them. Are these cults to be treated, then, as representative of divine immanence in the African traditional world? Cf. Noel King, Religions of Africa, pp. 47-61.

41. In 1941 eight Balokole leading students were expelled from Bishop Tucker Theological College because they refused to go

to theological classes, regarding them as "modernist" and "un-christian." Some of them are still alive and they are regarded as the pillars of the Christian faith among the Balokole group. Both theology and philosophy are also generally viewed with suspicion by the Church of Uganda hierarchy.

42. Mr. Antyeri Bintukwaga is 103 years old. He now lives at Kakoba, in Mbarara Town, East Ankole, Uganda. He is incredibly alert and strong for his age. His sight is failing, but his mental powers are undiminished. It was a very enlightening experience to interview him.

There were two 3-hour interviews held with Mr. Bintukwaga on March 27, 1982, and on March 29, 1982. He has a keen memory, and he is also respected as a knowledgeable and intelligent old man. He is one of the few people still alive that have lived in the pre-colonial times, the colonial era and post-colonial era. He says that he was 27 years old when the first Christian missionaries came to Ankole; therefore his recollections and information in this interview are very valuable and important.

43. Fr. F. Geraud, "The Idea of God," in Donald Denoon, ed., _A History of Kigezi_, p. 163.

44. Kazooba is more like the Word (Logos) as described in John 1:1-2, 4-5:

> In the beginning was the Word, and the Word was with God, and the Word was God. He was in the beginning with God. In him was life and the life was the light of men. The light shines in the darkness, and the darkness has not overcome it.

45. See Tempels, op. cit., pp. 17 ff., 44-69.

46. Whereas West Africa is generally rich in divinities, it is generally the reverse in East Africa; cf. Idowu, _African Traditional Religion_, pp. 165-173; Placide Tempels, _Bantu Philosophy_, pp. 44-70.

47. E.g., see A. Shorter, _Prayer in the Religious Traditions of Africa_, pp. 10 ff.

48. See, e.g., Y. K. Bamunooba, "Diviners for the Abagabe," _Uganda Journal_, XXIX:1 (1965), 95-97; Y.K. Bamunooba and F. B. Welbourn, "Emandwa Initiation in Ankole," _Uganda Journal_, XXIX:1 (1965), 13-25; F. B. Welbourn, "Some Aspects of Kiganda Religion," _Uganda Journal_, XXVI (September, 1962), 171-182; Noel King, _Religions of Africa_, pp. 32-48.

49. Because of Ugandan political complication by regionalism, tribalism and the military conflict between Buganda Kingdom and the Ugandan central government in 1966, all the four kingdoms in Uganda (Buganda, Ankole, Bunyoro and Toro) were subsequently

abolished by a new national republican constitution in the same year.

50. Cf. E. Bolaji Idowu, African Traditional Religion: A Definition, pp. 108-189, and John S. Mbiti, African Religions and Philosophy, pp. 8-18; also Tempels, op. cit., pp. 167-186.

51. Cf. Tempels, op. cit., pp. 18-70, 95-114; Newell S. Booth, ed., African Religions: A Symposium, pp. 32-68; Mbiti, African Religions and Philosophy, pp. 75-100, 166-193; Noel King, Religions of Africa, pp. 47-61.

52. Deviants are usually persecuted in the guise of witches and taboo violators. For instance, most of the people accused of witchcraft in this area are usually anti-social, unfriendly or very ugly individuals! See Africa, VIII:4 (1935) (whole number is devoted to "witchcraft"); J. Middleton and E. H. Winter, eds., Witchcraft and Sorcery in East Africa (London: Cambridge University Press, 1963).

53. Evil is considered to be what disrupts or destroys individual and communal peace and harmony (Obusingye), as this is the summum bonum in African thinking. Consequently, whatever enhances this perceived summum bonum as peace and harmony is, similarly, considered to be good. God is therefore not the measure of ethics and morality, but rather, the human being in the context of the community who is the measure. This is the reverse of the traditional Judeo-Christian approach to ethics and morality. Cf. Tempels, op. cit., pp. 18-69, 95-166; Mbiti, African Religions and Philosophy, pp. 194-215; Newell S. Booth, op. cit., pp. 4-10, 32-68.

54. See Tempels, op. cit., pp. 61-69; Mbiti, African Religions and Philosophy, p. 6.

55. It almost sounds like Genesis Chs. 1-3. The myth tells of the original perfect creation by God, the creation of man (Kintu) first and woman (Nnambi) to keep him company, and to reproduce and populate the earth. There is a divine commandment not to return to heaven, the woman (Nnambi) breaks it, and as a result death (Walumbe) comes into the world, not only for the woman who disobeys God, but for all humankind and all living creatures on earth, since they find their meaning and representation in the human being, and are therefore, inseparably bound to his/her fate.

56. Chicken is considered a great delicacy in Buganda. In this context, it can be said that chicken is for Nnambi what the fruit is for Eve in the Genesis "story of The Fall"; cf. Gen. 3:1-6. Both of them are desired for food, and lead to each woman's temptation and finally to the fateful disobedience and the violation of God's commandment that ushers death into the world.

57. Reminiscent of the Homo Mensura theory of the Sophist

School of Philosophy, whose main exponents were Protagoras and Heraclitus; cf. e.g., Gordin H. Clark, Thales to Dewey: A History of Philosophy, pp. 61-70.

58. Cf. John S. Mbiti, African Religions and Philosophy, pp. 2, 20, 92; Mbiti, Introduction to African Religion, pp. 39 ff.; Okot p'Bitek, African Religions in African Scholarship (Kampala: East African Literature Bureau, 1970), p. 109.

59. John S. Mbiti, African Religions and Philosophy, p. 21. See also New Testament Eschatology in African Background, pp. 24-62 (for the detailed East African application). However, some scholars like Tempels, Jahn and Kagame, whose words on Bantu philosophy predate that of Mbiti, tended to emphasize the Bantu concept of cosmic pervasive dynamism, creativity, or "vital force" (UNTU) as the only key for understanding African philosophy and traditional religions; see note 27 above. Nevertheless, each of these concepts, though providing a valuable tool for the understanding of the African thought and religion, provides an even better tool or key for such a purpose when combined and utilized as correlatives than being used singly in a mutual exclusion as Mbiti and his opponents seem to suggest or imply. Cf. Newell S. Booth, Jr., "An Approach to African Religions," African Religions: A Symposium, pp. 1-10, or Mbiti, African Religions and Philosophy, pp. 15-27; New Testament Eschatology in African Background, pp. 24-62; Tempels, Bantu Philosophy, pp. 17-114.

60. Cf. e.g. J. V. Taylor, The Growth of the Church in Buganda (London: S.P.K. Press, 1958), pp. 28 ff., F. B. Welbourn, East African Rebels: A Study of Some Independent Churches (London: C.M.S. Press, 1961), pp. 3 ff.

61. Cf. ibid., pp. 25 ff., for a slightly different version of this reckoning of time in Ankole.

62. Cf., e.g., Y. K. Bamunooba and F. B. Welbourn, "'Emandwa' Initiation in Ankole," Uganda Journal, XXIX:1 (1965), 13-25; Noel King, Religions of Africa, pp. 43-46.

63. Cf. Newell S. Booth, ed., African Religions: A Symposium, pp. 4-10, 15, 32-62; P. Tempels, Bantu Philosophy, pp. 44-64, 95-114; R. A. Wright, ed., African Philosophy: An Introduction, pp. 157-168.

64. Ibid. For the African, personal relationships that constitute the harmony and wholeness of the community have priority over everything else. This is because the individual is authentically constituted as "Omuntu" (a human being) by the living network of these interpersonal relationships of "I-Thou," in the context of the community (very much reminiscent of Martin Buber's book, I-Thou).

65. Consequently, it is generally considered unfriendly and

rude in Africa to ask someone coming to visit, "What can I do for you?"

66. Mbiti, African Religions and Philosophy, pp. 22-23. Mbiti's work on time is generaly recognized as a fairly accurate observation and interpretation of the traditional concept of time in East Africa.

67. Cf. Tempels, op. cit., pp. 61 ff. Tempels and Mbiti are in agreement here that Africans are oriented to creation or genesis in the Zamani period as the glorious human era of the "archipatriarchs" and direct human communication and socializing with God!

68. Cf., e.g., the story of Kintu, Nnambi and Walumbe in Buganda and the story of the Musingo woman whose excessive hatred for her mother-in-law led to the general loss of the divine gifts of the resurrection and rejuvenation (as told in both Kigezi and Ankole). In Ankole and Kigezi hatred is usually the evil root for witchcraft and murder.

69. It is almost similar to the traditional Catholic doctrine of the Original Sin as it finds its key expression in St. Augustine; e.g., see On Free Will, XVI-XX; Rom. 5:12:

> Therefore as sin came into the world through one man and death through sin, and so death spread to all men...

See also Tempels, op. cit., pp. 18-69, 95-114; Mbiti, African Religions and Philosophy, pp. 92-100, 194-215. (The Good News of Christianity for Africa is that these lost gifts, resurrection and eternal life in divine presence, have been restored in Christ, and therefore, the African can now look in the future with hope and anticipation of an eschatological resurrection and eternal life before God.)

70. It is thought that the enjoyable state of being "Omuntu" (a human being) ends with death. It is also thought that some human elements survive death in their new spiritual embodiment. However, this new state of being is thought to be less meaningful and less enjoyable than that of being "Omuntu." Consequently, death is thought of as an irrevocable great loss. Cf. Mbiti, op. cit., pp. 31-34, 107-118, 195-218; Noel King, Religions of Africa, pp. 62-82; Tempels, op. cit., pp. 18-64, 95-114, 187-189.

71. Cf., e.g., Eccl. 2:24, 4:11. This kind of attitude manifests a lack of a future dimension and probably helps to explain the general absence of permanent buildings in Africa South of the Sahara, an exception being the Zimbabwe stone walls, which were built for self-defense and protection from the surrounding "warlike," "savage" and even presumably cannibal tribes; cf. Roger Summers, "City of Black Gold: The Riddle of Zimbabwe," in Edward Becon, ed., Vanished Civilizations of the Ancient

World, pp. 33-54.

72. "Living-dead" is Mbiti's invented term to refer to the spirits of the recently departed, who are still regarded as part of the daily affairs of the community. For Mbiti, this is the stage of personal immortality, since the remembrance of the dead is still fully vivid and personal. See Mbiti, African Religions and Philosophy, pp. 107-118.

73. "Baishenkuru-itwe" should ideally be used to refer to ancestral spirits and others that are good. The term "Emizimu," if used appropriately, should refer to the malignant or evil spirits as the ghosts of the departed. Consequently there are no "good Emizimu" nor good ghosts, as this would amount to saying that there is a "good evil-spirit," which is self-contradictory. Cf. Noel King, Religions of Africa, pp. 32-46; P. Tempels, Bantu Philosophy, pp. 44-70, 115-165.

74. Cf. Tempels, op. cit., pp. 55, 61 ff.

75. The story of Khabengu as the expected eschatological Messiah of the Sonjo, that reads like the story of Jesus, is unique in Africa. See R. F. Gray, The Sonjo of Tanganyika (London: Oxford University Press, 1963); John S. Mbiti, African Religions and Philosophy, pp. 30, 250 ff. This Khabengu story illustrates clearly the nature of divine revelation in African traditional religion. It is possible that if foreign religions had not come to Africa, the African Traditional Religion would have become Messianic. This speculation is based on the emergence of Ryangombe and Khabengu cults in East Africa.

76. Even the Swahili language has no word that means "future." There is Zamani for "past" and Sasa for "now/present," but there is no single word to denote the future in its indefinite dimension. There is the word Kesho, which means tomorrow, and beyond that one has to describe the future time in terms of days, weeks, months or years. This is the same case with the other nine African languages of which I speak. See: Mbiti, New Testament Eschatology in African Background, pp. 24-61, and African Religions and Philosophy, pp. 19-35; Rechenbach's Swahili-English Dictionary (Washington, D.C.: Foreign Service Institute, 1967); H. F. Morris and B. E. R. Kirwan, A Runyankole Grammar (Kampala: EALB, 1957); C. Taylor's Simplified Runyankole-Rukiga English Dictionary (Kampala: EALB, 1959).

77. Therefore, basically more like the traditional Christian conception of God and time as found in St. Thomas; cf., e.g., Summa Theologiae, I:I q. 10, in contradiction to the Whiteheadian Process Philosophy, which claims that God does not know the future contingent events, as he is limited to the past and present actuality as well as those two dimensions of time, like us human beings; cf. Alfred North Whitehead, Process and Reality, Parts III and V:II. See also Alex Kagame, La Philosophie Bantu-Rwandaise de l'Etre, pp. 332 ff; Tempels, op. cit., pp. 49-70; R.

A. Wright, ed., African Philosophy An Introduction, pp. 149-156.

78. See P. Tempels, Bantu Philosophy, p. 64.

79. Ibid., pp. 18-70, 95-114. This material here is a basic key for understanding Bantu ontology or metaphysics. This is where Mbiti's claim that time is the key to understanding African religion and philosophy falls short. By itself, the African concept of time cannot explain Bantu anthropology or philosophy.

80. See John S. Mbiti, Introduction to African Religion, pp. 54-76. The human being through prayer to God and worship provides harmony and divine blessings to the world, and by human sin the world loses this harmony and divine blessing; cf. Booth, op. cit., pp. 8-9, 32-68; Tempels, op. cit., pp. 18-64, 95-114.

81. Cf. Newell S. Booth, African Religions: A Symposium, pp. 31-68. Booth's detailed analysis of Muntu is applicable to the Bantu people under discussion (with just a few minor modifications).

82. See Tempels, op. cit., pp. 64-66.

83. Cf. Booth, op. cit., p. 36: "'Muntu' properly refers only to one who is healthy. A sexually impotent person is not 'Muntu' but 'mufu'."

84. Almost functions like Whitehead's objective immortality" except that in African thinking the living people immortalize their departed rather than God; cf. Alfred North Whitehead, Process and Reality, Part III:I-IV, PART V:V-VII.

85. Booth, op. cit., pp. 7-10, 33-51. It is probable that killings of abnormal children still go quietly in the villages; cf. Emmanuel K. Twesigye, Death among the Bakiga of Uganda (Kampala: Makerere University Dept. of Religious Studies and Philosophy, 1971).

86. Cf. Booth, op. cit., pp. 7-10, 14-15, 33-51; Tempels, op. cit., pp. 18-70, 95-114; Kagame, op. cit., p. 53.

87. Cf. Tempels, op. cit., pp. 18-25, 39-61, 95-114; Booth, op. cit., pp. 13-16, 32-46.

88. Cf. Tempels, op. cit., pp. 18-21, 25, 54-62, 167-182; Kagame, op. cit., pp. 53 ff.

89. Booth, op. cit., pp. 1-10; King, op. cit., pp. 62-82; Tempels, op. cit., pp. 18-64, 95-165; Wright, op. cit., pp. 157-168; Mbiti, African Religions and Philosophy, pp. 100-110.

90. For instance, the African extended family includes several wives and children in a polygamous family, and their own relatives such as brothers, sisters, uncles, aunts, and several

degrees of cousins! Cf. Mbiti, op. cit., pp. 104-109, 142-144; Mary Edel, The Chigga of Western Uganda (London: Oxford University Press, 1957), pp. 20 ff.

91. African Religions and Philosophy, p. 141.

92. Cf. Tempels, op. cit., pp. 44-66, 95-114.

93. See note 65 above.

94. African Religions and Philosophy, p. 135. Based on this understanding, it should be easy to understand why tribalism and nepotism seem to be the major problems accounting for a great deal of instability in Africa today; e.g., see Colin Legum, "After the Amin Nightmare," Africa Report, January-February, 1983, pp. 15-22.

95. "Divine kings" in Uganda were still subject to the community and so were the religious leaders, i.e. priests and diviners; cf. Noel King, Religions of Africa, pp. 32-61.

96. Wholeness is a key concept in African philosophy and religion, as it is the central focus for all African total religious, cultural, moral and political activities as the desired goal and end-result of these activities. It is connected with the "holy," the "moral" and "ideal" state of being in the community.

Wholeness implies peace, harmony and general well-being. It also means good personal relationships between the individual and the following:

1. The community (neighbors and relatives).
2. The "living-dead"/ancestral spirits.
3. God (and the other intermediaries).
4. The physical environment.

Wholeness was symbolized in African traditional society by round houses, fences, decorations, etc. Wholeness as expressed in harmony is the present expression of divine eternity and human eternal life now in the present. It provides continuity between the past (Zamani) and the present (Sasa) and the future. Cf. Booth, op. cit., pp. 7-10, 36.

97. This concept of peace as wholeness and harmony (Obusingye) is considered as a divine categorial gratuitous offer of salvation to human beings right now. In other words, it is supernatural eternal life now for those enjoying this blessed state of wholeness, harmony and peace. This concept is very close to Whitehead's concept of peace as expressed in the last chapter of his book, Adventures of Ideas. See also King, op. cit., 47-61.

CHAPTER IV

A POSSIBLE DIALOGUE BETWEEN CHRISTIANITY AND THE AFRICAN TRADITIONAL MODALITY OF HUMAN EXISTENCE: AUTHENTICITY AND DIVINE SALVATION

The main constitutive elements of the African[1] Traditional Religion and Philosophy discussed in the preceding chapter indicate that the African people have both a cognitive or thematic and a prethematic knowledge of a triune supreme God (Ruhanga/Katonda). This supreme Being or God is conceived of and worshipped as the most transcendent incomprehensible nameless Mystery who is Nyamuhanga (the Creator), Kazooba (the Light, Sun, Enlightener, Guide and Savior) and Rugaba (the Giver/Provider of everything including life, talents and possessions).

This transcendent incomprehensible God is worshipped as the cause of life, well-being, peace, riches, harmony and the happiness that all human beings (Abantu) crave in all they do in hope that God will in his free loving grace be kind enough to bestow blessings on them as reward for their diligent search, godliness, hard work, and for having been considerate, kind, generous and loving to their relatives and neighbors; that is, having practiced the "Obuntu."

Since these people have accepted the divine Mystery and have also accepted their given humanity and that of others they interact with in the community as relatives and neighbors, and they even do respect and provide hospitality for the stranger or traveller without the hope of payment or reward in return except by God (Ruhanga) in heaven, who is attributed with the power of omniscience as the one who sees and knows all human actions even before they happen,[2] they have subsequently fulfilled the Christian conditions for "anonymous Christianity" which Karl Rahner, on behalf of the Catholic Church teaching states as follows:

> Now God and the grace of Christ are present as the secret essence of every reality we choose. Therefore it is not easy to opt for something without having to do with God and Christ either by accepting them or rejecting them, either by believing or not believing. Consequently, anyone who, though still far from any revelation explicitly formulated in words, accepts his existence in patient silence (or better, in faith, hope and love), accepts it as the mystery which lies hidden in the mystery of love...is saying "yes" to Christ even if one does not know it...Anyone who accepts his humanity... [that] of others, has accepted the Son of Man

> because in him God has accepted Man...whoever loves his neighbour has fulfilled the law, then this is the ultimate truth because God himself has become this neighbour.[3]

However, as in explicit Christianity, not everyone is an heir to eternal life, similarly, not all "anonymous Christians" are living in accordance with God's will either in its implicit or explicit giveness. As a result, in both explicit and anonymous Christianity, there are candidates for both heaven and hell. In other words, the life of salvation and that of damnation are both possible and co-exist with each other side by side in both explicit Christianity or in the historical Church and likewise outside it, depending on an individual's personal response to life, love and the Transcendent Mystery.

Furthermore, the kind of damnation that can be experienced by some members of the Church can be even more agonizing, since these individuals have been given a more explicit divine salvific gratuitous revelation which they have consciously and deliberately turned down with a resounding and a consequential "No," and therefore, incurring serious guilt due to this rejection of God's proffer of redemptive grace and its correlative divine salvation.

On the other hand, in traditional Africa, to be human is to belong to God and the community which is itself by nature religious. Subsequently, one had to say "Yes" to God publicly before the corporate community in its collective cultic worship, since deviance would not be tolerated by the community, as the traditional Africans thought that an irreligious member of the community would, invariably, bring divine displeasure, wrath and destruction of that community by God in his righteous retribution for the sacrilege committed by one of its members.

Like the Catholic Church which excommunicates an unrepentant notorious persistent sinner, (and in the past, even executed some of them), the African community also ostracized (Kucwa) notorious sinners until their repentance, propitiation and expiation of their sins. However, in cases of grave sins such as incest or pre-meditated murder, the individual would be put to death and the entire community would undergo ceremonial purification from the abomination.

In this light, Rahner would probably argue that the African Traditional Religion is a good example of a medium for "anonymous Christianity," which is endowed by God with supernatural gratuitous salvific grace, and as such, able to mediate supernatural salvation to its members according to God's unconditional infinite love, and his universal salvific will for all human beings that he has created, and that this is also the case with Islam, Buddhism, Hinduism and Judaism as the other possible media of this "anonymous Christianity."

According to the African Traditional view of religion and divine salvation, God's salvific activity is thought to be efficaciously universal. Consequently, there is no concept of missionary work in African traditional religion. Traditional Africans believe that all groups of people know God as their Creator and worship him as such.

This African view of God, universal divine revelation and salvation for whoever obeys God and loves the neighbor is very much in line with Rahner's own teaching on universal divine salvific will and the divine universal efficacious self-communication in free salvific grace for the salvation of every human being, regardless of race, color, creed, level of education and technology.

This Rahnerian Catholic inclusive teaching finds its best expression in his concept of "anonymous Christianity." By "anonymous Christianity" Rahner also means that God's salvific self-communication in gratuitous redemptive grace is universal. The purpose of this chapter is to demonstrate that such a divine redemptive revelation existed in the African Traditional Religion, and that it was effectively salvific for the African people who practised the African Traditional Religion.

The method adopted in this section is to compare and contrast some key concepts in the African Traditional Religion with those of Christianity as taught by the major main-line Church theologians, such as Karl Rahner, who is here regarded as the exponent of the Christian faith as both grounded and informed by revelation, holy Scriptures, tradition, doctrine (dogma) and Western scholarship. The assumption or hypothesis here is that since God is one and the ultimate salvific truth which manifests itself universally in the world, then at least, there should be a basic, mutual understanding of God, humanity, love and community between Christianity as explicated by Rahner and the African Tradition.

It is hoped that by this method it will be demonstrated that the Africans were practising the principles of Christianity long before historical Christianity itself was ever known. However, it will be maintained that although "anonymous Christianity" is efficaciously salvific, nevertheless, it still remains a deficient mode of Christianity that anticipates the coming of an explicit or historical missionary Christianity still required for its fulfillment and completion.

God as the Triune Mystery and the Ultimate Origin of Humanity

It is probably a surprise for some people to find a sound understanding of God among the Bantu people of Uganda that is in line with Rahner's main concept of God as the incomprehensible Mystery, which is by nature a self-subsistent intelligent creativity and the ultimate origin of all life and humanity and the Creator of all things that are in the cosmos which have "NTU" or being. God is regarded by both as the very ground and prerequisite of life and any form of being or existence.

For the African Tradition (Culture, Religion and Philosophy), God is such a Mystery that he is the unnameable Creator (Ruhanga). God is unnameable because he is considered as being the Incomprehensible, the Transcendent Mystery or "Abyss" who is beyond the grasp of the finite human intellect and understanding (omutwe n'obwengye), and as such, beyond the grasp of human language and thought; and therefore, beyond naming.

Since for these Africans a name is thought to be expressive of the essential identity and inner nature of the named person as expressed in the Bakiga proverb, "Eiziina niwe muntu" (the name denotes the person), God's name would, similarly, be expressive of his inner nature. This being impossible, since he is by essential nature an infinitely incomprehensible Mystery, consequently, he has no proper name given to him. Subsequently, he is known and called by his various activities and attributes, such as creating, and therefore Creator (Kuhanga--Nyamuhanga/Ruhanga).

Rahner's conception of God as Mystery is in harmony with this African view of God. For instance, Rahner refers to God in terms such as "the Incomprehensible," "the Infinite Mystery," "the Abyss," "the Ground of Being," "the Absolute," "the Transcendent," "the Horizon of human knowledge and human existence," and the like, which are not names of God, but rather, terms that express the transcendence, mystery and the incomprehensibility of God.[4] This Rahnerian Christian inclusive conception of God would be most appealing to the Bantu of Africa as a better articulation of what they already understood of God, as the holy Transcendent Mystery whose chief activity is creativity and divine salvation or preservation of creation.

This absolute Mystery which both Rahner and the African tradition designate and worship as God, is not the transitory finite mystery that is accountable for by human ignorance and gaps in scientific knowledge, or an illusion that will be consequently dispelled and banished from the human minds by more scientific knowledge, and anti-religious education and propaganda as the atheist Feuerbach speculated in his attacks on Christianity.[5] But rather, it is the infinite Mystery NTU/BEING that originated and constitutes life, the cosmos and its creative processes, that is both transcendent yet close; that is impersonal yet personally involved, loving, caring, creating and mindful of individual detailed uniqueness, needs specific fulfillments and happiness.

This is the Infinite, Creative Mystery at the center of the cosmos that sets the human being wondering at the beauty and life processes which surround him or her, such as the birth of a new healthy baby, the beauty and smell of the flowers, the glow of the stars, the beauty of the moon, the majesty of the sunshine as its modest warmth warms up the human complex body, brain and its functions, particularly, in thought processes and language. In addition, the delight of human love and community strike the human being as elements of that same unnameable impenetrable Creative Mystery that sets the human being indefinitely wondering, and questioning without ever arriving at any definitive final answer that explains it all fully and adequately for all time.

This is for Rahner the all-encompassing Absolute Mystery that faces the human being with the inner basic question about one's being itself, how complex it is, and where it ultimately originated, where it is ultimately destined, and whether there is any purpose for one's being and for existence in general. Questions such as: "Who am I?" "Why am I here?" "Does life have any purpose?" may not always be so well formulated or articulated, particularly, in the African Tradition. Nevertheless, they may be asked in any varied form as a result of the unique human encounter with an awareness of the Supernatural, Infinite, Creative Holy Mystery.

Therefore, these questions can be described as the questions of a dilemma, since they usually require the decision of saying "Yes" or "No" to this Transcendent Holy Mystery as the ground of one's being. The response of "Yes" affirms oneself, life, hope, love and God, whereas "No" leads to self-denial of one's being, one's meaning and the rejection of the a priori destiny in God as this Transcendent holy Mystery. However, in so doing the individual chooses separation from God, and subsequently, he/she has a self-imposed sentence to eternal damnation.[6]

This triune Mystery acknowledged by both Rahner and the African tradition is particularly interested in the human being as his special creation and representative on earth. And indeed in the rest of creation, as both the Rahnerian Christianity and the African Tradition seem to think that the human being is the only speaking and intelligent creature so far known to exist in the whole of the cosmos.

Whereas the African Tradition conceives Kazooba as the second person of the Trinity, and views him as the eternal Light (Sun) that enlightens and guides all human beings from error into truth and from the wrong path into the right one, and protects the individuals from pitfalls both physical and moral or spiritual, and also enables the righteous person to see through other people's shady motives, and therefore, be able to avoid evil company and the harm of enemies posing deceitfully and maliciously as friends, it nowhere claims that Kazooba became a human being in order to enlighten human beings by the way of identification and example, as Rahner following the Catholic Incarnational Christology, teaches.[7]

Nevertheless, this absence of the idea of the Incarnation does not in any way nullify the validity of the African Traditional Religion as a divine medium for mediating supernatural salvation. Rather, it should be regarded by the Church as God's own effective preparation of Africa for the eventual arrival and meaningful acceptance of the historical Christianity, thus turning and fulfilling this African "anonymous Christianity" into the explicit one.[8]

For historical Christianity, God's Mysterium tremendum includes the Incarnation by which the Logos (Word) of God became a human being, thus creating the irrevocable union of the human being with God by the indissoluble bond of the "Hypostatic Union." Therefore, for Christianity, in contrast to the African tradition, God is not only the Ultimate source of humanity as Creator, but he has also become permanently united with humanity, since God has become one with humanity by virtue of the Incarnation. In the Incarnation God's Word as God, has became the Ideal Man by uniting itself permanently with Jesus of Nazareth. By this incoprehensible "Hypotastic Union," God symbolically and irrevocably united himself with all human beings and in the same free act of redemptive free grace, has unconditionally also reconciled all human beings to himself in order to share in his own life of perfection, unconditional love and the cross of Christ by innocent suffering so as to serve or save others.[9] This is therefore, the "Good News" (Gospel) that Christianity has to bring to Africa, so as to complement and complete the divine salvific self-communication already given to the African via the traditional religion and moral law.

Since God and the human being have become one by virtue of the Incarnation, for Christianity, the human being has similarly become like God of whom he/she is the image, and therefore, meaningful cipher in this categorial world, and as such revelatory of God. The human being is, therefore, the intelligent co-Creator with God, and because God has in Christ become a human being, and therefore, our very close neighbor, being symbolically incarnated in every human being, our search for God and our acceptance and love for God are correlative with our search, acceptance and love for our fellow human beings, for God has become inseparably bound with them through Christ's Incarnation. Hence, Christ's summary of the divine law is to love God and to love our neighbor as ourselves.[10]

However, it is surpringly on this crucial point of gratuitous love for the neighbor that both Christianity and the African tradition appear to be in complete agreement. Nevertheless, both of these traditions realize how difficult it is for the human being to love others unconditionally without the hope for either reward or some kind of gain.[11]

The Uniqueness and Mystery of Humanity

Both Christianity and the African Tradition acknowledge the uniqueness and mystery of the human being as a special creature in the whole of God's creation. Christianity as taught by Rahner, its spokesman, uses terms such as "imago Dei," "human self-transcendence," "hearer of the Word," "supernatural existential," "Hypostatic Union," "co-knower" and "co-Creator" with God in order to express this uniqueness of the human being.[12]

Africans also affirm that humanity is unique in creation. They use terms such as "Omuntu aine obwengye" (the human being possesses intellect, reason, knowledge and wisdom), "Omuntu aine Orurimi" (the human being possesses a tongue/language and is capable of speaking), "Omuntu aine Omutima" (the human being possesses a heart, human emotions, understanding and has spirit), and "Omuntu aine obuntu" (the human being possesses humanity/humaneness, love, politeness and culture).

All these unique human elements are in contrast to the rest of creation, particularly the other animals, especially the higher primates such as chimpanzees, monkeys and gorillas since they are very close related to human beings in the biological evolutionary branch. It is clear that Rahner and the African Tradition are complementary to each other on this point. However, the African Tradition can benefit from Rahner's modern Christian understanding of anthropology and biological evolution.

Unique human specialized features such as the large brain and high intellect permit the human being greater capacity for logical thinking processes, or reason, memory, data or information gathering, data analysis, planning, sophisticated means of communication, learning, and progressive creativity as it is to be seen in poetry, fiction writing, scientific inquiry and technological inventions, which in turn, revolutionize human modes of life and thinking. As a result, human beings have exploited and modified their environment, changing it to fit their ideals, dreams and self-image, whereas animals generally seek to adapt themselves to their environment or migrate to a more favorable one.

This unique human ability to think and create new possibilities for better and improved conditions for human life, whether in the invention and processing of new drugs for treating deadly diseases or in the refinement of new medical diagnostic technology, new efficient surgical instruments and new surgical procedures, demonstrates the uniqueness, complexity and mystery of the human nature itself, which has become inseparably bound up with divine nature ever since the time of the Incarnation.

This state of affairs is probably best described by Rahner, who emphasizes the fact that human knowledge and human creativity are co-extensive with divine knowledge and divine creativity, and as such, make the human being the co-knower, co-Creator and co-worker with God in this world.[13] This Rahnerian understanding can also help us to understand the African view of "Omuntu" as being the "insider" of UNTU, which is BEING or God.

The mystery of the co-extension and co-existence of such a God-human relationship in knowing, creation and historical process in this categorial world is the very mystery of the Incarnation and "Hypostatic union" in Rahner's Christology. In the African Tradition this mystery is probably to be equated with the mystery of divine-human mediation through a chain of mediators, both human and supernatural, through whom and by which God is supposed to act in the categorial world. In both Rahner and the African Tradition, God and humanity have a special relationship that is wrapped up in mystery.

In the understanding of both, God is the Origin of human beings, although Rahner and the African Tradition differ in their accounts of how the human being came about. For instance, Rahner espouses the modern biological evolutionary theory as the divine method of bringing human beings into existence, whereas in most traditional African Creation Myths, which are almost similar to those found in the book of Genesis 1-3, God is said to have created the human being, Kintu in the case of Buganda, and later gave him a wife Nnambi who soon afterwards, by her disobedience to God's commandment, caused death (Walumbe) to come into the world which was previously perfect.

As a result of human disobedience, the world had lost its original order, harmony, peace and perfection. The entry of death or non-being had, subsequently, caused havoc in the world by pain, suffering, disease and inescapable death to all human beings together with all living beings as they find their central focus, expression, fate and value in the human being, in whom they have their access to God as the world's high priest.

As a result, in both Christianity and the African Tradition there is agreement on the understanding that the human being is such a special creature in the world to the extent that his/her actions have serious consequences in relation to God and the rest of creation. Both agree that the human action has cosmic consequences (both positive and negative) for the world.

For instance, in Judeo-Christianity and in the East African Creation and Fall Myths, human disobedience to God did not only bring divine retribution and punishment on the offending human beings, but on all creation. This religio-philosophical presupposition is based on the view that the human being is the head, mediator and symbol of all the created order, and therefore, being in agreement with Rahner that the human being is both the image of God and divinely appointed categorial representative in the categorial world and its historical processes. For the African this probably is best expressed in diviners, mediums, "Bafumu" (healer-priests) and divine kings.

The human being is regarded as the representative of God in the world because he or she of all creatures is the one that is the most intelligent and most equipped by God to fulfill such a role. The human being does not only possess a larger brain, intellect and more capacity for thought, freedom, creativity, memory, planning, a movable thumb and an upright posture to enable the hands to do work, according to Rahner, the human being is also ontologically attuned to God's Word and Mystery, _a priori_ in creation.

This ontological orientation towards God and permanent ordering of the human being in gratuitous grace by God towards salvation as _visio beatifica_ is what Rahner refers to as the "supernatural existential" that enables all human beings, universally, to become aware of God's invitation, and proffer of salvific grace and supernatural salvation, and to be able to respond or react meaningfully to this invitation with either a "yes" or "no" in responsible personal consequential freedom.[14] The study of the African Traditional Religion has attempted to demonstrate that the Rahnerian explication of Christianity enables us to call traditional Africans, "anonymous Christians," and to accept them honorably, as such members of God's universal interdenominational Church.

Human Prior Orientation to the Mystery in Creation and the Requirement for Faith

The Africans and Rahner believe that God's knowledge is deposited in the human being by God at creation. For instance, in relation to prior human orientation to God, Professor Mbiti points out the African proverb that "No one ever shows the child the moon," in order to illustrate that Africans take it for granted that the young are spontaneously aware of God by the presence of an inner divine illumination which is present *a priori* in the form of prethematic and uncognitive knowledge of God that is spontaneous and co-extensive with humanity.[15]

Even young children are known to ask embarrassingly of their parents questions about their own Ultimate Origin and Destiny. Young children very often ask questions such as: "Mummy, where did I come from?" Where was I before I was born?" "What happens when a person dies?" "Where do dead people go?" "Why do people die?" "Where does God live?" "What is God like?" "Does God love me?" "Does God hate me when I am naughty?" and the like.

These questions and others may not all be asked at one given time, but may be asked in the course of years as the child grows up and increases in knowledge and curiosity, due to the increased awareness of the all-encompassing mystery of life and human beings that the child is in daily contact with.

Human beings, apparently, never outgrow this question about the infinite mystery of the human origin, life, meaning and the ultimate destiny. As children grow older and their religious and scientific knowledge expands, these questions, instead of being definitively answered, rather become more complex both philosophically and scientifically more sophisticated in nature, and no definitive answers are ever found that could be empirically supported or permanently intellectually satisfying.

As a result, the human being is faced with the question of the infinitely incomprehensible Transcendent Mystery at the center of humanity and the cosmos that requires the response of faith in order to continue living meaningfully in face and in the presence of the infinite Mystery, that Rahner refers to also as the human Horizon of knowing and living that keeps on beckoning and motivating the human being to advance forwards towards it and yet itself remains ever receding.

However, although this Horizon is never near enough to be grasped by the human being, it is nevetheless never too far for the human being to be discouraged in his/her unending desire and attempts to struggle forward to try and get hold of it, in order to complete oneself in it. According to Rahner, the human being's pilgrimage and search for the truth, perfection in knowledge, personal completion, fulfillment and the attainment of happiness are tantalizingly reflected in and symbolized by this Horizon as God, which the human being requires for his/her authentic self-actualization and existence.

According to Rahner, this process by which the human being is ever moving forward towards the Mystery or God as the tantalizing ever-receding Horizon is what Rahner refers to as "human self-transcendence" (Vorgriff) that is the chief characteristic of all normal human beings. By this human self-transcendence (Vorgriff) the human being recognizes human finitude and the infinite beyond that which is enshrined in incomprehensible Mystery, yet recognized and required to give human life its meaning and direction towards the human fulfillment and destiny that are similarly hidden in this impenetrable Mystery. Consequently, faith is required on the part of the human being as the "courage to be" and to live in the hope that all will be well in this future blind destiny that lies deep in this impenetrable Mystery, the "Abyss" that is God or Ruhanga.

In this respect, faith is the courage to be a finite human being that is utterly threatened by finitude as non-being, and also being utterly unable to peep into the eventualities of the future that lie hidden in the darkness and incomprehensible Absolute Mystery that is known as God (Ruhanga).

Without this essential faith that is required of human beings, who are aware of their finitude and helplessness due to being utterly dependent on this invisible Absolute Mystery, one can get paralyzed by an all-pervasive and consuming fear, anxiety and despair (Angst); and as a result, will live in a state of "hell," whereas faith leads to a fuller human life here and now, despite the presence of the felt human vulnerability and uncertainty about the unknown future that is completely hidden in God as the Absolute Mystery and also as this Absolute Future that is the _a priori_ human destiny as _visio beatifica_, according to Rahner.

This Rahnerian exposition is on the whole consistent with the African understanding of God/Ruhanga as the Transcendent Mystery before whom human beings are to live in awe, obedience and trembling. In fact, it is a better articulation of what most Africans generally believe unreflectively.

Therefore, both Rahner and the African Tradition recognize that the human being is created by God in such a way that the human being is ever attuned and oriented to God's mystery as the mystery that ever beckons and guides the human being forward towards positive self-actualization, self-fulfillment, completion and happiness, both now here on earth and in the unknown future that lies hidden in God's mystery. Subsequently, both traditions agree that the appropriate human response to this divine Mystery that is operative in the world for the creation, salvation and well-being of the human being is faith alone; and that without this faith in the presence of this pervasive infinite Absolute Mystery which is at the center of humanity and the cosmos, normal human life that is aware of itself as utterly finite, contingent and vulnerable gets utterly crippled by the fear, anxiety and despair that are characteristic of living in hell and damnation, as is well described by both Soren Kierkegaard and Paul Tillich.[16]

Hence, it is quite clear that both Rahner and the African tradition are essentially in agreement that faith in response to the awareness of contingency on this all-encompassing infinitely incomprehensible Transcendent Mystery is the most appropriate human response and attitude to this Mystery as God, the Holy One, the Creator and Sustainer who is appropriately worshipped by all thankful intelligent creatures. This is implicitly or anonymously as one surrenders to the Mystery that is encountered both at the center of one's being, especially, as symbolized in the insatiable void at the core of the human being and the impenetrable Mystery at the center of the cosmos. It is also done explicitly in wonder, adoration, study, research, meditation, prayer and worship, both private and informal or collective and structured.

The Supernatural Existential and the "Obuntu"

Rahner's view is that human nature as we know it is already infused with the elevating divine gratuitous universal salvific grace that has elevated the original human nature from "pure human nature" to the one that we know now, which is in this sense "supernature" in that it is open and capable of freely responding to God's universal self-communication in grace for human salvation.[17] This is Rahner's way of explaining how it is possible for supernatural salvation to take place everywhere in the world where there are human beings, since God has freely in his unmerited grace created in them the permanent ontological openness and capacity for apprehending God's universal free salvific self-communication and disclosure in both non-cognitive, pre-thematic revelation and explicit revelation as in the case of the Scriptures and the Incarnation.

The Rahnerian concept of the human *a priori* "supernatural existential" helps us to explain the African traditional view that all human beings are freely and personally responsible for the kind of people they finally become before God. That is as "abantu" with a significant degree of "Obuntu" and as such bad, wicked people lacking a sufficient degree of humanization and therefore lacking in supernatural salvation, since supernatural salvation is for both the African people and Rahner considered to be coextensive and synonymous with humanization.[18]

The Rahnerian Christian concept of the "supernatural existential" enables us to view the whole cosmos as the arena of God's universal creative and salvific activity. If one views supernatural salvation as God's continuing creative activity, then one can also view it as the universal gratuitous divine invitation addressed to all human beings everywhere, to actualize themselves more positively and more fully in unconditional faith, and hope for a more abundant and more meaningful life that is still to come in the future. In addition, the divine invitation calls the human being to practice charity and unconditional love for the categorial neighbor so as to bring the very goodness and happiness to others in the same spirit and measure which we ourselves desire, and seek in both God and our fellow human beings. And in so doing, to experience these same fulfillments ourselves, by the same token, thus experiencing together the eschatological state of divine salvation, both individually and collectively, as a fellowship community of faith, love, brotherhood/sisterhood and righteous action.

For Rahner, the "supernatural existential" does not only enable the individual to be the "hearer of God's Word" of invitation to eternal life, and to respond to it freely and responsibly with a consequential "yes" or "no" to this proffer of gratuitous supernatural salvific grace, but it also makes the consequences of that "yes" or "no" to this divine invitation to salvation a historical reality. In other words, those who say "yes" to God are led further into the riches and mystery of God's life of grace and salvation, whereas those who reject him and the salvation he offers, subsequently, cut themselves off from the origin and sustenance of life. As a result, they often fall into a kind of paralyzing anxiety and despair (Angst). This anxiety tends to make living a meaningless hazardous venture full of unnerving fear and uncertainty making life or living unpleasant and hellish.

This is consistent with the African Tradition, where one cannot reject God and live, since God is regarded as the very ground and condition of human life itself, orientation to the world and action. For that matter, all notorious sinners were usually executed, since they were considered a danger to the life of the community as they offended God, its source. Therefore, both the Rahnerian concept of Christianity and the African Tradition essentially agree that the human life and its continued existence is entirely dependent on this human faith in God as the Transcendent Holy Mystery, by which this *a priori* life is accepted and appropriated by the human being by *living* it out in the presence of this Mystery and acknowledgment of this Mystery or God as both its Ultimate Origin and Sustainer.

Human Radical Awareness of Socio-Religio-Moral Responsibility and Guilt

Perhaps more so in the African Tradition than in Rahner, there is great emphasis placed on human socio-religio-moral responsibility as the ground for the right harmonious human relationships in the community that knit together an individual member of the community with other members of his/her immediate family, extended family, neighbors, friends, relatives, and general members of the community and finally total strangers such as foreign travelers.

This moral responsibility and kinship define the humane behavior expected of human beings in any given situation. For example, in traditional East Africa it was generally expected that one should give hospitality to a traveler who comes into the village late in the evening. This hospitality usually includes lodging, food, drink, conversation, treatment of any injuries or sickness the traveler might have suffered or contracted on the journey, protection, and helpful information regarding safe travel in the local area and its neighborhoods.

Failure to render a stranger such needed hospitality and unconditional humanitarian loving service, or maliciously causing harm to befall the stranger, such as misleading the stranger, so that he or she ends up hurt or traveling on the wrong path, is treated very gravely as a sin before God and an offense against the ancestral spirits, therefore to be confessed and atoned for immediately by both the offending member and his/her community so as to avert the divine wrath and punishment by allowing disaster, misfortune, disease or destruction to befall the sinning individual or his/her community. Consequently, in traditional Africa these manifestations of evil and human suffering, such as disease, epidemics, floods, famines, accidents, misfortunes, disasters and the like, are attributed to supernatural punishment and retribution due to human sin and guilt before God and the ancestral spirits or the departed.[19]

This is probably the main reason why in the African tradition so much attention and emphasis are put on the value and necessity of observing the customs, laws and taboos or avoidances, as these are supposed to ensure the maintenance of the right harmonious relationships within the community between various members of the community, the departed (ancestral spirits), and ultimately, God. Since failure in the observance of these relationships causes a breach within the community that destroys the balance and harmony which are required for the individual and the community to function well at any level, be it socio-political, economic or religious, the cause and breach have got to be diagnosed quickly so as to bridge it and restore the religio-socio-political harmony that is required for the African traditional community to function properly. The African authentic human existence hinges on the reverence and fear of God, the departed, religion, loving and harmonious relationships within the community and the correlative human moral responsibility as "Obuntu" that grounds right conduct and societal harmony.

If the cause of trouble or disharmony was not readily diagnosed by the affected individuals, then a religious expert or consultant was sought and consulted. It was usually a priest or a diviner or both working jointly in order to provide a more effective religious service to the community. The diviner, utilizing his/her special skills and special powers of supernatural vision by God's grace and permission, was supposed to peep insightfully into the otherwise impenetrable divine mysteries.

Consequently, the diviner was supposed to look into the past of the individuals and the community and be able to see the point and cause of breach in relationships, the nature of offense and its magnitude, and therefore, be able to prescribe a cure. This cure was usually prescribed in terms that would remove and expiate the offense so as to restore general well-being of the relationships and religio-social harmony and wholeness within the community. Therefore it is probably not an overstatement to claim as Mbiti does that the religious priest, who is usually also a herbalist or a medicine-man, and the diviner are as much God's gift to the people of Africa as the clergy and medical personnel are to the Western world.

In comparison to the African Tradition, Rahner can probably be said to be lacking in emphasis on human sin and its harmful consequences on human relationships within the community between individual members of the community, the departed, and ultimately with God as the veritable Ultimate Guarantor, Ground, locus and pivot of these human networks of relationships and interactions. This network of relationships can be said to constitute human beings as "abantu" endowed with "Obuntu" (humanity) and the human community, where human beings are called into being by God and set on their pilgrimage in quest of an authentic existence in the form of a personal meaningful self-actualization, self-enjoyment and fulfilling process of full humanization and completion as such.

For Rahner, the conventional church is the best form of the community for such a supernatural salvific process to take place. Nevertheless, he recognizes that this gratuitous supernatural salvific process can also take place with both validity and a measure of success outside the ecclesial community, as he affirms enthusiastically in his teaching on "anonymous Christianity."

However, Rahner tends to view this "anonymous Christianity" from the point of view of an atomic, individual "anonymous Christian" who responds positively to God inwardly in response to the inner divine *a priori* salvific revelation deposited at the center of the human being by God at creation. This being done in gratuitous divine grace and manifesting itself in the human being implicitly as human self-transcendence and ontological orientation to holy Mystery and by the gift of the "supernatural existential," being open and receptive to God's salvific Word which is given to all the human beings everywhere implicitly in non-thematic divine revelation, with the exception of where the Gospel has been preached, and therefore, the implicit revelation has been made explicit and thematic.

Consequently, these "anonymous Christians" are not yet members of any Christian community both explicit and anonymous, according to this Rahnerian conception.[20] Therefore, in this individualistic aspect the Rahnerian concept of "anonymous Christianity" can be attractive to traditional Africans who are basically social and community-oriented in their ideals. However, this problem would be overcome if the African traditional religion itself could be viewed as "anonymous Christianity."

The Human Community as the Special Arena of God's Salvific Activity

Rahner recognizes the Church as the special community and arena of God's salvific activity. He also views the whole world as God's general arena of salvific activity for the individuals who as "anonymous Christians" do not belong to the Church or other salvific community. This is a major weakness in Rahner's concept of "anonymous Christianity" that can probably be overcome by adopting the African concept of community as God's arena of creative and salvific activity inasmuch as it is the locus of human life, meaningful human relationships, sinning and forgiveness, hurting and healing; revelation and worship, cultic religious activity, learning, humanization, love, faith, trust, hope and immortality through posterity and the memorial of the departed members of the community as friends, neighbors, relatives or as ancestors.

The Rahnerian concept of the Church should be modified too, in line with his concept of "anonymous Christianity," so as to include the "anonymous Christians" in a kind of "anonymous Christian Community or Church." This is necessary because no human being is able to exist fully and authentically as such outside the human community, as it is the community that grounds and mediates God's activity of the creation of the individual human being, i.e. bringing that individual into being, and the divine salvation of that individual being partly constituted in the community's process of humanizing that individual who has been born into it.

In short, there is no humanity if there is no correlative community. Similarly, there cannot be salvation apart from the community, since salvation as authentic human existence and wholeness can only take place within the context of the community. This means that the traditional Catholic dogma of *extra ecclesiam nulla salus* can be still defended as valid and *true,* inasmuch as the term *ecclesia* is expanded to mean any human community that in some *major way* serves as the medium for divine self-comunication for the humanization or salvation of the individual members of that community.

Therefore, salvation as the complete humanization and human authenticity of both men and women is a historical process that can only take place in a categorial human community, and not outside it nor in total independence or opposition to the community. This is mainly because God works through ordinary human beings and the ordinary human community in order to address the ordinary situations of human beings at their level. In other words, the ordinary is the bearer of the extra-ordinary and the vehicle for the mediation of the divine. This vehicle or medium of divine activity is not always explicitly Christian, but is always explicitly associated with humanity and the human community. Therefore, Rahner has got to be challenged to go further in his concept of "anonymous Christianity" so as to include the "anonymous Christian community."

Furthermore, with the Incarnation, God has become a human being, and therefore, the extra-ordinary has become ordinary, and consequently, the human being has become the effective mediator and representation of God, and the human community has, likewise become the community of God, the very embodiment and mediation of God in this categorial world. Consequently, it can be affirmed that no one can find God and no one can ever be saved by God apart from humanity and the human community.[21] Therefore, on this basis Rahner's concept of "anonymous Christianity" can be said to be hollow and deficient. Subsequently, in the way it now stands, would be unattractive to those who find meaning and fulfillment in the corporate religious community as opposed to those few who delight in holy solitude, and delight in the path of individual direct quest for God, sought in solitary quiet contemplation, meditation and divine mediation leading to the beatific vision or the spiritual beatitude resulting from the spiritual ecstatic union with God.

Unconditional Human Love for the Neighbor as the Concrete Expression and Mediation of Divine Revelation and Salvation

It is perhaps on this topic of love that we find the most surprising similarity between Rahner and the African Tradition as regards the fundamental role that love plays in supernatural salvation. Perhaps most important of all, in both systems of thought and world-view, God is the Creator and Father of all human beings, and consequently all human beings are his beloved children (Abantu ba Ruhanga), and therefore to love him means also to love these other people as God's children of his macrocosmic extended family that includes all nations, races, colors, creeds and cultures.

According to the Africans (under study), one cannot love nor say that he/she loves a person whose children he/she hates. But rather it is said and believed that love for a particular parent can be expressed and mediated to that parent by being expressed to his/her children unconditionally. It is believed in Africa that the parents and their children are one and inseparable, as such. This is thought to hold true for God, too, namely, that one cannot profess to love the Creator (Ruhanga), and to respect him whereas he/she hates, disrespects and mistreats his creation, particularly the human beings who are usually regarded as the children of God (Abantu ba Ruhanga).

This is mainly why traditional Africans in Kigezi and other areas used to pray to God before going out on hunting expeditions, going to war or going to cut down a big tree or clear some virgin land for cultivation. These activities involved an apparent destruction of life, human in the case of war, animal in the case of hunting, and plant life in the case of clearing forests or cutting down trees. These activities were usually done carefully and prayerfully so as not to disturb the divinely given state of balance of nature and the harmony between the human being, the world and God, that is required to ensure this harmony and mutual wholesome contingent existence of both the human being and the world that are both themselves contingent on God as Creator, Sustainer and Protector of his creation.

However, for Western Christianity and the African Tradition though, the preservation of the environment and the world are important both to God and to the human being, who is dependent on them, they are nonetheless, secondary to the value and preservation of humanity itself. For the African Tradition, it is the human being from whom the rest of creation gains its value and importance as measured by its degree of utility to sustain human life or provide for human comfort, self-enjoyment, satisfaction and happiness. Therefore, whatever contributes to these human needs is valued, and conversely, what does not is thought to be of less value and importance.

It is generally recognized that the human being has needs that are both spiritual and physical. The physical needs, such as hunger, thirst, sex, shelter and clothing, can easily be satisfied to a reasonable level by providing the required material needs (except in remote African villages, where droughts can cause a severe shortage of both food and water). However, the spiritual needs, such as the need for security, love, recognition, self-worth, identity, freedom, sense of belonging and the like, are usually not easy to fulfill satisfactorily. Nevertheless, through love and the network of relationships, the community tries to meet these human psychological needs.

The African Traditional community, being aware of these two types of needs, took measures to provide an acceptable religio-social context within which these needs could be met. For instance, human sexual drives and needs were recognized and exogamous marriages were devised to make sure that incest and close kin sexual activity did not take place, as it would cause jealousy, rivalry and tension within the family unit itself, probably causing its breakup and consequently the general breakdown and disintegration of the community. The extended family was also generally the context for learning how to express gratuitous love and to practice charity. The idea that charity begins at home was very true here. The extended family, which was usually also polygamous in nature, was also usually full of tension and conflict and thus an ideal arena to train in patience, forgiveness and love.

Furthermore, the African practice of polygamy was encouraged to ensure that all the surplus marriageable girls were married off, so as to give them an acceptable context to meet their sexual needs and to bring up their own offspring within a marriage relationship, hence avoiding bastardism, which was regarded as a terrible scandal usually punishable by death for both partners and their illegitimate child.[22] In addition, polygamy was also valued for the new network of kinship relationships and alliances that it made possible, particularly, in pre-colonial tribal Africa, where intertribal fighting broke out very regularly due to the breakdown in alliances or willful and sinful violation of the human rights of one group by another group, usually as a result of failure in an unconditional love for other human beings, which was often enough to cause suspicion of strangers and concern to the African communities.[23]

The unconditional love for others, though the ideal, usually failed in the face of strong sense of kinship ties, extreme ethnocentrism (or tribalism), ethnic pride and arrogance; individual greed, selfishness; malice, hatred and brutality. Nevertheless, both Christianity and the African Tradition still insist that this unconditional love for the neighbor, though an apparent failure, is still nonetheless regarded as the authentic mark and full expression of the inner divine salvific activity in gratuitous grace as "Obuntu" in the case of Eastern Africa.

In this part of East Africa under discussion, the unconditional love for the categorial neighbor is treated as divine, a microcosmic expression of the macrocosmic one. This is primarily because to love the neighbor in traditional Africa usually required unconditional forgiveness and unconditional love for the neighbor, since the neighbor was usually the very person whose goats or cows ate up and destroyed your gardens, crops and banana plantations. It was also your neighbor's kids that sometimes killed your chickens or dog just for fun or out of malignant rivalry and malice. It was your neighbor that sometimes seduced your wife, spread malicious damaging gossip about you, or dug a portion of your land as his own without your consent.

In modern times it is the neighbor that often refuses you to pass a road, a water pipe, electric poles and wires through his/her land and tells you to get lost when you try to persuade him/her that he/she is being unreasonable and unneighborly. In short, your neighbor is usually the person that "drives you nuts," and yet, it is the very same person that you have to live with as peacefully as you can, even when he/she "is sometimes too much for you" and you would have probably been happier driving a spear or a knife in his/her heart rather than calling him or her to a neighborhood beer party and feasting.

Nevertheless, like Christianity and as expounded by Rahner and the African Tradition, this is the very neighbor that we are taught and called upon to love by our own religion and upbringing as Africans. For instance, in both Ankole and Kigezi, children were required to learn the following poem by heart in the African general context, telling of the necessity of unconditional love for the neighbor as one of the main basic foundations for the African philosophy of human existence:

Mutaahi wangye anshagiza Tindihemuka.	My neighbor drives me crazy But I will not lose my composure.
Akanterera omwana Owe ndyamushwererera.	He beat up my son But I will help his own son to get married.
Akanyokyeza enju Nyowe ndyamuha omuganda Nayombeka.	He burned down my house But I will give him timber To build his own house.
Akansisira bingi Kwonka Ruhanga we Aryabinyongyera.[24]	He destroyed a lot of my property and did me great harm But the loving God Will reward me greatly.

This Rukiga-Runyankole poem articulates the African version of the unconditional love for the neighbor, whereas at the same time it defines the neighbor that is to be loved. In this teaching context of the poem, the neighbor to be loved unconditionally happens to be the very person that beats up your own kids, maliciously burns your own house down, and does many other despicable things to you, "driving you crazy!" This definition of unconditional love for the neighbor is apparently in surprising harmony with the Scriptures and the Christian tradition. For example, James writes:

> If you really fulfill the royal law, according to the scripture, "You shall love your neighbor as

> yourself," you do well. But if you show partiality, you commit sin. (2:8-9a, R.S.V.)

John agrees and writes about love as a divine correlative:

> Beloved, let us love one another; for love is of God, and he who loves is born of God and knows God. He who does not love does not know God, and God is love. (1 John 4:7-8, R.S.V.)

Love in the African understanding is a matter of action and conduct. It is not a matter of verbal expression. For instance, it is very rare in traditional Africa to hear one person telling another that "I love you!" Where this is said explicitly it will usually be meant as a deceitful flattery, such as that involving two people in an illicit love affair in which the participants are "only fooling around."

However, if this relationship became serious, commitment, trust, faithfulness, considerate humane behavior and mutual generous exchange of gifts, and serious intimate personal conversations, and the like, would usually replace words as the authentic expressions of genuine love. In other words, love is acted out rather than being merely talked about. The East African Bantu people are on the whole generally action-oriented, and this also applies to matters of love and gratitude, which are generally expressed in action or get acted out rather than being verbalized.[25]

Similarly, therefore, in traditional East Africa, love for the neighbor generally means living in positive, humane and loving attitude toward the neighbor, exchanging daily greetings and detailed family and personal news, protecting each other's property, exchanging tools and food-stuffs, eating and drinking together regularly, helping each other in times of need, disease, disaster or death in the family.

In short, love for the neighbor means open living with the neighbor as if the neighbor were part of the family in its African traditional extended fashion. This kind of love for the neighbor is generally expected to be self-sacrificial, as it usually requires giving generously without counting the cost or expecting anything in return except God's supernatural reward in his mysterious ways. In some cases this appears to be the chief motivation for one's unconditional love, generosity and help for the neighbor.

However, the neighbor is treated as such because he or she happens to be a fellow human being that one is in contact with, in this way being symbolic of the microcosmic human representation of the macrocosmic total humanity and God, who is inseparably bound with the human being as ultimate Origin, Sustainer and absolute Future. Furthermore, according to Rahner's Christocentric theological teaching, God has also become inseparably bound with humanity by virtue of the Incarnation and the "Hypostatic Union," by which process God has become our close neighbor in Christ who as an incarnate human being is inseparable from the categorial neighbor.

Therefore, both in Christianity and the African Religion and Philosophy, it can be said that no individual human being can love God and experience God's love or forgiveness apart from the other people, the community, and especially apart from the categorial neighbor. Also, in both teachings, God is loved and known by us as we come to know and love the neighbor unconditionally. Similarly, divine forgiveness is experienced as we forgive others, particularly, the neighbor as the person we live closely with and come to know personally and interact with, offend or get offended by, resent and conflict with due to close proximity and constant interaction.

It is in this concrete and imperfect neighbor that God is, still nonetheless, incarnate and categorically present in the world. In this understanding, it can therefore, be affirmed that our unconditional love for the neighbor is the path or ticket to God our true humanity and happiness through our personal acts of unconditional love for him or her. Consequently, our fate as human beings is bound together with that of our neighbor, and as such, to love our neighbor is to love ourselves and to love God. Furthermore, each human being is, consequently, lost without the other. Rahner puts it insightfully as follows:

> The act of love of the neighbour is, therefore, the only categorized and original act in which man attains the whole of reality given to us in categories, with regard to which he fulfills himself perfectly correctly and in which he always already makes the transcendental and direct experience of God by grace. The reflected religious act as _such_ is always and remains secondary in comparison with this.... higher dignity than the reflected act of love of the neighbour, since both acts are necessarily supported by the (experienced by unreflected) reference both to God and to the intramundane Thou and this by grace (of the infused _caritas_), i.e. by that on which the explicit acts both of our relationship to God and of our neighbour 'for God's sake' reflect...

Rahner goes on to connect the love for God as correlative to the love of the neighbor:

> The love of God unreflectedly but really always intends God in supernatural transcendentality in the love of the neighbour as such, and even the explicit love of God is still borne by that opening in trusting love to the whole of reality which takes place in the love of the neighbour. It is radically true, i.e. by an ontological and not merely 'moral' of psychological necessity, that whoever does not love the brother whom he 'sees,' also cannot love God whom he does not see, and that one can love God whom one does not see only by loving one's brother lovingly.[26]

Salvation as the Process of Humanization or the Acquisition of "Obuntu"

It can be said that both Christianity and the African Tradition have an apparent basic unity in their general approach to universal salvation. Both systems of thought are grounded in the basic idea that whatever else salvation might be, it is first and foremost the process by which God turns the primate creature (ekintu), traditionally referred to in English as "Man," into a person or a human being (Omuntu) that possesses "Obuntu" (essential humanity), and therefore, the capability for moral responsible choice, being kind, humane, tolerant, patient, generous, loving, considerate and forgiving. In addition, he/she is expected to be also capable of awe, respect, freedom, responsibility, wonder, worship, awareness of sin and guilt in relation to the Holy Mystery that is God.

The process of the acquisition of these human elements (Obuntu), and this state of human self-transcendence is the process of deification which is the same as humanization. Both Christianity and the African Tradition identify this process with the divine salvific historical process. According to the East African Bantu understanding, the acquiring of "Obuntu" as those human qualities that make a person a person or that turn the primate creature into a human being, the very special creature of God that is described in the Scriptures as "God's image,"[27] is the same correlative divine joint process of both creation and transformation or salvation.

Salvation as the humanization of the human being can be said to begin at conception, and to increase with the level of human growth in virtue such as knowledge, love, self-control, generosity and self-sacrificial giving for the sake of others for their well-being and happiness. Modern examples include such activities as being a missionary or a voluntary technical worker in the remote rural parts of underdeveloped Africa so as to bring to the villagers there the good news of the Incarnation and the restoration of their God-given gifts of the resurrection that had been lost and also to help them develop from a subsistence agricultural economy into an efficient, modern, large-scale, mechanized farming, thus improving their quality of life and well-being, which can be regarded as categorial landmarks of salvation in this historical world.

In both the African Tradition and Christianity, as expounded by Rahner and others, such as Karl Barth, Emil Brunner, Teihard de Chardin and Hans Kung, true humanity comes from God alone, and Jesus Christ is the true embodiment of this humanity. What Jesus reveals about this authentic humanity, or what it means is to be an authentic human being the way God created us to be, was manifested in his being which was fully oriented to God, in being fully open and receptive to God's Word, other people, love, divine grace, humanization and divinization. Consequently, when Jesus said that "My Father and I are one," he meant this harmony of purpose and being between himself and God, his Heavenly Father.[28]

Therefore, inasmuch as it can be said that Jesus is the mediation of authentic humanity, it can also be claimed by African Christians that Christ is the divine medium of authentic humanity, inasmuch as he is both the medium and the embodiment of "Obuntu" (authentic humanity or humaneness).

Therefore, despite the explicit absence of the idea of the Incarnation in African Traditional teaching, there is an implicit anticipation for the Incarnation, inasmuch as there is this awareness and explicit teaching that "Obuntu," which is the human elements that are constitutive of authentic humanity or humaneness, comes from God himself, who is conceived in a trinitarian fashion.

According to this African teaching about God and salvation as the process of supernatural humanization of the "Abantu" (humanity), it can also be said that it probably anticipates Christ's Incarnation in order to reveal explicitly (in a categorial manner) in this temporal historical process, what it is actually like to be an authentic human being in the world, and also what it means to be complete in humanization, having acquired the fullness of "Obuntu" (essential humanity/humaneness).

Death as the Eternal Validation of the Human Life for Either Eternal Life with God or Eternal Rejection and Damnation

In the understanding of both Christianity and the African Tradition, death is not the end of the human being. Rather, it is the final definitive culmination of the human process of humanization and growth as a human being. Rahner calls it the climactic zero point that the human passes through to another kind of spiritual life.[29] The Africans refer to it as "departing this life," meaning that the individual has gone into a new kind of life.

However, this new life is not to be equated with eternal life, since traditional Africans believe that the opportunity for human resurrection and eternal life were lost through disobedience in the "Zamani" period, whereas for the Christians these divine gifts have been restored in the Christ-Event, and therefore, they can now look to the future with hope and anticipation for the resurrection and eternal life.

However, the impenetrable mystery of the future state of existence, the manner of life and usually the kind of pain involved in the dying process and the felt loss of those friends and relatives left behind, make death seem such a monstrous meaningless evil with no redeeming value. Nevertheless, for both Christianity and the African it is the climactic divine valuation point of each individual historical being that cannot be indefinitely shirked, not even by pious prayer, intercessions, modern medicine and medical technology, which all have their limits. But rather, death is to be accepted as a given, very much like one's own life at birth.

In this respect, one can probably question whether some forms of Christian belief in the resurrection are not, in fact, some kind of denial of death. That would indeed be contrary to the African view of death as a great tragedy and an irrevocable loss of humanity (Obuntu).

Most people in traditional Africa, like the Christians in the West, very often live in anticipation of this final event and prepare themselves socially and spiritually for this eventuality. In some cases, this acceptance and preparation for one's eventual death have a profound effect on the type of life the individual actually lives all his/her lifetime, namely, as a preparation for this eventual and unavoidable death. The Bakiga and the Banyankole believe that God both creates and "kills" by letting death befall the individual. They express this idea of God creating and then "killing" whenever he chooses in the proverb that "akaguhangire niko kagwata" (the Creator is also the Smasher). Therefore, for the African, both creation and its destiny are completely hidden in divine mystery in which the whole process, ultimately, originates and culminates.

However, whereas the individual can do little about his/her origin, he/she is aware that he/she can entreat God to prolong his/her life, thus temporarily keeping back death that is usually perceived as the ultimate enemy of his/her humanity. Consequently, in traditional Africa, death is important in shaping people's lives positively,[30] because, just as in Christianity, it is believed that one's life is definitively evaluated and eternally validated by God for all its total worth, depending on the condition and the state of goodness (Obuntu) or wickedness (Obubi) in which the individual died.

This condition is then ratified as that individual's permanent record and eternal validation of the individual's earthly life by God. For instance, it is believed that if the wicked and angry people die in that wicked state unrepentant, they subsequently, turn into "Emizimu" (ghosts and malignant evil spirits) that are eternally rejected by God, the ancestral spirits and the human beings. It is believed that subsequent to this judgment and rejection they are revengeful and ever plotting evil, harm and mischief against the community, and particularly, against the "good" human beings, whom they envy and seek to destroy or turn into disruptive evil people, so as to be like them and eventually join them in their human rejection, consuming hatred, malice and subsequently, eternal damnation.

On the other hand, the good people who possess "Obuntu" are said to be transformed into the good spirits that are usually referred to reverently as "ancestral spirits" in both honor and elevation to this important status by their own community because of their good and exemplary life, which the other human beings are encouraged to emulate in the same way that some Christians seek to imitate the life of Christ and the Saints.

In this respect, the spirits referred to as "ancestral spirits" are the African equivalent of the Christian "Community of Saints," particularly within the Catholic tradition and devotional practice. For instance, the ancestral spirits are invoked by Africans in prayer so as to act as their guardian angels and to mediate between them and God or other supernatural beings or even to mediate between them and some other people.

However, although in the African Traditional Religion there is a general absence of the concept of hell as "a place" or eternal punishment by God for one's sins not repented and expiated by the time of the individual's death. Heaven, in contrast, is "a place" of eternal blessedness and happiness as the reward for the righteous (as missionary Christianity teaches in Africa). It can be said that the African idea of instant transformation of the human being at the moment of death, the subsequent embodiment in a spiritual body, evaluation, and judgment by God and the ancestral spirits, and the consequent acceptance by the ancestors and God if judged as good or rejection if judged as unworthy for having lived a life of hatred, malice and lacking in "Obuntu," is probaly a viable alternative eschatological view to the traditional Chrisitan teaching on death, the resurrection, judgment, hell and heaven.

The African version should be studied further for the promise it holds for a new understanding and a possible reformulation of a new modern version of Christian eschatology that is more consonant with the African Traditional Religion and philosophy, while remaining true to the Scriptures, biological sciences, and modern scientific cosmology. In this way, the African Tradition can be given the full recognition, respect and opportunity to function effectively as the divinely provided African medium for God's revelation and gratuitous salvific activity of humanization (Bantuzation) of the human being.

However, since God's revelation and salvific activity have been concretized in historical process in the Incarnation and therefore, in Jesus Christ, the African tradition, though revelatory of God and mediating his love, grace and salvation, does so in a partial manner in the deficient mode that Rahner terms "anonymous Christianity," which anticipates explicit Christianity for fulfillment and completion.

This explains why Christianity is growing fastest in Africa, and why most Christians in Africa are Catholics. Catholicism has meshed in well with the African Religion, Philosophy and cultural traditions, whereas Protestantism has tended to view these negatively, and consequently has rejected and repudiated them. Nevertheless, Rahner warns us that this does not mean that all "non-Christians" who qualify to be called "anonymous Christians" will necessarily welcome historical Christianity itself. Then what is the value of "Anonymous Christianity"? This question will be implicitly answered in the next chapter.

NOTES

1. The term "African" here and in most of this work should be understood to refer to the African Bantu ethnic groups under study unless otherwise stated. Similarly, the term "African Tradition" will, likewise, have a similar limitation. Nevertheless, these concepts may have a wider African validity due to the underlying oneness and unity of the Africans despite their ethnic pluralism.

2. God is only God (Ruhanga), as far as these people are concerned, if he is also omniscient. Cf. Ch. III in the section on God for a more detailed discussion of this subject, especially in contrast to the Whiteheadian Process metaphysics that claims that God like human beings cannot know the contingent events of the future until they have occurred, thus becoming concrete historical knowledge with causal efficacy; e.g., see _Process and Reality_, Part I, Ch. I:VI, Chs. VII-X; Part II and Part V.

3. Karl Rahner, _Foundations of Christian Faith_, p. 228.

4. Ibid., pp. 14 ff., 84 ff.

5. The major ones being: _The Essence of Christianity_ (1841) and _The Essence of Religion_ (1845).

6. Cf., e.g., Karl Rahner, _op. cit._, pp. 90 ff.

7. Cf., Karl Rahner, _Foundations of Christian Faith_, pp. 178-321.

8. Ibid., pp. 203-228, 311-321. This might also explain the strength of Christianity in this area of Uganda in contrast to the North.

9. Karl Rahner, "On the Theology of the Incarnation," _Theological Investigations_ 4:107-120; "Christ the Mediator: One Person and Two Natures," ibid. 1:158-182; "Christology within an Evolutionary View of the World," ibid. 5:173-184.

10. Cf. Karl Rahner, "The Commandment of Love in Relation to the Other Commandments," _Theological Investigations_ 5:439-467; "Reflections on the Unity of the Love of Neighbour and the Love of God," ibid. 6:231-249.

11. In this part of Africa under study there is a strong sense of kinship that is central and regulatory of social life and human existence in general. This being the case, love tends to be stressed less as the basis of human interaction, since it is liable to mood fluctuation and failure. But whereas kinship might be a good system for regulating life in a small, closely

interrelated community, it fails to work in a larger society and produces the characteristic tribalism and nepotism that are seen in Africa today. (This subject will be discussed in more detail later.)

12. See, e.g., Karl Rahner, Spirit in the World, pp. 57-77, 202-236, 387-408; Foundations of Christian Faith, pp. 24-115.

13. Loc. cit.

14. See, e.g., Karl Rahner, "Relationship between Nature and Grace: The Supernatural Existential," Theological Investigations 1:306-315; "The Order of Creation and the Order of Redemption," The Christian Commitment, pp. 44-53; "Anonymous Christians," Theological Investigations 6:390-395.

15. See, e.g., Karl Rahner, Foundations of Christian Faith, pp. 116-175.

16. See, e.g., Soren Kierkegaard's Concept of Dread and Sickness unto Death; Paul Tillich, New Being and The Courage to Be.

17. Cf. O'Donovan, ed., A World of Grace, pp. 64-119. See also note 14 above.

18. In the African understanding "Obunbtu" as the constitutive essence of an authentic human being is freely given by God to all people, both inwardly as heredity, and outwardly in community as culture, religion, values and the like, which the human beings freely accept or reject as they grow up and become responsible for their own choices, actions, attitudes and behavior, both before other people in the community both living and dead, and also before God.

19. See John Mbiti, African Religions and Philosophy, pp. 50-118.

20. See, e.g., Karl Rahner, "Anonymous Christians," Theological Investigations 6:390-398; "Christianity and the Non-Christian Religions," ibid. 5:115-134; "Atheism and Implicit Christianity," ibid. 9:145-164; "The Appeal to Conscience," Nature and Grace (New York: Sheed and Ward, 1964), pp. 39-63.

21. See Karl Rahner, "The Commandment of Love in Relationship to the Other Commandments," Theological Investigations 5:439-467; "Reflections on the Unity of the Love of Neighbour and the Love of God," ibid. 6:231-249.

22. However, in precolonial Kigezi it was usually the pregnant girl who got killed. But the father of the girl or her brothers did not hesitate to kill the offending male partner if they found out who he was and if he refused to marry the girl, or if he was a close relative within the category in which marriage

is not permitted. The latter case would constitute incest in this respect, which was similarly punishable by death.

23. As frequent cases and the pervading fear of witchcraft, hatred, homicides, tribalism and its implications for the exclusion of other people clearly illustrate. This is the human existential problem of human self-negation and hatred that slowly consumes oneself, as in the case of being in hell, of which it constitutes for those people engaged in such human negations of their own essential being as "Abantu" with "Obuntu" and the negation of the humanity of others in their community whose harmony and stability they also seek to destroy just out of utter malice, hatred and inhumanity.

24. Katiti, Ninshoma (Kampala: School Readers, EALB, 1950), p. 28.

25. For instance, some people may just smile instead of saying "Thank you" to a person who has done them a favor, and others give gifts or perform another service for the person just to show gratitude and to act out "thank you." Of course this cultural trait leads to the rampant corrupt practice of bribery bedevilling the modern African governments today.

26 Karl Rahner, "Union of the Love of Neighbour and the Love of God," Theological Investigations 6:246-247.

27. Cf. Genesis 1:26-28.

28. See, for example, John 10:30 ff., 17:21-23.

29. See, e.g., Karl Rahner, Foundations of Christian Faith, pp. 434-443. Rahner argues that death is a transformation rather than a split of a person into a body that becomes a corpse and a spirit that departs. Rahner says that this kind of division is impossible because a human being is one united being, who cannot be split as such without being totally destroyed as a person. This argument is in line with the African idea that people are transformed at death into spiritual beings that are identical in complete continuity with their former lives which, unlike before, they cannot now modify or improve in any way except by divine approval.

30. Cf. P. Tempels, Bantu Philosophy, pp. 17-18.

CHAPTER V

ANONYMOUS CHRISTIANITY AND ITS IMPLICATIONS

FOR THE PEOPLE AND THE CHURCH IN AFRICA

To affirm the concept and the possible existence of "anonymous Christianity" is to affirm the gratuitous divine work of creation, sustenance and persuasive guidance toward meaningful self-actualization and fulfillment. In other words, it is to affirm the following Biblical teaching:

> In the beginning was the Word [Logos] and the Word was with God, and the Word was God. He was in the beginning with God; all things were made through him, and without him was not anything made that was made. In him was life [Zoe] and the life was the light of men. The light shines in the darkness, and the darkness has not overcome it...The true light that enlightens every man was coming into the world. He was in the world, and the world was made through him, yet the world knew him not.[1]

Since the "world knew him not" in the text refers to the Logos that was the medium of creation and the Savior as "the life" and "the true light that enlightens every man" and every woman in the world, it is quite explicit that the Gospel text is referring to the Logos as being incognito and anonymously present in the world and active in its categorial processes until the Incarnation, when this divine Logos, the pre-existent Christ, became explicit as a historical human being in Jesus of Nazareth.[2]

This Johannine text illustrates very clearly how God's process of creation in Christ can be coextensive and continuous with the universal elevation in free unmerited grace as "the true light that enlightens every man" in this world. Karl Rahner's helpful categorization of Christianity into:

(1) The implicit/anonymous Christianity, covering the period in which Christ's salvific work as the cosmic divine Logos is primarily incognito or anonymous.

(2) The explicit categorial revelation in the historical Christianity of the conventional and institutional church, is helpful in viewing God's universal gratuitous activity of redemptive self-communication to the world in two moments, the first moment being the "Universal Transcendental," which is non-cognitive, ethical and mystical, whereas the second moment is that of the Hypostatic Union, which is historical, cognitive, thematic, ethical and mystical. The second moment is complementary and

fulfilling to the first moment rather than being its abolition or negation, as Jesus himself affirmed: "Think not that I have come to abolish the law and the prophets; I have come not to abolish them but to fulfill them."[3]

Similarly, the writer of the Letter to the Hebrews also saw the continuity of these two moments of God's self-communication to the world and put it as follows:

> In many and various ways God spoke of old to our fathers by the prophets; but in these last days he has spoken to us by a Son, whom he appointed the heir of all things, through whom also he created the world. He reflects the glory of God and bears the very stamp of his nature, upholding the universe by his word of power.[4]

However, the second moment of God's self-disclosure, being cognitive and historical in nature, can only be mediated historically through the teaching of the Church and its missionary teachers and preachers. This is a very slow process as judged by the example of Jesus himself, who taught and made converts by the personal exemplary way of life of the teacher touching his students at the innermost core of their being by his own life, love, words and deeds.

In this sense the Gospel of God in Christ is also Incarnational in that it is the love of God addressed to human beings through and in the embodiment of another human being. This is slow and time-consuming, so there will always be people who will not yet be effectively reached by this Gospel message of the Incarnation.[5]

Nevertheless, these unreached people will not be in any way excluded from God's salvific grace, as it is already active world-wide in an impartial manner, inviting all human beings to come to him in his Mystery and as the very Mystery that guides each responding individual towards the fullness of authentic being and the full individualistic uniqueness of being a person.

Since this process is enabled by Christ as the Cosmic divine Logos that mediates and energizes this dual coextensive process of humanization and salvation and outside of which this process is unable to take place, Karl Rahner correctly designates those people who experience this divine humanization process as Christians and those responding to God at the level of the first moment of "implicit faith" as "anonymous Christians" and those responding in the second moment of the explicit faith in the Gospel as "explicit" or "confessing" Christians.[6] Rahner epitomizes this as follows:

> Until the gospel actually enters the historical situation of a certain person, a non-Christian religion contains not only elements of a natural knowledge of God mixed with depravation caused by original sin and human elements, but also supernatural elements, of grace. It can therefore be ac-

> knowledged to be a legitimate religion even though in different gradations...Non-Christian religion may be said "a priori" to contain supernatural elements of grace...As Christians, we must profess the dogma that God wills the salvation of all men even in post paradisal period of original sin. On the one hand this salvation is specifically Christian for there is no salvation apart from Christ ...God truly wants all men to be saved...Man is exposed to the influence of divine grace, which offers him communion with God, whether he accepts it or not...True we cannot hope that religious pluralism will disappear in the forseeable future; nevertheless, Christians themselves may well regard the non-Christian world as an anonymous Christendom.[7]

Rahner, having declared the non-Christian world to be an "anonymous Christendom,[8] goes on to repudiate the notorious Catholic doctrine of <u>extra ecclesiam nulla salus</u> as follows:

> It follows, therefore, that today the Church will not so much regard herself as the exclusive community of candidates for salvation, but rather as the avant-garde, expressing historically and socially the hidden reality which, Christians hope, exists also outside her visible structure. The Church is not the community of those who possess God's grace as opposed to those who lack it, but the community of those who can confess explicitly what they and the others hope to be.[9]

The Major Implications of the Existence of "Anonymous Christianity"

Undoubtedly, the affirmation of this concept of "anonymous Christianity" and, in light of the previous chapter, the affirmation of African Traditional Religion as part of this "anonymous Christianity" in Africa have serious implications for the people and the Church in Uganda and the rest of Africa, and indeed, the whole world, that is today seriously divided chiefly on the basis of religion, socio-economic ideologies and systems that are so deeply grounded in this religious milieu, yet sometimes expend so much energy and resources fighting each other on this religious basis.

Therefore, the affirmation of "anonymous Christianity," implies the correction and the negation of this myopic religious exclusivism and bigotry that both divides humankind and negates humanity itself.

If we are to avoid the deficient religious background which have created the crusades, the inquisition, jihads, religious divisions, communism, fascism, apartheid and the like, we have to develop a broader concept of God, Grace, humanity, sin, and salvation.

"Anonymous Christianity" as a Critique of Narrow-Minded Exclusive Ecclesiology: Taking Uganda as an African Example

Since our religious views shape our world-view, our mode of existence, our ideals, goals, values, hopes and utopias, in the same way, they also shape the nature of our dislikes, fears, egotism, guilt, associations and dissociations. In some extreme cases, this is done to the extent of religious fanaticism and bigotry. Unfortunately, religious fanatics and begots do not take seriously the religions of other people or different religious views, theological philosophies and religious practices other than their own, which are very often naively and exclusively conceived as the only orthodoxy, and consequently, are equated with the authentic divine salvific revelation.

In pre-Vatican II Catholic theology, this kind of attitude was articulated in the then acceptable guise of the doctrine of _extra ecclesiam nulla salus_ which was repudiated by the Vatican II, undoubtedly, at the prompting of the more open-minded Catholic theologians and ecclesiologists like Karl Rahner and Hans Kung, who were among the scholarly advisors at Vatican II. The type of Catholicism to be found in Africa, and particularly, Uganda today is still largely pre-Vatican II in nature, very conservative and reactionary. Ugandan Catholicism is so unorthodox and conservative, that in the rural parishes, converts from Anglicanism are still occasionally rebaptized; the reason being that the Catholics in Uganda, generally, do not regard Anglicans as authentic Christians.

The Catholics were taught to regard the Anglicans as protestant heretic sectarians who are heading for eternal damnation and hellfire! Unfortunately, the Anglicans were likewise taught to regard Catholics as heretic "papists" who worship "images" of the saints, Mary the blessed Mother of Jesus, and the Pope.[10]

This kind of background has led to religious hostility, rivalry and conflicts. And in the unforgettable past has led to real military confrontations between the Anglicans and the Catholics and between these two groups and the Muslims.[11] And it is no secret that the D.P. (Democratic Party) and U.P.C. (Uganda People's Congress) are disguised forms of an ancient religious-political rivalry, which is now a conflict between Catholicism and Anglicanism in an acceptable modern conventional warfare of modern times, and which is mitigated only by tribalism, especially in Buganda.[12]

Therefore, Rahner's inclusive, positive theology of the Church and the availability of supernatural salvation outside the conventional Church, make such exclusive religious bigotry and mutual anathematization seem a pathological anachronism. But as we know, this anachronistic religious understanding is not devoid of its potentiality for religious division and uncharitable conflicts or even a new kind of inquisition, especially among the fundamentalists such as the rigorous Balokole of Uganda.

Therefore, in a sense, Rahner's concept of the "anonymous Christianity" is very much a critique of the Church and its pride, its sectarian theology and ecclesiology, as well as a recognition and an acknowledgment of the universality of God's gratuitous activities of creation, and universal self-communication in gratuitous grace for the salvation of every human being, who will respond to this supernatural invitation to a fuller life of self-actualization and complete humanization by God. This is what is fully symbolized and articulated in Christ's incarnation and the Hypostatic Union as the divinization of the human being, since authentic humanity is possible only through the supernatural elevation of the human being by the divine salvific grace.

Since the historical Church cannot itself represent all the cosmic divine salvific activity, similarly, therefore, it cannot be the sole container and dispenser of God's salvation nor hold any valid claim to being the exclusive community, the sole divine medium, embodiment and dispenser of this supernatural salvation, which by God's gratuitous grace transcends time, human culture, technology, language, sins, understanding and exclusiveness.

As a result, no individual religious group can ever validly claim to possess salvation in its exclusive totality to the exclusion of non-members, who must join this one church group, denomination or religion in order to gain God's favor and access to supernatural salvation, which is somehow now thought to be encapsulated in this specific community, which usually has become analogous to "Noah's Ark,"[13] outside which nobody can obtain salvation.

Unfortunately, this has been the attitude and explicit enthusiastic teaching of some groups of Christians in Uganda, mainly the Balokole, who are mostly Anglican in origin and membership. For instance, the Balokole have made it known that non-Balokole will never go to heaven and that they are all candidates for hellfire! This has of course alienated the non-Balokole Anglicans in the same Church and the Catholics, who are even "hated" by the Balokole because, although they claim to be Christians, to the horror of the Balokole, they drink beer openly, dance and smoke! They do the very things which the Balokole have repudiated as deadly sins leading only to hell and not to heaven!

However, it can be argued that the Balokole have misunderstood the Gospel of Christ to mean self-denial for everybody, which is an error and uncharitably mean; they insist that all should confess their sins publicly and should become ascetic like them in order to gain their fellowship and, most important of all, in order to gain eternal life.

What is often overlooked, however, by the Balokole, like most of us human beings, is the Biblical warning not to judge anybody, as judgment is the sole prerogative of God, the holy impartial, omniscient Creator and gracious, redemptive God:

> Therefore, you have no excuse, o man, whoever you are, when you judge another; for, in passing judgement upon him you condemn yourself, because you, the judge, are doing the very same things. We know that the judgement of God...will be revealed. For he will render to every man according to his works: to those who by patience in well-doing seek for

> glory and honour and immortality, he will give eternal life; but for those who are factious and do not obey the truth...there will be wrath and fury. There will be tribulation and distress for every human being who does evil, the Jew first and also the Greek [everyone else], but glory and honour and peace for everyone who does good...For God shows no partiality.[14]

If God is the Creator, loving Savior and impartial, omniscient, merciful Judge of human beings, then anyone who usurps this divine prerogative is attempting some kind of <u>coup de Dieu</u>. We can never be completely sure that the individual <u>is totally</u> lost to God, even when society may condemn that very individual to death as a criminal, and therefore we cannot know who is "saved" and who is lost. The implication is that we should treat all human beings as potential candidates and heirs of supernatural salvation.

The values of God and the values of society might sometimes be opposed to each other and might be in conflict, and therefore in this case what would be regarded as a sin and a criminal offence by human beings might prove the reverse with God. For instance, Jesus was executed on the cross as a criminal by human beings. But the Scriptures consistently claim that he was innocent and that his trial and consequent execution were a travesty of justice.[15] The Scriptures also point out that one of the two criminals that were crucified along with Jesus was granted eternal life by Jesus, yet he was put to death for his sin and the crime of being a thief![16]

We also know that during his earthly ministry, Jesus was in constant opposition and conflict with the religious priests, scribes; and the rigorous, self-righteous and legalistic Pharisees who were pious adherents of the law, observing it diligently to its minor details. Nevertheless, Jesus instead commended sinners, the tax-collectors, harlots, and outcasts, because they were more open-minded and receptive to his teaching of the good news of salvation and were ready to be touched by his healing power that makes men and women new and whole by faith and hope.

For such a newness, wholeness and restoration is salvation in Christ. Like the anonymous woman in the crowd who touched Jesus in this faith and hopeful anticipation of wholeness and salvific healing and who was made whole, every man and every woman everywhere and any time, it may be inferred, can touch the same Cosmic Christ by faith and in hopeful anticipation for salvific healing of body, mind, relationships, hence restoration to newness and wholeness.[17]

Therefore, the affirmation of "anonymous Christianity" brings us back to the authentic teaching of Christ and the Apostles as we find it in the New Testament. Jesus and the Apostles never excluded other people outside their original small community from divine salvation. Indeed, the Jews and the Gentiles (pagans included) were all thought to be equal candidates for this supernatural salvation. For instance, St. Luke dramatizes this fact by recording the "Song of Simeon," known in the Anglican and Catholic liturgy as the "Nunc dimittis:"

> Lord, now lettest thou thy servant depart in peace, according to thy word; For mine eyes have seen thy salvation, Which thou hast prepared before the face of all people, To be a light to lighten the Gentiles, and to be the glory of thy people Israel.[18]

Or the "Song of the Lamb" (Dignus es):

> Worthy art thou For thou wast slain and by thy blood didst ransom men for God. From every tribe and tongue and people and nation and hast made them a kingdom. And priests to our God and they shall reign on earth.[19]

And the "Song of the Redeemed" (Magna et mirabilia):

> O ruler of the universe, Lord God, great deeds are they that you have done, surpassing human understanding. Your ways are ways of righteousness and truth, O King of all the ages.
>
> Who can fail to do you homage, Lord, and sing the praises of your Name? for you only are the holy One. All nations will draw near and fall down before you because your just and holy works have been revealed.[20]

These liturgical texts are sung or said for "daily office" in the in main-line churches, such as the Catholic and Anglican Churches. But how seriously are they taken or understood? It is probably amazing, then, that one can read these Biblical texts, sing them, meditate prayerfully upon them as it is supposed by the liturgy, and yet still remain blind to the fact that God's salvific activity is by nature and scope universal, proferred to all human beings everywhere in the world and through all the ages. This cosmic dimension of God's love compels us then, too, as his redeemed people, to think, to love and to act like our God in a cosmic fashion.

This probably means that we have to be more openminded, discerning, patient and tolerant in order to see and appreciate this divine cosmic dimension of God's salvific activity, as we have to look at the Traditional African Religion's believer, the Muslim, the Jew, the Hindu and Buddhist transcendentalist in order to see it, for that is where it is happening. It might not be the kind of spirituality with which we are familiar and expect to find. Nevertheless, there is something of God's work going on there, even when the forces of evil are also seen to be actively at work in the same locus.

Moreover, our own spiritual life can even be deepened by learning from other peoples and other religions: new religious truths, new ways of thinking, worship, meditation, or a fresh way of viewing the world and the supernatural. Similarly, these other religions and people, too, can learn from us, and therefore, be able to supplement their own deficiency to a certain extent (e.g. concerning unconditonal love for the neighbor, concern for human value and human rights, providing and taking care of those in need, such as the poor and the victims of disasters). Hopefully, through this process of mutual religious, socio-economic and political exchange and explicit missionary endeavors, the "anonymous Christendom" can gradually but significantly move toward explicit Christianity in its general outlook and socio-political basic emotional values.

The Problem of Christian Baptism

In the process of affirming "anonymous Christianity" beyond the historical Church, baptism, like circumcision in the early church, can become a theological problem and a hindrance, preventing the Church from seeing God's salvific activity that is taking place world-wide even among the unbaptized.

As we know, even in explicit Christianity it is recognized that conversion and the outpouring of the Holy Spirit and divine salvific grace can precede baptism, as St. Peter to his shock discovered at the house of Cornelius, a Gentile non-Christian whom he had regarded as an outsider to God's salvific community until God visibly contradicted him by sending the Holy Spirit upon Cornelius and the whole of his household, indiscriminately.[21]

This indicates how God's salvific activity can work apart from and independent of the Church and the sacraments such as baptism. Christians are like the ancient Jews, who were very reluctant to admit that God can and does act redemptively and graciously outside the covenant, which was marked by circumcision regarding Judaism and now by baptism as regards Christianity.[22]

Therefore, St. Pauls's remarks on the irrelevancy of the external Jewish rite of circumcision, in contrast to unconditional loving and good deeds as the essence of true religion, can also apply to baptism in our general argument and context of "anonymous Christianity." For instance, if Paul was writing his Letter to the Romans today, Chapters 2:12-3:2 would read as follows:

> All who have sinned without the Gospel will also perish without the Gospel and all who have sinned under the Gospel will also be judged under the Gospel. For it is not the hearers of the Gospel that are righteous before God, but the doers of what the Gospel teaches are the ones who will be justified. When non-Christians who have not yet heard the Gospel do by nature what the Gospel requires, they are a Gospel unto themselves, even though they do not have the written Gospel of Christ Jesus. They show that what the Gospel requires is written on their hearts, while their

> conscience also bears witness and their conflicting thoughts accuse or excuse them on that day when, according to my gospel, God judges the secrets of men by Christ Jesus.

Paul would probably continue his theological letter to the the well boastful Christians in Rome as follows:

> But if you call yourself a Christian and rely upon the Gospel and boast of your relation to God and know his will and approve what is excellent, because you are instructed in the Gospel, and if you are sure that you are a guide to the blind, a light to those in darkness...you then who teach others, will you not teach yourselves?...You who boast of the Gospel, do you dishonour God by not living according to the Gospel? For it is written, "The name of God is blasphemed among the non-Christians because of you."
>
> Baptism is indeed of value if you obey the Gospel; but if you disobey the Gospel your baptism becomes unbaptism. So, if a man who is unbaptized keeps the precepts of the Gospel will not his unbaptism be regarded as baptism? Then those who are physically unbaptized but keep the Gospel will condemn you who have the written Gospel and baptism but fail to live by it. For he is not a Christian who is one outwardly, nor is true baptism something external and physical. He is a Christian who is one inwardly, and real baptism is a matter of the heart, spiritual and not literal. His praise is not from men but God.
>
> Then what advantage has the Christian? Or what value is baptism? Much in every way. To begin with, The Christians are entrusted with the explicitly proclaimed Word of God and the written Gospel of Christ.[23]

If baptism by itself does not confer eternal life (ex opere operato) and neither does its absence exclude anybody from God's unconditional love and gratuitous universal efficacious salvific grace, then why should the Church insist on it? The answer to this difficult question may be found in sociology as well as theology. Sociologically the Church as a voluntary social community needs a "rite of passage" for making the initiation and entry of new members into its own community and membership.

The best illustration of the social element is perhaps infant baptism, which is usually a time of social gathering and party-making at the child's home.[24] The christening party following the infant's baptism has little religious significance, if it has any. It is on the whole just another social function like a wedding, Thanksgiving, Christmas or Independence Day.

Theologically, baptism is more difficult to discuss, as it is a very controversial subject within Christianity itself. For instance, some Christians such as the Baptists even contend that infant baptism is invalid as the candidate for baptism should be adult enough to make a personal decision for Christ as Lord, whereas in other major Christian traditions, such as the Catholic, Anglican, Eastern Orthodox churches' doctrines, infant baptism is strongly commended as if it was of an automatic intrinsic value in itself, thus functioning *ex opere operato* in the life of the baptized child until the child grows up to affirm his or her own faith in the confirmation ceremony.

However, the adoption of a more flexible view of baptism, as the concept of "anonymous Christianity" demands, requires the repudiation not only of the old-fashioned and anachronistic doctrine of *extra ecclesiam nulla salus*, but also of the underlying Augustinian view of the universality of the original sin that can only be cleansed by Christian ritual baptism.[25]

Nevertheless, the Augustinian predestination, if looked at from a cosmic point of view, need not be opposed to the view of "anonymous Christianity." It would rather enhance it in that in every age or nation God would have to find a way of saving those elected to supernatural salvation, including the era before the Incarnation and the arrival of the Gospel in each given area or individual people.[26]

Theologically, baptism is the initiation of a person into the mystery of Christ's life, passion, death and resurrection, and into communion of all those people that acknowledge Jesus as Christ the Lord and Savior.[27] This means that baptism, if clearly understood, is not a denominational entry rite or affair; rather it is a symbolic ritual entry into mystical union with Christ and the saints past, present and future, and a symbol that one belongs to a particular institutional church as categorial local expression of this universal belonging and union with the universal (Catholic) Church, which is the aggregate sum of all the presently divided traditional and denominational churches.

"Anonymous Christianity" as Possible Background for Ecumenism

African Christians, like in the case of the Ugandans, have to learn that they are all Christians, regardless of whether they are Balokole, Catholics or Anglicans. If they cannot accept each other as Christians who share one common baptism in the triune God, they cannot accept the authentic humanity of non-Christians as expressive of an "anonymous Christianity" and divine salvation.

In addition, if some Christians like those in Uganda, insist on the absurd idea that Anglicanism and Catholicism are two religions rather than two branches or denominations of the same Religion or Faith, and if they could affirm the existence of "anonymous Christianity," then they could find it easy to accept each other at least on the level of "anonymous Christianity"! This approach would circumvent the problem of doctrine, orthodoxy and heresy that have been a major stumbling block in the current ecumenical discussions.

Most of this bigotry and denominational pride and exclusiveness could be constructively dealt with if "anonymous Christianity" were affirmed and taught to the ordinary Christians in a way that would not cause them to lose their own faith but would enable them to see that God's incomprehensible, infinite Mystery and diverse cosmic activity causes pluralism in religious systems, knowledge, experiences, hopes, beliefs and practices; then people would be able to be more sensitive to and tolerant of the religious views and practices of the other people, even when they are apparently quite different or even seem to be opposed to our own reliigious or philosophical views and principles.

There is always a possibility that one's own religious beliefs and practices could be erroneous or distorted, too, so that the condemnation of the beliefs and practices of others could also be a condemnation of one's very own. There is no basis or guarantee on this crucial point that the religion, religious beliefs, hopes, objectives and practices of the other people will always be wrong and that our own will always be right.

Furthermore, we can always benefit by mutual exchange of ideas and by learning from each other, rather than engaging in negative and uncharitable mutual destructive behaviors such as resenting, hating and fighting with each other. Moreover, God does not seem to be bothered by diversity, since he has created it in plenty.

Therefore, there is no good theological reason why we should seek religious conformity rather than well-informed diversity in the unity of understanding and appreciation. Conformity can be understood to be mainly required by those people and groups who are insecure and afraid of variety or change, whereas the diversity of religious views and practices can only be accepted by those people and churches that are secure in their faith that is fully grounded in the triune Creator and Redemptive God that is the *mysterium tremendum* behind the beauty, variety, diversity and individuating uniqueness in the world.

Surely, such a God that is behind the rich variety and diversity in this world would not like to be understood, glorified and worshipped in the unison of religious conformity! Therefore, it would seem that religious fundamentalist rigorous conformity is preferably understood as a manifestation of human insecurity and lack of sufficient faith in God as the God of infinite unconditional love, gratuitous salvific grace, the very Creator and Redemptive God that desires us to become the unique selves that he has created us to be.

This is as true of individuals as it is of nations and races in their uniqueness and diversity in the unity of the all-embracing, one common humanity. Analogously, human religions, religious views, beliefs and cultic expressive practices are likewise ideally diverse within the unity of one common objective, namely, the worship and adoration of God as the Infinite Mystery at the center of our being and the cosmos, the Ultimate Source and Destiny of our lives, and the mediator of our own lives and those of others in the quest of meaning and direction for our immediate future action.

Ecumenism and the "Venture in Mission" to the "Anonymous Christians"

The implication for Christianity is that God can be served best by the Church when it is diverse in practice and theology, but united in faith, love, worship, witness and missionary outreach. Our own internal religious divisions, conflicts, fights and anathematizations are a great scandal and stumbling block in our Christian witness and missionary outreach in the world, since uncharitable deeds to each other negate words of God's love in Christ.

Christian ecumenism and unity will, therefore, not only enhance fellowship and love for each other as brothers and sisters in Christ, but it will also give more credibility in the world as a consequence of joint witness and venture in mission. Moreover, resources and expertise can be pooled in the cause of world Christian mission, so as to bring "anonymous Christianity" to cognitive explicit Christianity, and specifically to personal acknowledgment and confession of Christ as Lord and Savior and unconditional love of neighbor. This is the apex of explicit Christianity.

Therefore, "anonymous Christianity" should also be brought to full cognitive espousal in its mature, explicit Christian expression. In order to speed up this historical growth process, all missionary endeavors should be undertaken by the Christian Church so as to bring it about quickly.

However, the very notion of "anonymous Christianity" should serve to warn all Christian missionaries of the need for the appropriate missionary strategies that take into account the people's notions of integrity, dignity and freedom, local religious traditions and cultural religious practices. These local elements should be approached with respect as the prior divine groundwork preparation for the new, that is the Gospel, that has to be taught in light of this given background, and therefore, must be linked with the old that is already known.

Accordingly, all attempts should be made to avoid condemnation of what is found there, but rather, like St. Paul, to look for the "altar of the unknown God" as St. Paul did on his missionary journey in "pagan" Athens.[28] Certainly, Paul saw the numerous "pagan" temples, statues and idols that abounded in the city. But he chose not to start his preaching on a negative note by attacking or even possibly demolishing these idols and other false gods.

Paul being tactful, chose wisely, to begin positively by focusing local people's attention on the good news he was bringing them in fulfillment of what they already imperfectly and anonymously knew, had and worshipped as the Unknown God! So Paul, standing in the middle of the Areopagus, where the people were always gathered to hear enlightening public lectures and other educated kinds of discourses, said:

> Men of Athens, I perceive that in every way you are very religious. For as I passed along, and observed the objects of your worship, I found also an altar with this inscription, "To an unknown god." What therefore you worship as unknown, this I proclaim to you. The God who made the world and everything in it...[29]

The main objective for Christian missions should not be to make people feel more guilty than they already feel about their sins and failures. But rather, it is to bring them the good news of their free unmerited acceptance, forgiveness, hope and unconditional love of God in Christ's Incarnation, life, teaching, passion and resurrection.

This approach is certainly the reverse of the former missionary strategy and approach in Uganda. Missionaries like Alexander Mackay of the Church Missionary Society thought that everything that was African, such as dress, music, dance, names, marriages, religious pracitces, morals and customs, were all barbaric and pagan. This being the case, Mackay understood the Christian mission as the downgrading and destruction of the African culture, or at least to achieve local individual conversion, which he equated with the total break with the past and the encompassing and constitutive African culture that he equated with barbarism and heathenism.

In his own understanding, there was no divine activity going on prior to the arrival of the Anglican missionaries. He was convinced that the African Traditional Religion, Islam and Catholicism, which arrived two years later after the initial arrival of the Anglican missionaries in 1877, were all devilish! For instance, of the local East Africans, Mackay wrote the following in his letter to Wigram:

> East Africans are generally savage -- sunk in low state of barbarism, low intellect and low in

> morals. Their names are those of animals or deities or they bear some grotesque meaning on the face of them causing the owner to blush with shame when a European pronounced the word...It was necessary to make a clean break with names of 'things indecent and obscene.'[30]

Did it ever occur to Mackay that the Europeans terribly mispronounced these African names, causing a total change in the meaning, thus grossly changing the identity of the people who bore the names, and thereby causing them embarrassment?[31] It seems that in his ethnocentric missionary approach and fundamentalist Christian bigotry, he ignored the cultural and linguistic barrier and consequently there were frequent misunderstandings between the European missionaries and their local African converts.

Christian boarding school education for the young was one of the missionary maneuvers to cut the young converts from their relatives and community and so to uproot them from their African Traditional Religion and culture, that they regarded as unredeemably pagan, so as to make them "good Christians" or "Black-European Christians" at best! This missionary approach was similar to the French colonial policy of "assimilation" in Africa that proved a great failure, since the Africans naturally failed to turn into "Black Frenchmen" as it had been naively hoped. Similarly, Mackay's imperialist-missionary venture of turning the East Africans into "Black Anglican Englishmen" was bound to fail, too.

Mackay, being in charge of the Anglican Church Missionary Society's (C.M.S.) work in Uganda, was terribly upset that the Catholics, too, had decided to come and do some missionary work in the same country. Instead of welcoming them as allies and fellow Christian laborers in this wide unharvested vineyard of God, he got annoyed and resentful. Consequently, he lamentedly wrote back home to England as follows:

> It seems to me that God has allowed these false teachers to come...Oh, that we could and use the short time we have, more to God's story. We did what we could to keep the tares from being sown when the Papists [Catholic missionaries] turned up, but we failed and now they will settle in the country beside us. Well as Christ himself taught, let the tares grow up along with the wheat and on harvest day God will gather them separately.[32]

Christianity and the Church in Uganda were established in this background of religious rivalry, intolerance, exclusivism, hostility and bigotry that have bedevilled the people and Church of Uganda ever since. How was Mackay sure that the Catholic missionaries and their converts constituted the tares in the wheat? Were the Anglicans then the wheat? Could Mackay ever work together in love with the Catholics he regarded tares, and as such fuel for the eschatological hellfire?

Obviously, for Mackay the Anglicans and only "those born

again," (Balokole) were the wheat and the rest, particularly the Catholics whom he referred to simply as "the Papists," were the tares that the devil was sowing in Uganda by the mediation of the "anti-Christ" Catholic missionaries!

It is hardly surprising, therefore, that just ten years later, this religious intolerance, hostility and rivalry grew worse as the local converts to both these denominations that were mutually opposed to each other. Consequently, an open religious military conflict took place between the Anglicans and the Catholics, thus turning the previous religious, verbal "cold war" into a real, protracted, military and bloody one.

Obviously, the Lord's obligatory commandment for his followers to love one another and all human beings unconditionally, even inclusive of one's enemies, is the quintessence and the only veritable measure of authentic Christianity or any other truly redemptive religion. Therefore, unconditional love is the only true criterion of who is either an authentic Christian or a false Christian; and subsequently, a tare had been ignored by both Christian parties, instead, choosing the unchristian, mundane, uncharitable, wicked, bloody and contradictory method of violence, warfare and bloodshed, ironically enough, in order to demonstrate their personal deep commitment and love for both Jesus Christ and God his heavenly Father.

But did it ever occur to these missionaries or their converts that this religious warfare and bloodshed in the name of Christ/God might actually be the very negation of authentic Christianity? The same question is still valid today, since this religious milieu is still basically the same, despite the current positive attempts at ecumenism, joint translations of the Holy Scriptures, religious educational syllabi and educational programs.

These pioneering joint programs are a great Christian idea and positive godly witness that should be promoted so as to minimize the negative effects of the initial Christian missionaries, who sowed the harmful seeds of religious hatred, intolerance, division, bigotry, and war, instead of bringing the Gospel of the good news of forgiveness, unconditional love and reconciliation with God and the neighbor.

There is great hope that with good, positive, sound teaching of the Gospel and its underlying essential obligation for unconditional love for the neighbor, this uncharitable, harmful religious background that has been fatefully inherited from these European ethnocentric bigoted and factious Christian missionaries can be either neutralized or negated by our own African traditional orientation to love, openness, community and inclusiveness of diversity and religious pluralism. This noble African background has great potentiality for greater factual Christian successful ecumenism and Christian unity. However, at the moment this ecumenical process is still moving slowly because of the presence of large numbers of Western missionaries still in Africa.[33]

Therefore, the Church in Africa will do better to become independent of Western traditions and structures in order to distance itself from the entrenched Western Christian conflicts and denominational rivalry which Africa has no business getting engrossed in as if they were of its own creation. Christianity in Africa will become more meaningful, unitive, wholistic, reconciliatory and redemptive to the African people if it is allowed to become authentically African. In other words, if Christianity is contextualized and rooted in the African milieu, and therefore, in the African life itself, God will have become Incarnate in African life in Jesus Christ not as a Jew, but as an African, so as to address the Africans in their own language, symbols and cultural context.

"Anonymous Christianity" and the Universal Cross of Christ

"Anonymous Christianity" should not be looked upon with disdain or even rejected as "anti-Christian misssions" or an "easy back door to divine salvation."[34] Salvation may be gratuitously given to all human beings by God, regardless of what they are or where they are.

However, human beings have to work out their salvation daily in the course of ordinary day-to-day living with this divine assistance. Even then living is not easy, and this is precisely where the cross of Christ comes into focus in the process of human life and salvation. This pain of the cross that is encountered and experienced in the course of living, like "anonymous Christianity," transcends the barriers of conventional historical Christianity.

It can also be argued that in the same way "anonymous Christianity" was in existence even prior to the Incarnation of Christ, as preparatory anticipation of Christ's Incarnation, the cross was also implicitly present as an anticipation of the passion event. This means also that wherever and whenever human beings have stood up strongly for justice, righteousness, or truth, they often have been persecuted and sometimes even executed by their own communities that could not bear hearing them. Good examples are the Jewish prophets, and the most climactic of all, the crucifixion of Jesus as a blaspheming subversive religious teacher.[35]

Obviously, John the Baptist, the forerunner of Jesus, had been arrested, imprisoned and beheaded for his religious teachings and activities. He was not a conventional Christian, as he lived and died shortly before the founding of historical Christianity by Jesus his cousin. But can we then validly claim that John the Baptist never shared Christ's sufferings or experienced his cross because he preceded Christ, and that as such, he is lost to God? Only, a very naive person would answer this question in the affirmative.

But what about Mahatma Gandhi, whose life was entirely dedicated to the unconditional loving, self-scrificial non-violent mobilization for the freedom and independence of his own people of India that led to his unjust arrests, torture and imprisonment by the British imperialist officers in India? Can we say that he did not participate in the sufferings of Christ and experience of the cross of Christ just because he was a Hindu? The answer to these questions is definately, "NO!"

It would is theologically valid, therefore, to maintain that whenever and wherever human beings are persecuted for their stand for the truth, justice, human rights, equality, freedom, independence and self-determination in order to become what God has created them to become to be, then, there is the cross of Christ "being carried" and being experienced by these people through personal participation in the same kind of persecution, and innocent suffering Jesus underwent for the sake of divine truth, and love for fellow human beings.

In this noble venture, in which suffering is inevitable because of the presence of evil, human moral failure and sin in the world, is participation in the cross of Christ. This is true regardless of time, geographical location, creed, nationality, race and level of technology.

This is consonant with Christ's teaching that it is the doers of God's will and not the mere confessors of his name that shall enter the kingdom of heaven. For instance, St. Matthew reports Jesus' own words on this subject that are reminiscent of the proverb, "All that glitters is not gold":

> Beware of false prophets, who come to you in sheep's clothing but inwardly are ravenous wolves. You will know them by their fruits. Are grapes gathered from thorns, or are figs from thistles? So, every sound tree bears good fruit, but the bad tree bears evil fruit. A sound tree cannot bear evil fruit nor can a bad tree bear good fruit...
>
> Not everyone who says to me, "Lord, Lord" shall enter the kingdom of heaven, but he who does the will of my Father who is in heaven. On that day many will say to me, "Lord, Lord, did we not prophesy in your name, and cast out demons in your name, and do many mighty works in your name?" And then I will declare to them, "I never knew you; depart from me, you evil-doers."36

Therefore, conventional and confessing Christians who ignore the cross of Christ as it is carried and experienced in living in unconditional love for the neighbor and active self-sacrificial activity in the world processes in order to achieve freedom and justice for the oppressed, to feed the hungry, clothe the naked, defend the defenseless and to speak for the voiceless will have also ignored Christ and his mission, for that is where Christ and his redemptive work naturally belong.

Similarly, that is where Christ and his unconditional, loving, self-sacrificial salvific activity are to be found. Sister Theresa of Calcutta is a perfect modern example of this infinite loving selfless dedication and service to others. She diligently serves the poor masses and the needy streetdwellers of the overcrowded Indian cities in order to serve Christ in them.

This unconditional loving service to all human beings should be treated as the true bearing of the cross of Christ and the very criterion of authentic humanity and salvation. This is also the ultimate criterion for the irrevocable and definitive divine eschatological judgment. St. Matthew again reports the following words of Jesus about this subject:

> When the Son of Man comes in glory, and all the angels with him, then he will sit on his glorious throne. before him will be gathered all the nations and he will separate them one from another as a shepherd separates the sheep from the goats ...Then the King will say to those at the right hand,

> "Come, O blessed of my Father, inherit the kingdom prepared for you from the foundation of the world; for I was hungry and you gave me food, I was thirsty and you gave me drink, I was a stranger and you welcomed me, I was naked and you clothed me, I was lonely and you visited me, I was in prison and you came to me." Then the righteous will answer him, "Lord, when did we see thee hungry and feed thee or thirsty and give thee drink? And when did we see thee a stranger and welcome thee? And when did we see thee sick or in prison and visit thee?"

The parable teaches the principle or the idea of "anonymous Christianity" in the sense that the righteous seemed not to be aware that they were serving God and they were as surprised as the self-reghteous who found themselves very unexpectedly rejected. Jesus goes to give a definitive measure by which all human beings will be measured and judged when he answered the above question as follows:

> And the King will answer them, "Truly, I say to you, as you did it to me." Then he will say to those at his left hand, "Depart from me, you curse...for I was hungry and you gave me no food, I was thirsty and you gave me no drink, I was a stranger and you did not welcome me, naked and you did not clothe me, and in prison, you did not visit me." Then they also will answer, "Lord, when...?" Then he will answer them, "Truly, I say to you, as you did it not to one of the least of these [people], you did it not to me." And they will go away into eternal punishment, but the righteous in eternal life.[37]

This is the very quintessence and epitome of soteriology and Christianity in its overlapping two-fold dimensions, the explicit, cognitive and confessional Christianity on one hand, and the implicit, non-cognitive, unaware of itself, incognito or "anonymous" on the other. The latter may be anonymous to the world but it is not so with God the loving and merciful impartial judge, who does not judge by external appearances of human beings and their actions, but rather the true judge of human hearts and motives for their actions (deeds) both good and bad.[38]

The words of Christ quoted above reveal that the only sure key to unconditional love and charitable generous service and treatment of our fellow human beings, most especially during their time of need when they are most open and receptive to both God and their fellow beings. For this the opportune time when they are most eager to see, hear and experience the divine word of Love, Life and Hope acted out both in word and deed through us as Christ's missionaries and God's ambassadors of life, forgiveness, love, hope and reconciliation by the power of the Holy Spirit.[39]

However, in order to achieve this and to become God's effective missionaries and ambassadors in this categorial world of religious, cultural, economic, socio-political ideological pluralism, we have to be humble, flexible, open-minded, inclusive and loving to all human beings without any conditions.

This means working jointly with all men and women of good will regardless of their creed, race, color, political views, ideology and party or religious affiliation in the world, so as to serve God best and our fellow human beings (or our neighbor) more effectively. Above all, this approach will greatly insure global harmony, justice, peace and careful development and equitable utilization of the world's natural resources for the general welfare of all the earth's inhabitants.

The Affirmation of "Anonymous Christianity" Requires a New Theological Reflection

The affirmation of the existence of "anonymous Christianity" will inevitably require a new theological reflection in light of this new broad, universal context. It requires not only the repudiation of narrow and exclusive theological doctrines such as *extra ecclesiam nulla salus*, but it will also mean a review of other key doctrines on the sacraments, most especially baptism, the Eucharist and matrimony, questioning religious intermarriages.

Furthermore, there has to be an indigenous African theology expressive of the Gospel in a locally meaningful mode of thought, understanding, practice and liturgical worship. That means allowing the African man or woman to think, act and worship as an African Christian *vis-à-vis* the Western missionaries who brought Christianity to the local area. It is difficult for an ordinary African to worship God in a foreign liturgy and to sing Western hymns, even those with references to winter, snow and spring, when most Africans would have never seen snow!

For Christianity in its explicit form to become the meaningful and the divine vehicle or medium for daily salvific guidance and influence on the lives of the African masses, as the traditional religion still does, Christianity has to become African. It has to emphasize love, wholeness, healing, forgiveness and release from guilt. In addition, many would urge that Western missionary Christianity has to shed its superficial marks and trappings of the Western cultural elements that have no value or meaning in Africa, such as Western Christian art, music and musical instruments, architectural designs of church buildings, clerical robes, liturgical garments and vessels, wedding dress and order of ceremony, and the use of bread and wine for the Eucharist instead of local staple food and drink. These foreign practices, they would argue, can be adapted locally without necessarily making a radical change in theology.

However, the problem lies in human reluctance to change and, most of all, the lack of belief that the African cultural and traditional elements are truly fitting vessels and media for communicating God's Word in the proclaimed message and consecrated local food and drink to become by the power of the Holy Spirit the true efficacious symbols of Christ's mystical body and blood, for the maintenance of life now and, mystically, in the world to come.

Perhaps most important of all, Christology and the theories of the Atonement have to be reviewed in the light of "anonymous Christianity" and in a broader universal context as the arena of God's unconditional self-communication in efficacious grace for the salvation of every human being regardless of time and space, creed, tribe, nationality, race or level of technological development. Following the example of St. John, Christ's centrality in both creation and salvation would have to be strongly affirmed for all places and all ages.

Therefore, those people experiencing and enjoying salvation before the Incarnation and before the arrival of the explicit historical institutional Christianity can be validly termed "anonymous Christians," since their salvation is possible only through and by the presence and mediation of Christ, as there is no salvation possible anywhere except through Christ as the cosmic pre-existent divine creative and redemptive Logos/Word which is the very Logos of God that became categorial in the Incarnation and was historically manifested to the world in history as Jesus of Nazareth.[40] It is this categorial Logos as Jesus that becomes the founder of historical Christianity which will be gradually and historically mediated to all human beings through personal contact and deliberate church organized missionary outreach.

However, until then there will be a mutual co-existence and overlapping of "anonymous Christianity" that is only aware of the cosmic, transcendental and pre-Incarnate Christ as the divine Logos and the explicit Christianity that is grounded in the Incarnation, life, teaching, passion, death, resurrection and ascension of Jesus Christ, the latter being, particularly well outlined in the Gospels and the Letters to the Romans and Hebrews, as being the ideal form of Christianity, but both of them possessing salvific efficacy despite the glaring deficiencies to be found in "anonymous Christianity."

It is, therefore, mandatory that Christian missionary activity should be undertaken by the Church in order to remedy these dehumanizing shortcomings in the world. In this way the institutional Christian Church, being the categorial embodiment as well as the historical redemptive mediation of the fullness of God's unconditional love, would be the main categorial divine medium of the fullness of freedom, authentic humanization and supernatural salvation in this world.[41]

NOTES

1. John 1:1-5, 9, 10. There are many texts in the Bible that can be used to support this concept of "anonymous Christianity," since it was always affirmed that the God of Israel is the only God that has created the world and all the people in it and that he will judge them all, too; Gen. 1-12:3, Isa. 52-61, Rom. 1-5.

2. John 1:1-5, 9-14.

3. Matthew 5:17.

4. Hebrews 1:1-3a.

5. According to David Barrett's statistics in World Christian Encyclopedia: A Comparative Survey of Churches and Religions in the Modern World, A.D. 1900-2000, only 33 percent of the world is Christian. Even more sinister, he found that whereas Christianity was on the whole growing in terms of numbers, it was losing in terms of percentage of world population growth! For a quick analytical summary of Barrett's major findings, see James Munson's review article entitled "First World Survey of Christians a Mammoth Undertaking," Canadian Churchman (National Newspaper of the Anglican Church in Canada), 108:6 (June, 1982), p. 5.

6. Rahner acknowledges the problem of the term "anonymous Christianity" but also criticizes his critics, such as Kung, Jungel and Henri de Lubac for not coming up with a better term that would include all human beings experiencing God's salvation without being objectionable or offensive to anybody. See Rahner, "Observations on the Problem of the 'Anonymous Christian'," Theological Investigations 14:280-294, and Karl-Heinz Weger, Karl Rahner: An Introduction to His Theology, pp. 112-141.

7. Karl Rahner, Grace in Freedom (New York: Herder and Herder, 1969), pp. 83-85.

8. David Barrett, loc. cit.

9. Rahner, Grace in Freedom, pp. 85-86.

10. E.g., see Ssemakula Kiwanuka, A History of Buganda, pp. 155-180.

11. Ibid.

12. For instance, during the Ugandan national elections of 1980, most of the Baganda, regardless of political party or religious affiliation, voted D.P. mainly for tribal reasons, and

in protest against Dr. Obote, who is a Northerner and from a non-Bantu ethnic group.

13. Cf. Genesis 6-11 and Cyprian's epitome of the doctrine of _extra ecclesiam nulla salus_ in his _De catholicae ecclesiae unitate_, 6: _He cannot have for his father who has not the Church for his mother_. If anyone was able to escape outside of Noah's ark, then he also escapes who is outside the doors of the Church.

14. Romans 2:1-3, 6-11.

15. Cf. Luke 23:13-25; Matt. 27:1-31; Mark 15:1-20; Acts 3:13-14, 18:38-40, 19:14-15.

16. The story of Jesus and the criminal who got redeemed on the cross should keep us all humble. The thief went to heaven according to this story whereas the religious Pharisees and the priests were found acting on the side of the devil!

17. Cf. Luke 8:43-48.

18. Luke 2:29-32.

19. Rev. 5:9-10.

20. Rev. 15:3-4.

21. See Acts, 10.

22. See, e.g., Rom. 1-4.

23. I have taken baptism in Christianity to be a "dynamic equivalent" of circumcision in Judaism, similarly, Gentile to be the equivalent of "non-Christian," the Jewish Torah/Law to be the Christian equivalent of the Gospel, especially as it is epitomized in the Lord's commandment to love God and the neighbor unconditionally. Cf. Luke 6:27-36; John 13:34-35, 15:9-17; 1 Cor. 13; 1 John 4:8-21. We can never love unconditionally all human beings too much.

However, we are always in danger of loving too little or of being loving only to our friends and kindred, just like as mere "pagans" (cf. Luke 6:27-36). Love is the key to natural life and the supernatural life of salvation, and therefore, without it both kinds of human life are almost impossible or are greatly impoverished.

24. This is a true and common practice in Uganda. The Church has not made any attempt to discourage this attitude, partly because baptism is regarded as supernatural birth, and like a natural birth, is regarded as a time for rejoicing and festivity in order to celebrate the addition of new life to the particular family and the community as a whole.

25. E.g. see Augustine, _On Free Choice of the Will_, 19-25;

<u>Confessions</u>, X; <u>De Civitate Dei</u>, X.

26. Cf. Augustine, Epistle 217 (427) to Vitalis (which deals with prevenient grace) and his treatment of irresistible grace in <u>De corruptione et gratia</u>; <u>De dono perseverantiae</u> (428).

27. Cf. Rom. 6:3-11; Col. 2:6-15.

28. See Acts 17:22-32.

29. Acts 17:22-23.

30. Asavia Wandira, <u>Early Missionary Education in Uganda: A Study of Purpose in Missionary Education</u> (Kampala: Makerere University Department of Education, 1972), p. 109.

31. For instance, the religious name "Hategikimaana," which means "God reigns," if mispronounced with a short <u>a</u> in the last syllable, changes the meaning to "the vagina reigns"! This applies to all the names ending in "-imaana", which abound in Kigezi and Rwanda. Such other names, include "Buhooro" which, if mispronounced, means either "leftovers" or "knives," instead of "peace."

32. Kiwanuka, op. cit., p. 171.

33. For instance, in 1976 Hastings estimated that there were more than 40,000 Christian foreign missionaries in Africa, of which 25,000 were Roman Catholic missionaries; cf. Hastings, <u>African Christianity</u>, pp. 20-21, 31-34. This large Catholic number of missionaries represents a serious Catholic effort which has been equally rewarded with African converts to Catholicism.

34. As Hans Urs von Balthasar claimed in protest to Karl Rahner's concept of "anonymous Christianity," which Balthasar saw as a move towards the unacceptable Christian relativization; see Karl Heinz Weger, <u>Karl Rahner</u>, pp. 118 ff., Rahner, "Observations on the Problem of the 'Anonymous Christian,'" <u>Theological Investigations</u> 14:280-294; "Anonymous Christians," <u>Theological Investigations</u> 6:390-398; "Anonymous Christianity and the Missionary Task of the Church," <u>Theological Investigations</u> 12:161-178.

35. See, e.g., Matt. 22:66-71, 26:61-68, 27:32-50.

36. Matthew 7:15-23.

37. Matthew 25:31-46. having personally lived in exile for more than five years, I know from personal experience that help in time of my greatest need has usually come from unexpected quarters. My greatest horror was at Eldoret town in Kenya, where my wife and I got stranded on our flight from Idi Amin of Uganda in early 1977 because our fare to Nairobi was short by half a dollar. To our disillusionment, a white Roman Catholic sister veiled in white uncharitably refused to aid us. Ironically, it

was an anonymous poor man on the street who aided us.

Since then, I have realized that people are not essentially what they usually appear or claim to be and that they are a total mystery only known to God and to human beings through self-expressive and revelatory action (act or deed).

38. Cf. Romans 2:1-11.

39. Cf. 2 Cor. 5:16-20: "From now on, therefore, we regard no one from a human point of view...If anyone is in Christ, he is a new creation, the old has passed away. All this is from God who through Christ reconciled us to himself and gave us the ministry of reconciliation, that is in Christ God was reconciling the world to himself, not counting their trespasses against them, and entrusting to us the message of reconciliation. So we are ambassadors for Christ, God making his appeal through us..."

40. Cf., e.g., John 1:1-5, 9-14.

41. See Karl Rahner, "Anonymous Christianity and the Missionary Task of the Church," _Theological Investigations_ 12:161-178; "Church, Churches and Religions," _Theological Investigations_ 9:30-49; "The Church's Commisssion to Bring Salvation and Humanization of the World," _Theological Investigations_ 14:295-313.

CONCLUSION:

UNCONDITIONAL LOVE FOR THE NEIGHBOR AS THE KEY TO AUTHENTIC HUMAN EXISTENCE AND DIVINE SALVATION

An attempt has been made to show the centrality in both Rahner's Christian teaching and the African traditional mode of existence, of the concept of love for the neighbor. This concept is implicit in the human community with its complex network of interpersonal relationships, and it is explicitly manifested in societal norms, values, taboos and the moral teaching of the young.

Both Western Christianity and the African Religion and philosophy are in apparent agreement that love in its various dimensions (such as friendship, "blood-brotherhoods," marriage, family, neighborliness and the like) is the most powerful force that gives meaning to humanity, thus giving human beings the ideal motivation and goal for living, namely, to love and be loved.[1]

Rahner's great emphasis on the important role that love plays in the supernatural process of humanizing humankind and the world, and particularly, the role of unconditional or gratuitous love for one's concrete neighbor, has been brought to the forefront in this book because it offers a broad-based Christian soteriological framework that seems more relevant to the kind of religious pluralism that prevails in our modern world and Africa in particular. Unconditional love for the neighbor is for Rahner, as for Jesus, Paul and John, the fulfillment of the divine moral law in relation to both God and to one's fellow human beings.[2]

In this respect unconditional love for the neighbor is to be considered as the key to human authenticity as salvation, since it bridges the gulf with the Infinite Mystery that is God and also bridges the gap between the individual and his/her fellow human beings, who may feel alienated for a variety of reasons. Furthermore, love makes it easier for one to love his/her neighbor because of the implicit capability for forgiveness that love usually engenders.

Love heals "broken hearts" and broken relationships, as it enables gratuitous forgiveness and reconciliation. Love can therefore be said to be part of the divine process of creative transformation and the humanization of humankind and the world, as Rahner expounds at great length.[3] Consequently, for Rahner, love orients humankind to themselves, to other people and to God and therefore, to heaven. Conversely, therefore, the absence of love negates this process and leads to real "lostness" or hell.

It can therefore be claimed that, if for Kierkegaard a meaningful life in face of the prevailing *Angst* can be achieved by a "leap of faith," for Hegel through "absolute knowledge," for

Karl Marx through a secularized classless society, and for Karl Rahner through a truly meaningful life, then authentic human existence can be gained anywhere and any time, irrespective of creed, nationality and level of technological sophistication, by loving the neighbor without condition.[4]

For Rahner, unconditional love casts out fear and suspicion of fellow human beings, traverses the "natural" barriers of sex, race, color, nationality and other superficial barriers such as ideology, religious affiliation, and socio-economic class. Rahner further claims that love is also the basis for social justice and human rights.

Rahner argues that unconditional love for the neighbor will inevitably lead to concern for the well-being of the neighbor and his/her freedoms and rights, and furthermore, to a desire to act appropriately in order to safeguard these wherever they are in jeopardy and to seek to restore them when they have been unjustly violated or taken away. This kind of logic naturally leads to Rahner's conclusion that the Christian Church has to be a voice to speak on behalf of the silent voiceless masses and to be the organized fight against evil.[5]

It has been shown how one can understand some people in the African traditional society, like some Muslims and other people of non-Christian religions, to exemplify an "anonymous Christianity" which, though salvific, is nevertheless still a deficient mode of Christianity and therefore require an explicit Christian missionary effort to bring about a deeper understanding of divine unconditional love and forgiveness. In addition, it has been pointed out that we too could become the channel of divine grace and salvation if we unconditionally love all people and treat them with respect in order to minister to them without violating their sense of worth, dignity and freedom or incurring guilt in them.

Rahner's insistence that one's unconditional love and service for the categorial neighbor in this world as the measure of the individual's love and service to God is bound to cause a stir among those people (especially Christians) who probably would like to evade or even to repeal this commandment of Jesus Christ to his followers to love the neighbor uncondtionally as they love themselves. But Rahner's insistence on this unconditional love for the neighbor as the criterion for piety and authentic human existence is also intimately grounded in his "Incarnational Christology."

Rahner argues that, since God has in unconditional love for humanity become a human being and therefore our categorial neighbor, that subsequently, in order to love God we have to love our fellow human beings, since God in Christ has become present in every human being by virtue of Christ's permanent "Hypostatic Union."[6]

In short, Rahner argues that human authentic existence as divine gratuitous salvation, which is also the divine humanization of the human being, is universally given freely by the loving God, the Transcendent Infinite Mystery, to every human being who lives in full openness to the world and loves the neighbor, and that such a person is in essence an authentic human being saved by God, regardless whether he/she calls himself/herself a Muslim, a Hindu, a pagan, a communist or even an atheist.

In addition, Rahner believes that such a person should be termed an "anonymous Christian," because this salvation occurs through the pre-existent, cosmic divine Logos that also becomes incarnate in the categorial world and history in Jesus Christ, and that such a divine universal self-communication in gratuitous grace constantly takes place for the salvation of every human being, everywhere in the world and in every age, in order to enable human beings to become ever more loving, forgiving, humane, generous, creative and personally responsible.

The affirmation of this Rahnerian inclusive Christian concept of "anonymous Christianity," though seemingly radical for a "conventional Christian," is actually in line with the biblical message of gratuitous divine salvation. It can even amplify Jesus Christ's teaching, particularly, on constant forgiveness and the unconditional love for God and one's fellow human beings, including even one's enemies. Jesus' teaching on the Good Samaritan and association with the traditionally non-acceptable people, such as the "tax collectors and sinners," can be viewed as laying the foundation for such a broad and inclusive Christian teaching on the universal divine free salvation, as Karl Rahner seeks to expound by his controversial Christian teaching on "anonymous Christianity."

This Rahnerian inclusive Christian teaching is, particularly, attractive to those who are trying to discern how God's gratuitous salvific activity could have been previously at work in East Africa prior to the arrival of Western Christian missionaries at the end of the last century. Furthermore, this Rahnerian Christian teaching may help them to realize that God is even at work among our Muslim neighbors "in a mysterious way his wonders to perform,"[7] and that even some people like the Karamajong and the Masai, nomadic cattlekeepers who are still largely "unreached by the Gospel of Christ," are not entirely lost to God, either. Probably most important of all, the affirmation of "anonymous Christianity" requires that we view all human beings as children of God, irrespective of creed or color and treat them all with love and respect.

This acceptance of all human beings as the redeemable children of God can in itself be a factor of great value, as it can serve as a common unitive philosophical theological ground for handling religious and socio-political pluralism at national and international levels to enhance dialogue, mutual understanding, reconciliation and mutual peaceful co-existence.

However, unconditional love for the neighbor is still required to enable this mutual peaceful co-existence to endure the challenges of conflicts that usually arise in such a pluralistic context. Since it also appears that the world is getting even more pluralistic, both religiously and socio-politically, it can be also argued that there should be a great emphasis placed on Johannine and Rahnerian types of Christo-centric unconditional love for the neighbor and, co-extensively, the realization that each human being is potentially a "child of God" and is to be treated as such.

In the final analysis, this book represents an attempt to explicate, defend and adopt Rahner's Christian teaching for Africa, today. To this noble end, I have drawn quite a lot from Rahner's broad teaching on God's universal self-communication in gratuitous salvific grace, and unconditional love for every human being, in order to effect the individual's process of humanization and growth in love, humaneness and personal responsibility in the exercise of personal freedom.

Rahner's term for those people who have responded to this universal divine call to an authentic humanization and meaningful human existence, characterized by constant openness to the transcendent Infinite Mystery in hope and love for the neighbor, is "anonymous Christians." Although this term itself is problematical and controversial, it can be discarded in favor of a better terminology.

Nevertheless, what "anonymous Christianity" stands for is attractive to those who are interested in finding an inclusive Christian soteriological understanding that takes seriously the world's religious pluralisms into theological account, yet without compromising the uniqueness of historical Christianity and its special message of the Incarnation, and Jesus Christ's commandment of unconditional love for the neighbor.

Subsequently, this book has attempted to show that for those who seek to discern God's free salvific activity in traditional Africa, Rahner's inclusive Christian concept of "anonymous Christianity" can be a useful guide for their own inquiry, and theological contextual reflection, without negating the central message of the Bible and the Gospel of Christ.

This is particularly true since the emphasis is on Jesus Christ's commandment of unconditional love for the neighbor as the quintessence of Christianity. In this view, the only possible viable universal criterion and measure of a God-centered or an authentic human existence and true Christianity, is considered to be the personal self-expressive exercise of responsible freedom and unconditional love for the neighbor, inasmuch as it is true that "love is of God, and one who loves is of God and knows God ... for God is love."[8]

NOTES

1. Cf., e.g., Waldo Beach and H. Richard Niebuhr, _Christian Ethics_ (New York: John Wiley & Sons, 1973), pp. 183-193, 221-226, 436-442; Soren Kierkegaard, _Works of Love_ (Princeton: Princeton University Press, 1949); Immanuel Kant, _Groundwork of the Metaphysics of Morals_, trans. and analyzed by H. J. Paton (New York: Harper & Row, 1956), pp. 61-132. For Kant, love is the authentic categorical ground for ethical behavior and it imposes a "categorical imperative" and "duty"/"obligation" on human beings to act. However, Nietzsche negates Kant and proposes hatred, brutality, selfishness and lawlessness as manifested by his _Ubermensch_, to constitute authentic humanity and an ideal goal for humanity; see Nietzsche, _Thus Spake Zarathustra_, trans. R. J. Hollingdale (Great Britain: Penguin Books, 1969), pp. 1-66, 71-77, 84-106; _The Joyful Wisdom_, trans. Thomas Common (London: Cambridge University Press, 1910), pp. 283 ff.: "Live dangerously! ...Live in war with your equals and with yourselves. Be robbers and spoilers the Christian ideal of love for the neighbor as a guise for both weakness and cowardice!

2. For instance, it can be argued that for Jesus, John and Paul that unconditional love for the concrete neighbor or for one's fellow human beings is the authentic manifestation of both godliness and authentic humanity, and correlatively a manifestation of the divine or theophany in this world of strife; cf., e.g., Luke 6:27-36; 1 John 4:7-21; 1 Cor. 12:27-14:1.

3. See, e.g., Rahner, "The Commandment of Love in Relation to the Other Commandments," _Theological Investigations_ 5:439-467; "Reflections on the Unity of the Love of Neighbour and the Love of God," _Theological Investigations_ 6:231-249.

4. Ibid. Unconditional Love for the Neighbor is the only true religious test for both godliness and religious authenticity or worth of any religion including Christianity itself!

5. Cf., e.g., Karl Rahner, _Grace in Freedom_, pp. 261 ff.; "The Peace of Christ and the Peace of the World," _Theological Investigations_ 10:371-388; _Christian Foundations_, pp. 398 ff.

6. Cf. Karl Rahner, _Grace in Freedom_, p. 261.

7. _The Hymnal of the Protestant Episcopal Church in the United States of America_, 1940, #310 (written by William Cowper, 1774).

8. 1 John 4:7-8. One feels almost compelled to say a resounding AMEN! The Bible has put definively that God is LOVE, and that those who do not love do not know God. It is very clear that those who love like God loves are his redeemed people, and

it is of no consequence to what Church or even religion these people belong to! Wherever and whatever they are, they are God's own choosen, obedient and redeemed people, and nothing can change that except God himself.

We may be Christians, Jews, African Religionists, Muslims, Hindus, Monks, Nuns, Cab-drivers, Soldiers, Janitors or Kings, but the religious test and requirement for salvation is the same, namely, the unconditional love for both God the neighbor. And whoever has fulfilled this requirement is the one truly saved or redeemed by God's free grace, regardless of condition!

APPENDIX:

A KEY TO AFRICAN WORDS

(Most of these words are Bantu words taken from Rukiga-Runyankole unless otherwise noted).

Abafumu: Medicine-people, prophets and visionaries. These are attributed with supernatural powers to heal, bless or curse.

Abantu: Human beings. This category includes only those who are alive.

Balokole: Luganda word meaning literally "the saved ones" or those "born again." The Balokole are the major Evangelical group in East Africa.

The Balokole tend to be fundamentalist and religiously conservative. They are like most Southern Baptists in the U.S.A.

Bantu: Human beings; the African people ofmost of East Africa, Central and South Africa who speak related languages employing the root word NTU for a human being or another form of being.

Buntu: Human qualities that make human beings humane, such as, love, kindness, patience, and gentleness.

Cwezi: The legendary founders of the ancient East African kingdoms. They are now part of the Traditional Religious cult in most of Uganda, Rwanda and Burundi, serving the benevolent role of watchfull ancestral spirits and guardians of statehood.

Dini: Religion. This word was introduced by the Arabs because the Africans generally lacked a word for religion. This was because to be human being was for them the same as being religious since each person was in their own understanding, by nature a religious being.

Subsquently, the African Religion has no name. Its name and identity is the same as that of the people since they are one and the same inseparable dimensions of African human existence and consciousness.

Eiguru: Sky or heaven; God's dwelling place.

Emizimu: The spirits of the dead. The bad ones are those of the dead wicked people. These possess people in order to carry out their malicious activities or vengeance and the Bafumu are consulted to come amd bust them. Africa has always had its own "Ghost Busters" in the form of Bafumu.

Ensi: World, the Earth; land as opposed to sky or heaven; the human dwelling place.

Juju: A kind of West African form of Voodoo.

Katonda: Luganda word for the Creator or God.

Kucwa: To curse; to ostracize or excommunicate a guilty person.

NTU: Being; the underlying reality; God; the totality of all beings; existence.

Obuntu: The same as "Buntu."

Omuntu: Singular of "Bantu."

Omunsi: In the world; belonging to the world; mundane.

Omwiguru: In heaven; belonging to the heavenly or divine.

Ruhanga: The Supreme Being; the creator; God.

Sasa: Swahili word meaning the present time. Sasa convers several months. It covers both the vivid or immediate past as well as the immediate future. This is the very arena of African life. For the African, life is meaningfully lived within this perimeter of time. Too far in the past or in the future is meaningless and has no appeal for the average African.

Zamani: Swahili word meaning the past. This may refer to the events of just afew years or the antiquity. John S. Mbiti's contention is that African life is Zamani oriented to the glorious lost paradise before the human rebellion, sin and the fall or expulsion by God from the realm of immortality, perfection, happiness and plenty to the life of imperfection, finite, disease, pain, scarcity and death.

Subsquently, in Africa, there are more glorious stories of the past, the despair at the present and little planning for the unseen future. Most of the serious problems of Africa today are largely due to poverty, poor education and poor planning. Most of these problems can be dealt with more effectively if Africa shifts from a Zamani oriented life to a future oriented life.

BIBLIOGRAPHY

Primary Works by Karl Rahner

Christian at the Crossroads. New York: Seabury Press, 1975.

Encyclopedia of Theology: The Concise Sacramentum Mundi. New York: Seabury Press, 1975.

Faith Today. London: Sheed and Ward, 1967.

Foundations of Christian Faith. New York: Seabury Press, 1978.

Grace in Freedom. New York: Herder and Herder, 1969.

Hominisation: The Evolutionary Origin of Man as a Theological Problem. New York: Herder and Herder, 1965.

Karl Rahner: A Reader. Edited by Gerald A. McCool. New York: Seabury Press, 1975.

On the Theology of Death. New York: Herder and Herder, 1961.

Opportunities for Faith. New York: Seabury Press, 1974.

Prayers and Meditations. Edited by John Griffiths. New York: Seabury Press, 1980.

Revelation and Tradition. New York: Herder and Herder, 1966.

Spirit in the World. New York: Herder and Herder, 1968.

Theological Investigations 1: "God, Christ, Mary and Grace." London: Darton, Longman and Todd, 1961.

Theological Investigations 2: "Man in the Church." London: Darton, Longman and Todd, 1963; New York: Seabury Press, 1975.

Theological Investigations 3: "The Theology of the Spiritual Life." London: Darton, Longman and Todd, 1967; New York: Seabury Press, 1974.

Theological Investigations 4: "More Recent Writings." London: Darton, Longman and Todd, 1966; New York: Seabury Press, 1974.

Theological Investigations 5: "Later Writings." London: Darton, Longman and Todd, 1966; New York: Seabury Press, 1975.

Theological Investigations 6: "Concerning Vatican Council II." London: Darton, Longman and Todd, 1969; New York: Seabury Press, 1974.

Theological Investiagtions 7: "Further Theology of the Spiritual Life 1." London: Darton, Longman and Todd, 1971; New York: Seabury Press, 1972.

Theological Investigations 8: "Further Theology of the Spiritual Life 2." London: Darton, Longman and Todd, 1971; New York: Seabury Press, 1972.

Theological Investigations 9: "Writings of 1965-1967 1." London: Darton, Longman and Todd, 1972; New York: Seabury Press, 1973.

Theological Investigations 10: "Writings of 1965-1967 2." London: Darton, Longman and Todd, 1973; New York: Seabury Press, 1973.

Theological Investigations 11: "Confrontations 1." London: Darton, Longman and Todd, 1974; New York: Seabury Press, 1974.

Theological Investigations 12: "Confrontations 2." London: Darton, Longman and Todd, 1975; New York: Seabury Press, 1975.

Theological Investigations 13: "Theology, Anthropology, Christology," trans. David Bourke. New York: Seabury Press, 1975.

Theological Investigations 14: "Ecclesiology, Questions in the Church, The Church in the World," trans. David Bourke. New York: Seabury Press, 1976.

Theological Investigations 16: "Experience of the Spirit; Sources of Theology," trans. David Morland, O.S.B. New York: Seabury Press, 1979.

Theological Investigations 17: "Jesus, Man, and the Church," trans. Margaret Khol. New York: Seabury Press, 1981.

Theological Investigations 20: "Concern for the Church," trans. Edward Quinn. New York: Seabury Press, 1981.

Ed., Sacramentum Mundi: An Encyclopedia of Theology. 6 vols. New York: Seabury Press, 1968-1970.

SELECTED GENERAL BIBLIOGRAPHY

Abbott, Walter M., S. J., and Gallagher, Very Rev. Msgr., eds. and trans. The Documents of Vatican II, with an Introduction by Lawrence Cardinal Shehan. Chicago: Association Press/Follet Publishing Company, 1966.

Abraham, W. E. The Mind of Africa. Chicago: University of Chicago Press, 1962.

Achebe, Chinua. Arrow of God. New York: John Day, 1964.

Aquinas, Thomas. Providence and Predestination. Indiana: Regnery/Gateway, Inc., 1961.

-------. Summa theologica. 4 vols. Rome: Vatican Press, 1948.

-------. Summa contra gentiles. Rome: Vatican Press, 1934.

Athanasius. "On the Incarnation of the Word." In Christology of the Later Fathers. Edited by Edward Rochie Hardy. Philadelphia: The Westminster Press, 1954.

Atterbury, A. P. Islam in Africa. New York and London: G. P. Putnam's Sons, 1899.

Baeta, Christian Gonsalues. Christianity in Tropical Africa. London: Oxford University Press, 1968.

Banks, John G. Healing Everywhere. Richmond: St. Luke's Press, 1980.

Barnette, Donald and Njama, Karari. Mau Mau from Within. London: MacGibben and Kee, 1966.

Barr, J. Fundamentalism. Philadelphia: The Westminster Press, 1978.

Barrett, D. B. Schism and Renewal in Africa: An Analysis of Two Thousand Independent Churches. Nairobi: Oxford University Press, 1968.

------, ed. World Christian Encyclopedia: A Comparative Survey of Churches and Religions in the Modern World A.D. 1900-2000. London/New York/Nairobi: Oxford University Press, 1982.

Barrett, David B. African Initiatives in Religion. Kenya, Nairobi: East African Publishing House, 1971.

Barrett, William. Irrational Man: A Study in Existential Philosophy. New York: Doubleday & Co., Inc., 1962.

Barth, Karl. Church Dogmatics: A Selection. Introduction by Helmut Gollwitzer. Translated by G. W. Bromley. New York: Harper & Row, 1961.

-------. Church Dogmatics. Vol. 3. New York: Scribner's Sons, 1960.

-------. Dogmatics in Outline. London: S.C.M., 1949.

-------. The Epistle to the Romans. London: Oxford University Press, 1933.

------. Evangelical Theology: An Introduction. New York: Holt, Rinehart and Winston, 1963.

-------. The Humanity of God. Richmond, Va.: John Knox Press, 1960.

-------. Protestant Theology in the Nineteenth Century. New York: Harper & Row, 1959.

Bascom, William. Ifa Divination: Communion between Gods and Men in West Africa. Bloomington: Indiana University Press, 1968.

Baxter, P. T. W. "The Kiga," East African Chiefs. Edited by Audrey I. Richards. New York: Praeger, 1959.

Beattie, John, and Middleton, eds. The Banyoro. New York: African Publishing Corporation, 1964.

------, eds. Spirit Mediumship and Society in Africa. New York: African Publishing Corporation, 1969.

Beetham, T. A. Christianity and the New Africa. New York: Frederick A. Praeger, 1967.

Beier, Ulli. African Mud Scripture. Cambridge, England: Cambridge University Press, 1963.

-----. African Poetry: An Anthology of Traditional African Poems.

------. Contemporary Art in Africa. Pall Mall Press, 1968.

------. Introduction to African Literature. London: Longmans, Green, 1967.

p'Bitek, Okot. African Religions in Western Scholarship. Kampala: East African Literature Bureau, 1970.

------. Religion of the Central Luo. Nairobi: East African Literature Bureau, 1975.

------. The Song of Lawino. Nairobi: East African Publishing House, 1960.

Booth, Newell S. African Religions: A Symposium. New York: NOK Publishers, 1977.

Brother-Andrew. Battle for Africa. London: Marshall Morgan and Scott, 1977.

Brwon, Colin. Philosophy and the Christian Faith. Downers Grove, Ill.: Inter Varsity Press, 1968.

Brunner, Emil. Man in Revolt. Philadelphia: Westminster Press, 1948.

------. Moral Man and Immoral Society. New York: Scribner's Sons, 1960.

Buttmann, Rudolf K. Modern Theology: Selections from Twentieth-Century Theologians. Edited with Introduction and Notes by E. J. Tinsley. London: Epworth Press, 1973.

------. Jesus and the Word. New York: Charles Scribner's Sons, 1934.

-------. Kerygma and Myth. New York: Harper & Row, 1961.

-------. Theology of the New Testament. New York: Charles Scribner's Sons, 1955.

Buscaglia, Leo. Love. New York: Fawcett Crest, 1972.

Chadwick, O. The Victorian Church: An Ecclesiastical History of the Church. London: Oxford University Press, 1950.

Church, J.E. Awake Uganda. Kampala: Uganda Bookshop Press, 1954.

Clark, Gordon H. Thales to Dewey: A History of Philosophy. Massachusetts: The Riverside Press, 1957.

Cobb, John. Christ in a Pluralistic Age. Philadelphia: The Westminster Press, 1975.

-------. Christian Natural Theology: Based on the Thought of Alfred North Whitehead. Philadelphia: Westminster Press, 1965.

-------. God and the Word. Philadelphia: Westminster Press, 1969.

-------. The Structure of Christian Existence. Philadelphia: Westminster Press, 1967.

Cousins, Ewert H., ed. Hope and the Future of Man. Philadelphia: Fortress Press, 1972.

------, ed. Process Theology: Basic Writings by Key Thinkers of a Major Modern Movement. New York: Newman Press, 1971.

Desai, Ram, ed. Christianity in Africa as Seen by Africans. Denver: Allan Swallow, 1962.

Dewart, L. The Foundations of Belief. New York: Herder, 1969.

Dickson, Kwensi, and Ellingworth, P. Biblical Revelation and African Beliefs. London: Lutterworth Press, 1969.

Dumery, Henry. The Problem of God in Philosophy of Religion. Translated by Charles Courtney. Northwestern University Press, 1964.

Edel, M. M. The Chigga of Western Uganda. London: Oxford University Press, 1957.

Evans, Christopher Francis. Is Holy Scripture Christian? London: SCM Press Ltd., 1971.

Evans-Pritchard, R. Nuer Religion. Oxford: Oxford University Press, 1956.

------. Theories of Primitive Religion. Oxford: Clarendon Press, 1965.

Fagg, W. B. African Tribal Images. Cleveland: Cleveland Museum of Art, 1968.

-------. Tribes and Forms in African Art. New York: Tudor, 1965.

Fagg, W. B., and Elisafon, Eliot. The Sculpture of Africa. New York: Praeger, 1958.

Fallers, Llyod A., ed. The King's Men: Leadership and Status in Buganda on the Eve of Independence. London: Oxford University Press, 1964.

Farley, Edward. Ecclesial Man: A Social Phenomenology of Faith and Reality. Philadelphia: Fortress Press, 1975.

Feuerbach, Ludwig. The Essence of Religion. Translated by Ralph Manheim. New York: Harper & Row, 1967.

Findlay, John. Hegel: A Re-examination. New York: Oxford University Press, 1958.

Finney, G. Revivals of Religion. London: SCM Press, 1954.

Forde, Daryll, ed. African World: Studies in the Cosmological Ideas and Social Values of African Peoples. New York: Oxford University Press, 1968.

Fortes, Meyer, and Dieterlen, G., eds. African Systems of Thought. New York: Oxford University Press, 1965.

Foucault, Michel. The Order of Things: An Archaelogy of the Human Sciences. New York: Vintage Press, Random House.

Froelich, Jean Claude. Les Musulmans dans l'Afrique noire. Paris: Editions de l'Oriente, 1964.

Fuller, R. H. The Mission and Achevement of Christ. London: SCM Press, 1959.

-------. Foundations of New Testament Christology. New York: Charles Scribner's Sons, 1965.

Gaba, Christian. Scriptures of an African People: The Sacred Utterances of the Anlo. New York: NOK Publishers, 1973.

Gelpi, Donald, S. J. Light and Life: A Guide to the Theology of Karl Rahner. New York: Sheed and Ward, 1966.

Gilkey, Langdon. Catholicism Confronts Modernity: A Protestant View. New York: Seabury Press, 1975.

-------. Message and Existence: An Introduction to Christian Theology. New York: Seabury Press, 1980.

Graham, B. World Aflame. New York: The Worlds Word, Ltd., 1966.

Green, M., ed. The Truth of God Incarnate. London: Hodder and Stoughton, 1977.

Greenburg, J. The Influence of Islam on a Sudanese Religion. New York: J. J. Augustin, 1947.

Guilleband, L. A Grain of Mustard Seed. London: C.M.S. Press, 1959.

Guthriew, W. K. C. The Greek Philosophers: From Thales to Aristotle. New York: Harper & Row, 1950.

Gutierrez, Gustavo. A Theology of Liberation: History, Politics and Salvation. Translated and edited by Sister Cardidad Inda and John Eagleson. New York: Orbis, 1973.

Hardy, Edward R. Christology of the Later Fathers. Philadelphia: The Westminster Press, 1954.

Harold, B. Twice-Born Men: A Clinic of Regeneration. New York: Fleming H. Revelle Co., 1909.

Harrelson, Walter. The Ten Commandments and Human Rights. Philadelphia: Fortress Press, 1973.

Harris, Lyndon P. Islam in East Africa. London: Universities' Mission to Central Africa, 1954.

Hartshorne, Charles. The Divine Relativity: A Social Conception of God. New Haven: Yale University Press, 1978.

Hastings, A. African Christianity. New York: Seabury Press, 1976.

-------. Christian Marriage in Africa. London: S.P.C.K., 1959.

-------. Church and Mission in Modern Africa. London: Burns and Oates, 1967.

-------. The Faces of God. London: Geoffrey and Chapman, 1975.

Hatch, Edwin. The Influence of Greek Ideas on Christianity. Gloucester, Mass., 1970.

Hayward, Victor E.W., ed. African Independent Church Movements. London: Edinburgh House Press, 1963.

Hegel, G. W. F. The Christian Religion: Lectures on the Philosophy of Religion Part III (The Revelatory, Consummate, Absolute Religion). Edited and translated by Peter C. Hodgson, based on the edition by Georg Lasson. American Academy of Religion: Scholars Press, 1979.

-------.Phenomenology of Spirit. Translated by A.V. Miller, with analysis of the text and Foreword by J. N. Findlay. New York: Oxford University Press, 1977.

Heidegger, Martin. Being and Time. Translated by John Macquarrie and Edward Robinson. New York: Harper & Row, 1962.

-------. The Question Concerning Technology and other Essays. Translated and with Introduction by William Lovitt. New York: Harper & Row, 1977.

-------.What Is a Thing? Translated by W.B. Barton, Jr., and Vera Deutsch. Analysis by Eugene T. Gendlin. Chicago: Gateway, 1967.

Hick, John. Evil and the God of Love. New York: Harper & Row, 1978.

-------, ed. The Myth of God Incarnate. Philadelphia: The Westminster Press, 1977.

Hewitt, G. The Problems of Success: A History of the Church Missionary Society 1910-1942. London: C.M.S. Press, 1960.

Hillman, E. Polygamy Reconsidered. London: Orbis, 1975.

Hobley, Charles W. Bantu Beliefs and Magic. London: Franklin Cass, 1967.

Hodgson, Peter C. Jesus--Word and Presence: An Essay in

Christology. Philadelphia: Fortress Press, 1971.

-------. *New Birth of Freedom: A Theology of Bondage and Liberation*. PHiladelphia: Fortress Press, 1976.

Holmes, Urban T. *To Speak of God*. New York: Seabury Press, 1974.

-------. *What is Anglicanism?* Wilton, Conn.: Morehouse-Barlow Co. Inc., 1982.

Hughes, Langston, ed. *Poems from Black Africa*. Bloomington: Indiana University Press, 1963.

Hunter, David E., and Whitten, Philip, eds. *Encyclopedia of Anthropology*. New York: Harper & Row, 1976.

Idowu, E. Bolaji. *African Traditional Religion: A Definition*. Maryknoll, N.Y.: Orbis Books, 1973.

-------. *Towards an Indigenous Church*. London: Oxford University Press, 1965.

Ignatius of Loyola, St. *The Spiritual Exercises of St. Ignatius*. Edited by Louis J. Puhl. Chicago: Loyola University Press, 1951.

Ilogu, Edmund. *Christianity and Igbo Culture*. New York: NOK Publishers, 1973.

Jahn, Jahnheinz. *Muntu: An Outline of the New African Culture*. New York: Grove Press, 1961.

James, William. *The Varieties of Religious Experience: A Study in Human Nature*. Introduction by Reinhold Niebuhr. New York: Collier MacMillan Publishers, 1974.

Janzen, John and MacGaffey, Wyatt. *An Anthology of Kongo Religion*. Lawrence, Kans.: University of Kansas Press, 1974.

Jessop, T. E., Brunner, Emil, et al. *The Christian Understanding of Man*. New York/Chicago: Willett, Clark & Co., 1938.

John of the Cross, St. *The Collected Works of St. John of the Cross*. Translated by Kieran Kavanaugh and Otilo Rodriguez. Washington: Institute of Carmelits Studies, 1960.

Johnston, William. *The Inner Eye of Love: Mysticism and Religion*. New York: Harper & Row, 1978.

Jones, R. B. *Rent Heavens*. London: S.C.M. Press, 1955.

Kagame, Alexis. *La Philosophie Bantu-Rwandaise de l'Être*. Brussels: Academie Royale des Sciences Coloniales, 1956.

Kaggwa, Apolo. The Kings of Buganda. Translated with an Introduction by S. Kiwanuka. East African Publishing House, 1971.

Kant, Immanuel. Groundwork of the Metaphysic of Morals. New York: Harper & Row, 1956.

-------. Prolegomena to Any Future Metaphysics. Indianapolis: Bobbs-Merrill Educational Publishing, 1979.

Kasemann, E. New Testament Questions for Today. Philadelphia: Fortress Press, 1969.

Kaufmann, Walter. Existentialism from Dostoevsky to Sartre. New York: A Meridian Book, New American House, 1975.

-------. Systematic Theology: A Historical Perspective. New York: Charles Scribner's Sons, 1968.

Kenyatta, Jomo. Facing Mount Kenya. New York: Vintage Books, Random House, 1962.

Kierkegaard, Soren. Philosophical Fragments. Translated and introduced by David Swenson. Princeton: Princeton University Press, 1974.

King, Noel Q. Religions of Africa: A Pilgrimage into Traditional Religions. New York: Harper & Row, 1970.

Kivengere, F. When God Moves. Accra: Asempa, 1970.

Kiwanuka, S. M. A History of Buganda from Early Times up to 1900. Nairobi: Longmans, 1972.

-------. Mutesa. Nairobi: East African Literature Bureau, 1968.

Kiwanuka, Semakula. A History of Buganda: From the Foundation of the Kingdom to 1900. London: Longman Group Ltd., 1971.

Kritzeck, James, and Lewis, William H., eds. Islam in Africa. New York: Van Nostrand-Reinhold, 1969.

Kung, Hans. The Church. New York: Image Books, Doubleday & Company, Inc, 1976.

-------. On Being a Christian. Translated by Edward Quinn. New York: Pocket Books, 1966.

Lanternari, Vittorio. The Religions of the Oppressed: A Study of Modern Messianic Cults. New York: Knopf, 1963.

Latourette, S. K. The Expansion of Christianity. Vols. 6 and 7. London: Zondervan, 1970.

-------. A History of Christianity. London: Eyre and Scottiwoode, 1954.

Laye, Camara. The Dark Child. London: Collins, 1955.

Leakey, Louis S. B. Mau Mau and the Kikuyu. New York: John Day and Co., 1952.

Leaver, Robin A. Luther on Justification. St. Louis: Concordia Publishing House, 1975.

LeFevre, Perry, ed. Philosophical Resources for Christian Thought. New York/Nashville: Abingdon Press, 1968.

Lienhardt, G. Divinity and Experience; the Religion of the Dinka. Oxford: Oxford University Press, 1961.

Lewis, I. M., ed. Islam in Tropical Africa. London: Oxford University Press, 1966.

Lonergan, Bernad. Method in Theology. Darton: Longman and Todd, 1972.

-------. A Second Collection. Darton: Longman and Todd, 1974.

Low, A. D. Buganda in Modern History. London: World University Press, 1970.

Macquarrie, John. Principles of Christian Theology. New York: Charles Scribner's Sons, 1977.

-------. Twentieth Century Religious Thought. London: SCM Press, 1976.

Mair, Lucy P. An African People in the Twentieth Century. New York: Russell and Russell, 1965.

-------. Witchcraft. London: World University Press, 1969.

Malik, Charles H. The Wonder of Being. Texas: World Book Publishers, 1974.

Maquet, Jacques. Africanity: The Cultural Unity of Black Africa. London: Oxford University Press, 1972.

Martin, Marie-Louise. Kibangu. London: Blackwell, 1975.

Matthews, R. English Messiahs. London: Methuen, 1936.

Maududi, Sayyid Abul A'LA. Islam: Towards Understanding. Beirut: Dar Al-Koran Al-Kareen, 1975.

Mbiti, J. S. African Religions and Philosophy. London: Heinemann, 1969.

-------. Akamba Stories. Oxford: Clarendon Press, 1966.

-------. Concepts of God in Africa. New York: Praeger, 1970.

-------. New Testament Eschatology in African Background. London: Oxford University Press, 1971.

-------. The Prayers of African Religion. New York: Maryknoll, Orbis Books, 1976.

McGavran, A. D. Understanding Church Growth. Grand Rapids, Mich.: William B. Eerdams, 1970.

McVeigh, Malcolm J. God in Africa: Concepts of God in African Traditional Religion and Christianity. Cape Cod, Mass.: Claude Stark, 1974.

Melland, Frank H. In Witch-Bound Africa. London: Seeley, Service and Co., 1923; Frank Cass, 1967.

Mendelson, Jack. God, Allah, and Juju: Religion in Africa Today. New York: Nelson, 1962.

Merriam, Alan P. An African World: The Basongye Village of Lupupa Ngye. Bloomington: Indiana University Press, 1974.

Metz, J. Theology of the World. New York: Herder and Herder, 1969.

Middleton, John, and Winter, E. H., eds. Gods and Rituals. Garden City, N.Y.: The Natural History Press, 1967.

--------. Magic, Witchcraft and Curing. Garden City, N.Y: The Natural History Press, 1967.

-------. Myth and Cosmos. Garden City, N.Y.: The Natural History Press, 1969.

-------. Witchcraft and Sorcery in East Africa. London: Rowledge and Kegan Paul, 1963; New York: The Natural History Press, 1967.

Moltmann, Jurgen. Man: Christian Anthropology in the Conflicts of the Present. Translated by John Sturdy. Philadelphia: Fortress Press, 1979.

Montagu, Ashley, ed. Culture and Human Development. Englewood Cliffs, N.J.: Prentice-Hall, 1974.

Moore, Basil, ed. Black Theology, the South African Voice. London: Hurst, 1973.

Mulago, Vincent. Une Visage Africaine du Christianisme. Paris: Presence Africaine, 1962.

Niebuhr, R. H. Christ and Culture. New York: Harper & Row, 1951.

-------. The Purpose of the Church and Its Ministry. New York: Harper & Row, 1956.

------.The Social Sources of Denominationalism. Cleveland: World Publishing Median Books, 1965.

Niebuhr, Reinhold. The Nature and Destiny of Man. 2 vols. New York: Charles Scribner's Sons, 1964.

Neill, S. C. Christian Missions. London: Pelican, 1966.

-------. Colonialism and Christian Missions. London: Lutterworth Press, 1966.

-------. Twentieth Century Christianity. London: Collins, 1962.

Neill, Stephen. The Christian Society: Theology and Philosophy.

Neuner, Joseph, and Roos, Heinrich. The Teaching of the Catholic Church as Contained in Her Documents. Edited by Karl Rahner. New York: Alba House, 1965.

Newlands, George M. The Theology of the Love of God. Atlanta: John Knox Press, 1980.

Ngugi, James. A Grain of Wheat. London: Heinemann, 1967.

-------. The River Between. London: Heinemann, 1965.

-------. Weep Not Child. London: Heinemann, 1964.

Norris, Richard A., Jr., trans. & ed. The Christological Controversy. Philadelphia: Fortress Press, 1980.

Northcott, Cecil. Christianity in Africa. London: S.C.M. Press, 1963.

Nygren, Anders. Commentary on Romans. Philadelphia: Fortress Press, 1980.

O'Grady, John F. Christian Anthropology: A Meaning for Human Life. New York: Paulist Press, 1976.

O'Donovan, Leo J., ed. A World of Grace: An Introduction to the Themes and Foundations of Karl Rahner's Theology. New York: The Seabury Press, 1980.

Oliver, R. The Missionary Factor in East Africa. London: Longmans, Green and Co., 1952.

Osthuizen, G. C. Post Christianity in Africa: A Theological and Anthropological Study. Grand Rapids: William E. Eerdmans.

Outler, A. C. The Christian Tradition and the Unity We Seek. New York: Oxford University Press, 1957.

Pannenberg, Wolfhart. Human Nature, Election, and History. Philadelphia: The Westminster Press, 1977.

-------.Jesus--God and Man. Translated by Lewis L. Wilkins and Duane A. Priebe. Philadelphia: The Westminster Press, 1968.

-------. What Is Man? Contemporary Anthropology in Theological Perspective. Translated by Duane Priebe. Philadelphia: Fortress Press, 1970.

Pannenberg, Wolfhart, et al. Spirit, Faith and Church. Philadelphia: The Westminster Press, 1970.

Parker, William R., and Aldwell, Enid. Man: Animal and Divine. Los Angeles: Scrivener & Co., 1970.

Parrinder, Edward Geoffrey. African Mythology. London: Paul Hamly, 1967.

-------.African Traditional Religion. Westport, Conn.: Greenwood Press, 1970.

-------. Religion in an African City. London: Oxford University Press, 1953.

-------. West African Religion. London: Epworth Press, 1961.

-------.Witchcraft: European and African. New York: Barnes and Noble, 1963.

Patricia, St. John. The Breath of Life. London: Norfolk Press, 1971.

Pelikan, Jaroslav. The Christian Tradition: A History of the Development of Doctrine, vol. 1: The Emergence of the Catholic Tradition (100-600). Chicago: The University of Chicago Press, 1971.

Pittenger, Norman W. The Christian Understanding of Human Nature. Philadelphia: The Westminster Press, 1964.

Ramsey, M. A. An Era in Anglican Theology: From Gore to Temple. New York: Charles Scribner's Sons, 1960.

Ramsey, M. A., ed. The Charismatic Christ. New York: Morehouse-Barlow Co., 1973.

Ranger, T. and Kimambo, I. N., eds. Christian Independence in Tanzania. Dar Salaam: Historical Association of Tanzania, 1970.

-------. The Historical Study of African Religion. Berkeley: University of California Press, 1972.

Ranger, T., and Weller, J. The African Churches of Tanzania. Dar Salaam: Historical Association of Tanzania, 1969.

-------. Themes in the Christian History of Central Africa. London: Heinemann, 1975.

Ray, B. C. African Religions: Symbol, Ritual and Community. Englewood Cliffs, N.J.: Prentice Hall, 1976.

Richardson, C. C., ed. Early Christian Fathers. New York: MacMillan Publishing Co., 1970.

Robertson, E. H. Man's Estimate of Man. Richmond, Virginia: John Knox Press, 1958.

Roberts, Louis. The Achievement of Karl Rahner. New York: Herder and Herder, 1967.

Rogers, Carl. On Becoming a Person. Boston: Houghton Mifflin, 1961.

Rome, Sydney, and Rome, Beatrice, eds. Philosophical Interrogations of Martin Buber, John Wild, Jean Wahl, Brand Blanshard, Paul Weiss, Charles Hartshorne, and Paul Tillich. New York: Harper & Row, 1970.

Roscoe, J. The Baganda. London: Frank Cass, 1965.

-------. The Bagesu and Other Tribes. Cambridge: Cambridge University Press, 1924.

-------. The Bakitara or Banyoro. Cambridge: Cambridge University Press, 1923.

-------. The Banyankole. Cambridge: Cambridge University Press, 1925.

-------. The Northern Bantu. Cambridge: Cambridge University Press, 1915.

Russell, Bertrand. Has Man a Future? Baltimore: Penguin Books, 1961.

-------. Why I Am Not a Christian and Other Essays on Religion and Related Subjects. New York: Simon and Schuster, 1957.

Russell, J. K. Men Without God. London: The Highway Press, 1966.

Sabatier, Auguste. The Religions of Authority and the Religions of the Spirit. New York: Williams & Norgate, 1904.

Sangree, Walter H. Age, Prayer and Politics in Tikiri, Kenya. New York: Oxford University Press, 1966.

Sawyer, Harry. God: Ancestor or Creator. London: Longman, 1970.

Schleiermacher, Friedrich. On Religion: Speeches to Its Cultured Despisers. Translated by John Oman. Introduction by Rudolf Otto. New York: Harper & Row, 1958.

-------. The Christian Faith. Edited by H. R. Mackintosh and J.S. Stewart. Philadelphia: Fortress Press, 1976.

Shepherd, William C. Man's Condition: God and the World Process. New York: Herder and Herder, 1969.

Shorter, Aylward. African Christian Theology. London: Geoffrey and Chapman, 1975.

-------. African Culture and the Christian Church. London: Geoffrey and Chapman, 1973.

-------. Prayer in the Religious Traditions of Africa. London: Oxford University Press, 1975.

Sithole, Ndabaningi. Obed Mutezo, the Mudzimi Christian Nationalist. London: Oxford University Press, 1970.

Smith, Edwin, ed. African Ideas of God, A Symposium. London: Edinburgh House Press, 1961.

Smith, Huston. The Religions of Man. New York: Harper & Row, 1965.

Speck, Joseph. Karl Rahner's Theologische Anthropologie: Eine Einfuhrung. Munchen: Kosel Verlag, 1967.

Stock, E. A History of the Church Missionary Society. London: C.M.S. Press, 1899.

Stott, J. Men Made New. London: I.V.P., 1966.

Sundkler, Bengt. Bantu Prophets in South Africa. London: Lutterworth Press, 1948.

------. The Christian Ministry in Africa. London: S.C.M. Press, 1960.

------. Zulu Zion. London: Oxford University Press, 1976.

Tanner, Ralph E. S. Transition in African Beliefs: Traditional Religion and Christian Change. Maryknoll, N.Y.: Maryknoll Publications, 1967.

Taylor, J.V. Christianity and Politics in Africa. London:

Harmondsworth, 1957.

-------. The Christians of the Copperbelt. London: S.C.M. Press, 1963.

------.The Church Growth in Buganda. London: C.M.S. Press, 1958.

-------. The Cross of Christ. London: MacMillan and Co., Ltd., 1956.

-------. The Primal Vision. London: S.C.M. Press, 1963.

Teilhard de Chardin, Pierre. The Phenomenon of Man. New York: Harper & Row, 1975.

-------.The Prayer of the Universe. New York: Harper & Row, 1973.

Tempels, P. Bantu Philosophy. Paris: Presence Africaine, 1959.

Temple, William. Nature, Man and God. London: MacMillan, 1934.

TeSelle, Eugene. Christ in Context: Divine Purpose and Human Possibility. Philadelphia: Fortress Press, 1975.

-------. "Nature and Grace in the Form of Ecumenical Discussion." Journal of Ecumenical Studies 8 (1971), 539-559.

Temu, A. J. British Protestant Missions. London: Longman Group Limited, 1972.

Thomas, O.C. Introduction to Theology. Cambridge: Greeno, Hadden & Co. Ltd., 1973.

Tillich, Paul. The Courage to Be. New Haven: Yale University Press, 1969.

-------. Dynamics of Faith. New York: Harper & Row, 1957.

-------. The New Being. New York: The Scribner's Sons, 1955.

-------. Systematic Theology. 3 vols. Chicago: Chicago University Press, 1960.

Tracy, David. Blessed Race for Order: The New Pluralism in Theology. New York: Seabury Press, 1978.

Trimingham, J. S. The Christian Approach to Islam in the Sudan. London and New York: Oxford University Press, 1948.

-------. Christian Church and Islam in West Africa. London: S.C.M. Press, 1955; New York: Friendship Press, 1955.

-------. The Influence of Islam upon Africa. New York: Praeger, 1968.

-------. Islam in East Africa. New York: Friendship Press, 1962.

-------. Islam in Ethiopia. New York: Barnes and Noble, 1965.

-------. Islam in the Sudan. New York: Barnes and Novble, 1965.

------. Islam in West Africa. London: Oxford University Press, 1961.

Troeltch, E. Writings on Theology and Religion. Atlanta: John Knox Press, 1977.

Tucker, A.R. My Eighteen Years in East Africa. London: Edward Arnold, 1908.

Tuma, Tom, and Mutibwa, Phares. A Century of Christianity in Uganda, 1877-1977. Nairobi: Uzima Press Limited, 1978.

Twesigye, Emmanuel K. "Anonymous Christianity" and Human Existence in African Perspective: A Study Based on Karl Rahner's Philosophical Theology. Ann Arbor and London: UMI, 1983.

Vidler, A. R. The Church in an Age of Revolution. London: Penguin, 1961.

Vorgrimler, Herbert. Karl Rahner: His Life, Thought and Works. Translated by Edward Quinn. London: Burns & Oates, 1965.

Warren, A. M. Revival: An Inquiry. London: C.M.S. Press, 1954.

-------. Social History and Christian Mission. London: S.C.M. Press, 1967.

Weber, M.The Sociology of Religion. Boston: Beacon Press, 1964.

Webster, J.B. West Africa Since 1800. Ibadan: Longmans, 1968.

Weger, Karl-Heinz. Karl Rahner: An Introduction to His Theology. New York: The Seabury Press, 1980.

Welbourn, F.B.East African Christianity. Nairobi: Oxford Press, 1967.

------.East African Rebels: A Study of Some Independent Churches. London: S.C.M. Press, 1961.

-------. Religion and Politics in Uganda, 1952-1962. Nairobi: Oxford Press, 1965.

Welbourn, F.B. and Ogot, B.A. A Place to Feel at Home. London: Oxford University Press, 1965.

Welch, Claude. Protestant Thought in the Nineteenth Century, Vol.

1: 1799-1870. New Haven: Yale University Press, 1972.

Werner, A. Myths and Legends of Bantu. London: Oxford University Press, 1933.

Whitehead, Alfred North. Adventures of Ideas. New York: MacMillan Publishing Co., 1933.

-------. Process and Reality. New York: MacMillan, 1978.

-------. Religion in the Making. New York: MacMillan, 1926.

-------. Science and the Modern World. New York: MacMillan, 1925.

Willet, Frank. African Art: An Introduction. New York: Praeger, 1971.

Williamson, Sihey George. Akan Religion and the Christian Faith. Accra: Shane University Press, 1965.

Willis, J. J. An African Church in Building. London: C.M.S. Press, 1925.

Willoughby, William Charles. The Soul of the Bantu: A Sympathetic Study of the Magico-Religious Practices and Beliefs of the Bantu Tribes of Africa. Garden City, N.Y.: Doubleday and Doran, 1928.

Wilson, Bryan R., ed. Magic and the Millennium: A Sociological Study of Religious Movements of Protest among Tribal and Third World Peoples. New York: Humanities Press, 1975.

------. Patterns of Sectarianism: Organization and Ideology in Social and Religious Movements. London: Heinemann, 1967.

------.Religious Sects. London: Weidenfield and Nicholson, 1970.

Wilson, C. J. Uganda in the Days of Bishop Tucker. London: MacMillan & Co., 1955.

Wilson, Monica. Communal Rites of the Nyakyusa. London: Oxford University Press, 1949.

------.Good Company: A Study of Nyakyusa Aged Villagers. Boston: Beacon Press, 1963.

------. Rituals of Kingship among the Nyakyusa. London: Oxford University Press, 1949.

------. Religion and the Transformation of Society: A Study in Social Change in Africa. Cambridge: The University Press, 1971.

Wiredu, Kwasi. Philosophy and African Culture. London/New York:

Cambridge University Press, 1980.

Wright, Richard A., ed. African Philosophy: An Introduction. Washington: University Press of America, 1979.

SELECTED DISSERTATIONS, THESES AND RESEARCH PAPERS

Bamunoba, Y. K. "The Confrontation between Christianity and Ankole Traditional Religion since 1899." Occasional Research Paper No. 13, Department of Religious Studies and Philosophy, Makerere University, 1973.

-------."Diviners for the Abagabe," Uganda Journal 29: 1 (1965), 95-97.

Bamunoba, Y. K., and Welbourn, F. B. "Emandwa Initiation in Ankole," Uganda Journal 29: 1 (1965), 13-25.

Burtner, R. W. "Justification and Sanctification: A Study of the Theologies of Martin Luther and John Wesley." S.T.M. Thesis, Union Theological Seminary, 1948.

Hardy, D. W. "The Doctrine of Sin." S.T.M. Thesis, General Theological Seminary, 1963.

Healy, J. "The Development of the Doctrine of Grace and Some Implications in Light of Contemporary Thought: Karl Rahner, Johannes Metz and Alfred North Whitehead." S.T.M. Thesis, General Theological Seminary, 1972.

Horton, Robin. "African Traditional Thought and Western Science," Africa 37 (1967), 50-71, 155-187.

-------. "Destiny and the Unconscious in West Africa," Africa 31 (1961), 110-116.

-------. "Ritual Man in Africa," Africa 34 (1964), 85-105.

Jones, B. E. "Conversion: An Examination of Human Change," Ph.D. Dissertation, Columbia University, 1969.

Maari, E. "The Balokole Movement in Nyabushozi County of Ankole," in vol. 22, Occasional Research Papers, Department of Religious Studies and Philosophy, Makerere University, August, 1974.

Mason, C. E. "John Wesley's Doctrine of Salvation." S.T.M. Thesis, Union Theological Seminary, 1940.

Rhys, J. H. W. "Redemption in the Fourth Gospel." S.T.M. Thesis, General Theological Seminary, 1949.

Robins, C. A. "'Tukutendereza': A Study of Social Change and Sectarian Withdrawal in the 'Balokole' Revival of Uganda." Ph.D. Dissertation, Columbia University, 1975.

Twesigye, E. K. "The Ahmadiyya Muslim Hospitality: A Challenge to the Christians," New Day, September, 1969.

-------. "Anonymous Christianity and Human Existence in African Perspective: A Study Based on Karl Rahner's Philosophical Theology." Ph.D. dissertation, Vanderbilt University, 1983.

-------. "Christian Persecution in Uganda under Idi Amin's Dictatorship." Paper presented at the University of the South, Fall, 1978.

------."Christians and Social Change," The Franciscan, November 1970.

------."The Concept of Atonement among the 'Balokole' of Uganda." S.T.M. Thesis, University of the South, 1979.

-------. "The Context for Theology in the Third World." Paper presented to the International Clericus Conference, New York, June 16, 1981.

-------. "Death among the Bakiga of Western Uganda." Occasional Research Paper, Department of Religious Studies and Philosophy, Makerere University, 1971.

------. "The Death of a Mukiga," in Creative Moments, edited by Jacob Matovu. Church of Uganda Publishing House, 1972.

-------. "The Evangelical Revival Movement in England and Church Planting in Uganda." M.A. project, Wheaton Graduate School, 1978.

------. "Practical Theology in the Third World." Paper presented to the International Clericus Conference, New York, June 16, 1981.

-------. "The Revival Movement in Uganda up to 1941." Occasional Research Paper, Department of Religious Studies and Philosophy, Makerere University, 1971.

------."The Role of Christians in Politics." Occasional Research Paper, Department of Religious Studies and Philosophy, Makerere University, 1970.

------."Africa: The Origin of Western Civilization and Religion." Research Paper presented, Fisk University, October 1985.

Wilson, T., and Katarikawe, J. "The East African Revival Movement: History, Beliefs and Practices." Joint Master of Missiology Thesis, Fuller Theological Seminary, 1975.

SOME JOURNALS CONTAINING VALUABLE AFRICAN MATERIALS

Affer. Gaba/Elodoret: AMECEA Pastoral Institute.

Africa. London: Oxford University Press.

African Affairs. London.

African Studies Review. Los Angeles: African Studies Association.

Africa Theological Journal. Makumira, Tanzania: Lutheran Theological College.

Cahiers des religions Africaines. Zaire: Universite de Zaire, Centre d'etudes des religions Africaines.

Dini na Mila: Revealed Religion and Traditional Custom. Kampala: Makerere University.

Ghana Bulletin of Theology. Legon: University of Ghana.

Journal of Religion in Africa. Leiden: E. J. Brill.

Orita: Ibadan Journal of Religious Studies. Ibadan: Ibadan University Press.

Uganda Journal. Kampala: Institute of Social Sciences.

INDEX

Mary E. Giles

THE POETICS OF LOVE
Meditations with John of the Cross

American University Studies: Series VII, Theology and Religion, Vol. 18
ISBN 0-8204-0321-0 177 pp. hardcover US $ 28,00

Recommended prices - alterations reserved

The Poetics of Love is a meditative commentary on John of the Cross's celebrated poem, the "Spiritual Canticle." The author responds to John's expression of the journey to God and unitive love by turning to everyday events to see them as context for an inner development which is truly mystical. Commenting strophe by strophe on the mystical process, she shows the potential for mystical consciousness in such experiences as falling in love, writing a poem, studying the stars and riding a horse. Desire, suffering, paradox, ecstasy, compassion, metaphor, virtue, solitude and joy are among the twenty-one subjects that mark the journey. The scholar will find in the meditations an example of reader response criticism while the student of mysticism may be encouraged to celebrate human relationships, nature, art and science as revelations of the divine.

PETER LANG PUBLISHING, INC.
62 West 45th Street
USA - New York, NY 10036